GOD
IS
REAL

*A Testament in the Form of
an Autobiography*

DALLAS BILLINGTON

DAVID McKAY COMPANY, INC.

NEW YORK

MANUFACTURED IN THE UNITED STATES OF AMERICA

VAN REES PRESS • NEW YORK

GOD IS REAL

*A Testament in the Form of
an Autobiography*

Genesis 18:14

Is any thing too hard for the Lord?

Luke 1:37

For with God nothing shall be impossible.

Joshua 1:5

There shall not any man be able to stand before thee all the days of thy life: as I was with Moses, so I will be with thee: I will not fail thee, nor forsake thee.

Philippians 4:13

I can do all things through Christ which strengtheneth me.

MY GOD AND THESE SCRIPTURES HAVE MADE ME WHAT I AM

Dedication

This book is dedicated to my wife, NELL STOKES BILLINGTON, who has made it possible for me to live my life and write this book to the Glory of God. I would also like to dedicate this book to my son, Charles; his wife, Eileen; and my two grandsons, Charles Franklin Jr. and Dallas Robert; and to all the members of the Akron Baptist Temple, who are the dearest people on earth to me.

Foreword

SITTING HERE IN MY HOME IN FLORIDA, WHERE THESE words are being written, my mind wanders back down the halls of memory to a night in the Arlington Street Baptist Church in Akron, Ohio, more than thirty years ago, where I was conducting a revival.

A young man, just from the hills of Kentucky, joined the church and was baptized. He had been saved for some time, but perhaps this was the point in his life which was to mark the beginning of a ministry unequaled in this generation.

If there were no more evidence of the existence of God, the life and ministry of Dr. Dallas Billington would convince the most skeptical that "God is real."

Perhaps no man has been more closely associated with Dr. Billington, or known him more intimately than I. As you read *God Is Real,* you will discover something of the secret power of this unusual man. You will not read far until you feel the spirit of the author.

Dr. Billington is, first of all, a man of God, wonderfully saved and especially endowed with great business and administrative ability as evidenced in the building of the great Akron Baptist Temple, with a membership of over sixteen thousand and the largest Sunday school in the world with missions and churches around the globe.

Dr. Billington—preacher, teacher, author and world-traveler —sends this book forth to the Christian world with a prayer that in its pages the lost may find Christ; the weary, rest; the discouraged, hope; and all come to the knowledge that, "God is real."

—B. R. LAKIN, D.D., LL.D.

Purpose of this Book

HAVING TRAVELED ACROSS THE COUNTRY PREACHING IN revivals in every state in the United States, in many cities and towns both large and small, and also in many foreign countries, I have developed my own way of telling stories to explain Bible lessons. I most generally close a message with a story that has either happened to me in my life or in another minister's life. My son has urged me to write a book that he and other young ministers might have a record of my style and manner of preaching.

In answer to thousands of requests from preachers, laymen, and friends of mine I have attempted to write the book they asked for.

It is my prayer to God that this book will be used to the Glory of God, for the salvation of a million souls, and make happy the lives of many who shall read its pages.

D. B.

My Sincere Thanks

FIRST AND ABOVE ALL, I WANT TO THANK GOD FOR SAVING my soul through the blood of the Lord Jesus Christ, calling me to preach the gospel, trusting me with the Holy Bible, and giving me the privilege and knowledge to write this story.

I wish to thank Nell Stokes Billington, my wife, whose interest and prayers have been a constant source of inspiration to me. My own son, Charles Billington, has helped me in many ways to make the book possible. A lot of credit for the book goes to Mrs. Buster Garner, who transcribed every line of the book from the disk to the written page. My thanks also go to Mrs. Howard Wright, another secretary at our church, who has helped me gather data and recall to mind many things which have happened over the years. Of course, I wish to thank all the secretaries and other ministers of the church who did the regular work of the church while most of my time was used in writing the book.

The Akron *Beacon Journal*, Mr. John Knight, the publisher, Ben Maidenberg, executive editor, Mr. Lloyd Stoyer, feature writer, and many other newspapermen have helped me get national publicity. I shall not forget our Akron radio station, WAKR, Mr. Bernard Berk, and Roger, his fine son, for their help through the years.

It has been through friends like these and the Wondrous Goodness of God toward me that I have been permitted to publish this book. If this book in any way has been a blessing to you, nothing could encourage me more than to have a card or letter from you. Simply address your mail to Dallas F. Billington, Akron Baptist Temple, Akron, Ohio.

Contents

II. We Build God's House

III. Our Trip to the Holy Land

IV. The Harvest Years

V. How the Bible Can Remake Your Life

I

The Path to the Ministry

1. Kentucky Childhood

I WAS BORN ON JANUARY 23, 1903. MY PARENTS WERE James Monroe Billington and Margaret Kelly Billington. My grandparents were of the old Wesleyan Methodist stock on the Billington side. My mother's people came from Ireland and were of the old Presbyterian stock. Through them, my background has been religious for at least five generations back. In that time there have been preachers and educators as well as people of practically every walk of life in my family. Today, I sincerely thank God for Christian parents who taught me to believe in an Almighty God.

My birthplace was actually a log house in West Kentucky. It was not a log cabin like some, but a house. I was born the tenth child and the seventh son. My home was close to a place called Kirksey, where there were one grocery store and the old-type blacksmith shop where they built wagons, shod the horses, and where the crowds met on Saturday afternoons to pass the time away.

It was the custom of my parents to dedicate their children to God at birth. Instead of taking them to some cathedral or church and having them sprinkled and their names enrolled, my father, being a devout Christian man, and my mother, a wonderful Christian woman, always had this dedication service at their home. There was no fanfare—just the mother and father simply giving each child back to God as each was born. My father would sit at the foot of the bed, raise the

3

child up in his arms, and prayerfully give him back to God.

At the age of two weeks, I am told that I was seriously ill with pneumonia fever. My parents and the family doctor, Dr. Otis Jingles, did not expect me to live. However, it was the custom of my father when there was sickness, not being a divine healer or ever known as such, to pray for his own family. When the word was noised abroad that Dallas, the two-week-old baby, would perhaps not live, the doctor was asked if this were true. When asked this, the doctor said the baby would probably be all right. He said he had seen the baby's father, Jim Billington, out beside the barn (meaning the stock barn, of course) praying; "and you know how these Billingtons are, when things are serious, they go to God in prayer." The doctor believed that I would recover, because my father had gone to God in prayer. My parents always called the family doctor in case of sickness. Then, too, they went to God in prayer, as I have been taught from the cradle.

When I was six months old, we moved from our place south of Kirksey in Calloway County to a place known as Newburg, Kentucky, about fourteen miles east of Murray. At that particular time the place was called Blood. I stayed down on the big Tennessee River in East Calloway County from the time I was a child of six months until I was seventeen.

My first school days began when I was about five and a half years old. School started in July and ran until Christmas. We had the six months' school term, and eight grades met in the same one-room schoolhouse. When I was ten years old I was in the same class with others who were twelve. At the age of twelve I finished grade school or the eighth grade. My diploma, written on just a common piece of paper, merely stated, "This is to certify that Dallas Franklin Billington has finished the eighth grade," and was signed by the teacher and three trustees of the school. I am sorry now to say that I was never too proud of the diploma and thought it not worth keeping. For this reason, I do not have it in my files to show.

Our nearest high school was five or six miles away. We did not have a fine school bus to pick us up and bring us back. Instead the only means of transportation was to ride a mule or a horse to and from school. This meant that the horse or mule would have to remain tied until the school was over. Therefore, my father decided that since he was not able to send all of his children through high school, he would not attempt to send any.

This meant that at the age of twelve I had ended my school days for the time being. As it turned out, my formal education was ended for all time. My next five years, from the age of twelve to the age of seventeen, were spent on a large farm that had been a slave farm. On this farm, known as the old Coleman farm, were two Negro cemeteries—one on top of a ridge and the other on top of a high hill—and a large bottom area where we farmed. During the slave days, a man by the name of Mr. Coleman owned the place. The rains would come from the south and rush down through his farm, destroying crops. Mr. Coleman used his slaves to bring large rocks from many parts of the country. They built a large dam across the wide bottom area to hold back the water that came in from the south, off the hill regions and farms. When he had the farm land settled the way he wanted it, we were told by people who lived in those days, he had a dance and a big party with hard liquor to drink to celebrate the completion. The party lasted way into the night. Mr. Coleman was known not to be a Christian, and he all but defied God and told everyone that his dam had been finished and he could hold back the water from the farms south of his. That night during the dance, we were told, it started to thunder, and the people were compelled to stay the night at the big Coleman farmhouse (which was back off the main road where my home place was as I grew to manhood).

I sat as a boy and listened to older men tell this story. They said that after the rain began to fall and the cloudbursts came seemingly one after the other, the horses, hitched outside with the carriages, became terrified by the lightning, broke loose and ran. Until this day, large boulders can be found scattered hither and yonder, where they were carried like matchboxes crushed beneath the hand of God, proving to Mr. Coleman and all his friends that when the hand of God moves, no one can stop it. Thus the dam was crushed, the water went down, and huge sand piles were carried out into the fields, to prove to all who had witnessed the building of it for six years that truly the hand of God had moved. Therefore, we boys were often reminded by our father, whenever we said something about the rain or the drought, to take a look at the boulders and remember the story told us by the aged people.

If you will read the 5th chapter of the Book of Daniel, you will read the story of a man by the name of Belshazzar. He had all heart could wish for, and he too had defied God by bringing from the temple of God the vessels likened to our communion sets and laughing and making fun, like Mr. Coleman. The Bible says that in that same night Belshazzar's kingdom was taken from him.

My purpose in writing this book is that I might, through God's eternal grace and the Word of God, persuade you who read this chapter that there is a God in Heaven who rules in the hearts of men, who sets up kingdoms and sets them down. My prayer is that you will read Romans 10:13, which says that whosoever shall call upon the name of the Lord shall be saved.

2. Early Church Days

MY FATHER WAS A TRUSTEE IN THE METHODIST CHURCH at Russell's Chapel, approximately three and a half miles from our home. Our only means of transportation in those days was what we called the old hay wagon. My father would put the old frame on the wagon and cover it with hay straw. Then he would cover this with quilts before we climbed in ready to go to church. We always attended the Methodists' revivals at the old Russell's Chapel church. It was a common thing to hear a man preach on everlasting judgment without God. We would hear him read from the sixteenth chapter of Luke, where it says men are lost who die without God. Of course, during the series of meetings there would be a message on Heaven. We would be told of God's wonderful grace and of a home prepared for loved ones to gather in perfect happiness. We also attended all the revivals at the Sugarcreek Baptist Church. It was located five miles from our home. The old hay wagon covered with straw and quilts carried us there and back. Even though we knew the work waited for us early each morning on the farm, still we went to church, returning late at night.

My mother, being Presbyterian, took us to the revivals of the Presbyterian church known as the Liberty Church. Further away there was the old Ledbetter Baptist Church. One can readily see that my early days were spent in a very religious home. My father would read the Bible to us at night and talk to us about the way we should live. When Sunday came there was no such thing as our going to the swimming hole. We were told that was for six days a week but not Sunday. We were never allowed to go to ball games on Sunday. They had sandlot ball games, and others were permitted to go—but not us. We were never allowed to have playing cards. The only game of amusement allowed in our home was checkers. Some of the friends we had would often say, "Don't you think your parents are too strict?" We never took sides with those who would criticize our parents. A square dance or play party was never known in our home. Of course, we were not saints, and once in a while we did slip off and go to some of the play parties and square dances. We were human, just as you are. Especially as we grew into teen-agers and had our own horses and buggies, we went out nights and went to places that were not the wishes and will of our parents.

Whenever I came in at night, I would try my very best to slip in and oftentimes take my shoes off so as not to be heard. I knew that my father prayed for me, but at night it was only my mother I would hear pray for me. My father's custom was to slip out beneath the old cedar trees or by the stock barn and there talk with God. Nevertheless, they waited each night for us, and a dim light would be left burning until they knew all the boys were home and in bed.

Somehow, I passed up those tender years and never became a Christian. I well remember one night in the old Sugarcreek Baptist Church when I was a lad aged eleven. I am sure God spoke to my heart for the first time and convinced me by the Holy Spirit that I was lost. Someone is going to ask, What do you mean by the word "LOST"? The Bible speaks of being SAVED. That means that if you are to be SAVED you must first be LOST. When I refer to the word "LOST," I mean lost in sin, as the children of Israel were lost to wander for forty years. The wilderness was a type of sin. Therefore, at the young age of eleven, I well knew that night, when old brother Gregory preached the message and said perhaps three or four times, "Young man, God will find you out," that I was LOST. From the age of eleven, by the dealing of the Holy Spirit with me, I have known that God is real.

After that, when revival meetings were held and I attended those meetings and heard them sing "There Is a Fountain Filled with Blood" and "My Mother's Prayers Have Followed Me" I would think seriously of becoming a Christian. However, after the first year went by and I turned twelve and then thirteen, I found it easier each time to say no to God.

I remember one time, when I was perhaps fifteen, that I would have given all I had if I had only known Jesus as my Saviour. A girl by the name of Fannie Scott, who had gone to school with me and was the same age—though not a sweetheart or girl friend, for I had never dated her—became very ill; and my father, being a close neighbor of the Scotts, visited them. It was customary in those days to sit up with the sick. It was a rare thing for anyone ever to go to the hospital. You were born at home and you died at home. We knew nothing of cancer in those days, but we knew and dreaded t.b. If you contracted the disease, you simply stayed home and the doctor came once a week. If you became worse, the doctor came more often. If you were not too far away, he would come every other day. He would tell the family to call him if you should pass away in the meantime.

My father was down at Mr. Scott's home when he came in and said he was sure that Fannie was dying. We children went down to the home and went into the living room where they had moved Fannie. Seemingly very rationally, this young girl asked each one that came in the door, "Would you pray for me? I am not a Christian, I am not saved."

I realized then at the age of fifteen that surely it must be a dreadful thing to die without God. However, I am convinced that Fannie Scott is in Heaven today, for, after having been saved and reading the Bible for many years and understanding that God said that whosoever calls upon the name of the Lord shall be saved, Fannie Scott prayed about two hours before she passed away, asking God to save her and forgive her sins. As long as there was breath left in her body, she kept saying, "God, save me and forgive my sins."

The 23rd chapter of Luke, the 42nd verse, tells us that the thief, realizing that he was dying, said, "Lord, remember me when thou comest into thy kingdom." Jesus said, "To day shalt thou be with me in paradise." As you read this chapter may you realize that death is coming to you. It is coming to me and to everyone. As long as God lets me live, my purpose in living is that I may be a soul winner for Jesus, that I may be used of God, that I will never have to stand by another person's bed and see him die begging for help and not be able to help him or at least point him to One who can. I will show him the Bible with its cross and tell him of Jesus, who loved him and died to save him from his sins. My prayer is that you will become a Christian if you read this book unsaved. If you are a Christian, read your Bible, learn to know God well, so that you may introduce Him to others. After all, the only things that you and I will ever see in Heaven are the souls who are won for God. We will not take our houses, land, gold, or silver; but if you and I, while on life's journey home, will have patience and grace, the Lord will permit us to take many souls with us—the greatest treasure of all.

Do not say that because people are of another faith or another race there would be no use to talk to them. When I think of my own life as a boy of eleven until the age of twenty-two, I remember so many people who talked to me about my soul. My mother, one of my sisters, brothers, and many others talked to me, and I wonder how I could have gone so long without accepting Christ. They had the patience and grace for which I pray each day, and I pray that I may have life and strength like Moses of old, that my eyesight will not fail me, that my strength will not leave me until I have become able, through foreign missionaries, tracts, television, newspapers, and the publishing of books, to say one day, by God's grace, there are a million souls in Heaven because God saved me.

Will you bow your head where you are and accept Christ as your Saviour? Will you trust Him? If you will, the greatest joy that will ever come to your life is not your wedding day, not the birth of your firstborn, not your son coming home from the war—for these things I have experienced—but the greatest joy you will ever experience is the hour you first believe.

3. Leaving the Farm

WHEN I WAS SEVENTEEN YEARS OLD, ON FEBRUARY 8, MY father and two of my younger brothers and myself were planning to burn what we called plant beds to sow tobacco seed and raise another crop. About ten in the morning I laid down my ax and said to my father and brothers that I was going to leave the farm. I put on my sweater and made plans to go. My father asked me what I was going to do to live. I told him I planned to go to the city and get a job. I wanted to go to school at night and study in order to obtain a higher education. My father pointed out that the summer months would be over quickly and, like the prodigal son, I would return in the winter. I agreed with my father, but if I never attempted to do better for myself, no one would do it for me.

There was an old suitcase which an older brother owned that I packed my clothes in, and then I asked a friend who had an old car to take me to the county seat, Murray, if I would pay for the gas. We arrived at the county seat, and I went into the station and bought my ticket to Paducah, Kentucky, just fifty miles away. I had heard that people were able to secure jobs in a shoe factory there. There were also hosiery mills, railroad shops, and many other jobs available to men.

Upon arriving in the city, I asked a cab driver about a hotel where I could stay, it being my first trip away from home all alone. I chose the second hotel I looked at, where board and room was one dollar per day.

After I had my room and key and all seemed well, I walked across two blocks to the International Shoe Factory. There were four lines of men, and at the head of each line there was a foreman seated at a desk, doing his own hiring. I walked up to the desk of Mr. Evans, who was over the lasting department and the stitching machines located on Second Street off of Broadway. Standing in the line, I had heard the usual questions asked by someone employing others. The men were asked their age and if they had experience, and many were told, "We can't use you."

Mr. Evans looked at me, a tall, thin young man, and it was easy to understand why he called me "Slim." I was over six feet tall and weighed 140 pounds. He said to me, "Slim, where did you come from?" I told him that I came from the farm. He asked me if I had ever had any experience in a shoe factory, to which I replied no. He told me he could not use me, but I asked him if no one had ever hired him, would he be sitting behind a desk today as a foreman, hiring and telling people what to do. I shall never forget the look on his face. He dropped his chin for a moment and then looked me straight in the eye and asked if he gave me a job, would I stay with him. I promised him I would stay with him, for I was tired of the farm. He examined my hands, which showed that they were used to work. This was my first job in a big public place.

That night, all alone in my room, I realized that I was on my own. I tried to sit there in the room and think things out for myself. The following morning I was to have my vaccination for smallpox. Perhaps this was my first taste of homesickness. A few days later, when a combination of the smallpox shot and homesickness made me feel miserable, pure determination to make good kept me on the job. Giving God the glory, I did make good on my job. I was told that if I kept up the good work, I could expect to be taken off the lasting machines and put on the stitching machines. Within four weeks I was keeping up with experienced workers. After seven weeks, with some of the stitchers ill, Mr. Evans, my new-found friend, came to me and asked me to watch the stitchers; and within a short time I was stitching more shoes than any man on the line.

Since a child, I had always been taught to go to church. I

began to look around for a church, but the churches were
not conducted as I was used to and so I did not go to any.
The next thing I did was to borrow books at the library. I
had one ambition in life. It was real with me. I had often said
to my parents and brothers and sisters that I would like to
become governor of the state of Kentucky. I was interested in
one subject and that was political science. Anything that I
could find pertaining to government, whether it be county,
state, or federal, I read. I read about political campaigns and
how they were conducted and how to win. I took many cor-
respondence courses. These courses were in public speaking
and English. My studies kept me off the streets, and many,
many nights were spent reading books. Of course, I read the
Bible. This was not new to me, for I began to read the Bible
when I was nine years old. The Bible was interesting to me
for the wars and history it contained.

With my job at the factory and my studies at night, I gave
very little thought to church. I became acquainted with a
few cab drivers in town, and on occasion I would ride with
them on their runs; once in a while they would ask me to
drive for them when a fill-in was needed. To drive a cab, you
had to know the good and the bad. Travelers coming in
expected you to know all places and take them where they
would be satisfied. There was one place known as Leader
Bottom, where they made moonshine liquor. I am proud to
say that I never made or sold one pint of whisky, but I am
guilty of driving people to the places that did make it and
sell it. I learned early in life both sides of life. At the age of
seventeen the sinful life looked like glamour. I knew many
kinds of men; many policemen were my friends. I was never
arrested for any crime or misdemeanor but, as I will tell you
later on, I was arrested for preaching the gospel later in life.

I was far from perfect, living ungodly, sinful, and away
from Christ. I had two sisters who lived in Paducah, and
both were in church every Sunday. They too had jobs at the
shoe factory. However, while they were attending church on

Sunday, I remained at home and read the newspaper. I was eager for current events and read the paper thoroughly. I was never interested in the funny pages or jokes, but I could lose all track of time reading the news stories to the very last line. It was not uncommon for me to read every line of news in Sunday's newspaper.

Many of my friends then and now are Masons. I had known a Mason back home by the name of Mr. Fent Highland. He had good books, which he permitted me to borrow and read before I left home. My parents, of course, worried about their boy going to the big city and thought of me as their prodigal son. The morning I left home, my father took me by the right hand and, knowing that I was not a Christian, told me they would never stop praying for me.

4. The Next Four Years

THE NEXT FOUR YEARS WERE PRETTY MUCH A ROUTINE. Upon one or two occasions, being laid off at the shoe factory, I worked at a tobacco factory. There I met a good friend of mine, Mr. Bob Kirk, who had lived close to us in Calloway County. There I learned much about business, as oftentimes he let me help him in supervision and some book work. There I learned the art of getting along with people. As the years went by, I learned quite a few different jobs. Mr. Evans of the International Shoe Factory told me if I would stay with him, he would teach me a trade and I would have a lifetime job. Mr. Evans had started with a shoe factory somewhere in St. Louis when he was my age. Somehow, I was not impressed with the offer that he made me, for I still nourished the hope of being in public office. I loved people and enjoyed talking with them.

Even though I had dated several girls with whom I had attended school and like all boys had certain ideas about marriage, I really had never thought seriously about getting married. At least, I wanted to have a good job, money in the bank, and perhaps even own a car before taking a bride. Since my fortunes were not favorable, I did not let myself think seriously of marriage. I made it a practice not to date the same girl too often.

One night I met Nell Stokes. When I asked her to go driving with me, she refused and told me she went to the Emanuel Baptist Church. Now, I had not been to church more than five times in the last four years. After I met this girl, even though I kidded her about angels walking the streets of Paducah, I did not forget the name of her church; and the next Sunday morning I found myself at church looking for this girl whom I loved from the moment I saw her. Meeting her was the turning point in my life.

In the year of 1924 there came to our city a man by the name of Howard S. Williams. He had formerly been a newspaperman at Hattiesburg, Mississippi. He was then an evangelist and came to the church to tell us how sin had wrecked his life at the age of forty-five. Even his own family felt that he was a disgrace to them because of his drinking and gambling. My sweetheart, Nell Stokes, asked me to go with her to the tent meeting. The big tent was put up on Tenth and Broadway, and more than ten thousand people attended the revival. They had good music and a large choir from various churches. The churches had united to make the revival a success.

This man was a plain gospel preacher. He preached Christ on a cross, in order that people might be saved from their sins. He told us that our sins would find us out. In our city, previous to this, two men had raped a girl and had killed her. In the process of this awful sin, the two men had gagged her with a red bandana, and one of them had lost his cap near the scene. The posse brought bloodhounds to the scene, and they trailed the men as far as the railroad, where they had escaped in a boxcar. Later, twenty-five miles away at Mayfield, Kentucky, there was a burglary of a grocery store. The same bloodhounds were sent for. When one of the bloodhounds got the scent, her owner and trainer told them she was after a murderer. They followed the dog to a lumberyard in town, and there they found one of the men, who confessed it was the other man who had killed the girl.

The preacher took this story from the newspaper and read from the Book of Galatians: "Be not deceived; God is not mocked: for whatsoever a man soweth, that shall he also reap." He pointed out that if a man who has committed murder cannot get away from a dog, how do you expect to get away from God. After attending these meetings several nights, one night I heard the preacher say, people will go on kidding themselves believing that they are getting by, when the stars above and the sun and the rain prove God. Each night I would return to my hotel room and read the Bible which had been given me when I left home. Then I realized fully that all men are LOST. Men who have normal minds know right from wrong; they have a conscience which the animals of the field, birds of the air, or fish of the sea do not have. We are the only creatures whom God created with a conscience that will smite us when we do wrong and encourage us for every good thing.

One night Mr. Williams said that Jesus had become my sin-bearer. He pointed out that I had been scheduled to die or condemned to die, and Jesus had taken my place as a substitute. I was lost, unsaved, wicked, and I knew it. He only reminded me; already my conscience had told me. He would hold up the Bible night after night and say, "This is the supreme authority for all courts. This Bible is the high record of Heaven's court. Men are lost without God, and to die LOST means to be cast into a place called Hell, not for just a few days, months, or years, but for eternity, forever." The preacher read from the Book of Mark where it says that it is better for you to have your hand cut off and cast away or your eye or your feet and go into Heaven halt or maimed than to keep your hand, eye, and feet and be cast into Hell forever.

It seemed to me that the preacher and his message were all directed to me. There I stood, thinking about the many times I had gone to church on the hay wagon. I remembered hearing Mother pray for me and pondered over life and tried seriously to decide if it would be better to be some great worldly leader or to turn my face and become a Christian. I know that there are many statesmen and great leaders who are devout Christians, but the thing I was weighing in my balance was whether I would dedicate myself completely, without compromise.

The evangelist told us all we could do to be saved was to trust in God. Believe in the Lord Jesus Christ and ask Him to save you. Jesus took your place at Calvary but you must trust Him and believe. You must ask Jesus to forgive your sins. There, standing beside the girl I was to marry, Nell Stokes, while the choir was singing "I'm Praying for You," without a shadow of doubt, I was saved. God's great love and mercy came into my soul. You have heard people ask, "Is it true that the lights shine brighter when you get saved?" They ask, perhaps, "Did you hear angels sing?" The lights did not seem brighter nor did I hear angels sing, but how can mere words describe the perfect peace I felt in my heart? Fear had been cast out. The fear which I had had since I was a boy of eleven in the Sugarcreek Baptist Church was gone. The burden and desire to be a better boy and to live right had finally become a reality. I was saved. The peace which I have in my heart comes only from trusting that Jesus can be yours if you will only ask Him. If you will simply say— and earnestly mean it—Lord, save me and forgive my sins, you, too, can be saved. I John, chapter 1, verse 9, says, "If we confess our sins, he is faithful and just to forgive us our sins, and to cleanse us from all unrighteousness."

5. First Year in Akron

AFTER A YEAR OF COURTSHIP, NELL AND I PLANNED TO get married. We decided that the wages I was earning at the shoe factory were not sufficient. I had a sister and a brother-in-law living in Akron, Ohio, and quite a few friends had gone to Akron to gain employment. I was told the wages were much higher and employment plentiful in Akron. In February of 1925 I made up my mind that I would go there. After the plans were all made, I boarded the train at Paducah. When I arrived in Akron, it was snowing. I had on a summer suit and no topcoat. I shall never forget my very cold reception at the rubber capital of the world.

I found room and board on East Market Street, and the following morning I went to the Goodyear Tire and Rubber Company employment office. Fortunately, the first day I was hired. The job which I had was known as transportation.

It did not take long for me to see that people of the North thought nothing of calling one any kind of a name. For a while it was hard for me to take, and then I found if I were to behave as a Christian, I would have to put aside anger created by what men said or did to me.

The men with whom I worked took their social glass, talked freely of their poker games, and then proceeded to tell me of what church they were a member. This was all contrary to my concept or belief in what a Christian should be. Yet, I was really a baby in Christ. I was less than a year old as a Christian. I started on the first Sunday to visit churches, and I visited many churches. However, those which I attended did not seem to be what I understood my church ought to be. They preached the Bible and talked about Jesus as a good man. They had good singing, but I believed that the Bible taught an altar. I read in the Old

Testament that Abraham and Moses had altars. I found in the Old Testament where blood sacrifices were offered. When I read the references in the Bible, I found where Christ, too, had been offered as a sacrifice for me. Going from church to church, I did not find the type of church that I liked or one that I would want to attend regularly. I wrote a letter to my intended wife, Nell Stokes, and told her that when we were married and she and I could make our home in Akron, we would have to start a church of our own.

I think I knew then that God was calling me to be a minister of the gospel. I spent late hours reading and searching the Bible for the truth of what God wished me to do and His plan for my life. It was not long until I began to talk to the men in the factory and in a kind way rebuke them for their sinful ways.

One night a man was using profanity. I heard him, and knowing that he was a married man with two children, I stopped and talked with him. I called him by name and said, "Joe, I thought you had two children." He said, "I do, so what?" I asked him if he used that kind of language around those children. He sneered and said, "Oh, I suppose you are a Bible believer." I answered that I did believe in the Bible. He asked if I believed that the whale swallowed Jonah. I told him that if the Bible said it, I would believe it, for if there was anything impossible with God, then He could not be my God. God then would be like a false god or a wooden god of the heathens in faraway lands. I could see that he was beginning to be concerned. I have always carried the nickname Billy. He called me Billy and said he was sorry, for he did believe the Bible. He said that he did not mean what he said. This same man is a Baptist preacher now. For the next year we had fellowship at lunchtime and talked about the Bible and Jesus. I got him to go to church, and he was saved and baptized. He later attended a Baptist seminary, and I have heard that he is a wonderful preacher.

There came a time in the factory when there had to be

some Sunday work. I did not believe in working on Sunday. I still do not believe in working on Sunday; however, I do realize it is sometimes a necessity. If our doctors and nurses or firemen and policemen were to say that they would not work on Sunday, many lives would be in danger. The kind of Sunday work to which I am opposed is the kind which is not necessary. Each time they asked me to work on Sunday and I refused, I was told that if I did not work I would have to get someone to take my place. I told my foreman one day that I could not ask someone to do something that I myself did not believe was right. How was I going to witness to an unsaved man and ask him to do what I felt in my heart was wrong? How would I then make him believe that God is real? So when it fell my lot to work Sunday, I did.

After a year had passed and, with God's help, I had gained the respect of many of the men, one day one of the men came to me and asked me what I really thought of Sunday work. I asked him if he had ever read the New Testament. He told me that he had not read the Bible very much. I told him to read in the Book of John where Christ was on trial before Pontius Pilate. Jesus told Pilate that they that believed in the truth, believed in Him. Pontius asked Jesus what truth was. Jesus said they that believe the truth, come to Him. Jesus also told him that they that brought Jesus to him had the greater sin. I worked for this company on Sunday because they asked me to. I did not believe God would hold it against me for working. I was working to keep from asking an unsaved man to take my place. The company would be responsible, not "Billy." "This answer," he said, "would be accepted in Heaven"; and he walked away.

I am happy for the privilege that I have had in life to talk about Christ to men with whom I have worked. God has given me grace to rebuke sinful ways, but never in an unkind way so as to offend or embarrass them and perhaps lose their souls to Christ forever. You should rebuke sin harshly, perhaps, in the public pulpit, but when you are talking to an individual, be firm but gentle in pointing out his or her sinful ways. My days spent in Akron in the factory were the beginning of my seeking out lost souls. Wherever it was possible, at the mill, at lunch or any time that Jesus led me, I tried to win men for Christ. I tried to be wise as a serpent but as harmless as a dove. My first souls won for God were in the factory. It wasn't too long before those who had made fun of me and called me names like "preacher, rabbi, priest" would come to me and say their babies or wives were in the hospital and would I pray for them. I well remember one young man who came to me and told me that his wife was in the hospital and needed blood. I went to the hospital and found him there, and he had given a transfusion to his wife. This man was not a Christian, and I began to talk to him. Because he could understand giving his blood out of love for his wife, I told him Jesus had done the same for him. The Bible says that Jesus gave His life's blood to cleanse you and me, and there in the waiting room of the hospital I had the great privilege of seeing this man believe on the Lord Jesus Christ.

You might ask me how did I know that he believed. I believe that after you see the tears come because of sorrow and then you see the smile break, you can tell that it is the release from sin and judgment to life in the Lord Jesus Christ.

Thus began my work in the city of Akron in the rubber factories. There I was not ashamed to tell others that Jesus loved them and would save them. You will find throughout this book a verse of Scripture referred to, which I have learned to love—Acts 16:31: "Believe on the Lord Jesus Christ and thou shalt be saved." Believe even *now* and be saved.

6. Working Together

IT WAS THE CUSTOM IN FACTORIES FOR MEN TO WORK in pools. I was in a pool with five other men. My buddie and I drove hand trucks called jitneys, and the other four loaded the rubber and stacked it in the factory. One night the other four men decided to have some fun, and, since they knew I was from Kentucky, where men had the reputation of being hotheaded and quick to defend their honor, especially if they were called a bad name, they planned to have my buddie give me a beating. After the shift had started and my buddie and I had begun our regular routine of running our jitneys onto the elevators, one after the other, I would only see my buddie as we exchanged places at the elevator, while one was coming off the elevator and the other going on. About the middle of the shift that evening, my buddie came off the elevator and came at me in a very angry mood. He was holding a knife in his hand, and he called me a bad name. He said that I had been talking about his being lazy and not doing his part of the work.

We would carry the handles of our jitneys when we left the elevator or when we went to the elevator to ring for it. I looked at him and smiled, with this heavy weight in my hand, which could easily have killed a man, had a man the desire to kill. I called him by the nickname I had given him and told him I was sure that if he knew my sweetheart mother, weighing about 105 pounds and every bit a wonderful person, he would not have called her that name. He said that he had not called my mother anything, but I told him he had called me the son of ———. Then he asked me if I had said these things about him and I told him no. Very shortly after that he went out to talk to the other four men, and the shift foreman was called into the discussion. It was not easy to stand there and let this man abuse me, and before I became a Christian I would have fought bitterly. Only Christian people know what happens to your heart when Jesus comes to dwell in it. He changes your mind, your heart, and your thinking. I can say that I had no desire to become angry with him and it never crossed my mind to strike him. I believe that night brought me more close friends, for the foreman brought the men together and told them that they had had their fun and their day with Billy by calling him names, and even with their fun-poking I had taken it all in my stride. He asked them to refrain from making fun of me and the God I served.

That night when I got home I remember reading the Book of Daniel, which has always been a favorite of mine. Daniel was not only a man of God but he was a Christian statesman, and many, many things happened to him while he, too, was away from home. The Scripture teaches us that Daniel was carried away from Jerusalem to the city of Babylon when he was perhaps a boy of fourteen.

I bowed my head that night and thanked God that when someone had wished to anger me I had had enough Christian love in my heart to forgive him and control my fists. God gave Daniel many friends because he trusted in God, and under almost unbearable conditions he always turned to God. God had given me grace to smile amidst my tears. The more I thought about this the happier I became. I think there are men still living who can remember the episode of that night; and from that factory, including some top officials, came many members to the church of which I am now the pastor.

We read where Jesus said that if we would do good to our enemies, we would be pouring coals of fire upon their heads.

Another thing that I remember well about the days in the factory is about one of the men who worked with me in the calender room. He went to cross the street one morning and was struck down by an automobile in front of the gatehouse. He was taken to the hospital and pronounced dead. I always tried to be very careful but, knowing this man to have been a Christian and a churchman and liked by many, I used this example to point out to other men, if they had been taken in like manner, where would their souls be tonight.

It was my great and happy privilege to get to talk to men about their souls and tell them that life is uncertain but death is sure. I well remember asking one man, who worked on a calender, if he knew that the Scripture says it is appointed once for men to die, and after this the judgment. He asked where that was found in the Bible. I told him in Hebrews 9:27. Some two or three days later he came into the factory and, seeing me, stopped and told me that he had started to read his Bible. He had read all of the chapter in Hebrews. It had a lot to say about our sins and the sacrifices in the Old Testament. It wasn't long until he told me that he had read the entire Book of Hebrews through. From just one remark which I had felt laid upon my heart to say, I heard this man say that he was now going to church regularly. He thanked me for talking to him. Daily I labored for the Master.

I found in reading my Bible that Paul was a tentmaker by trade. Oftentimes, because Paul did not have finances to live on without working with his own hands, he would make tents. Like Paul as he labored, I talked about my Saviour.

The Bible tells us that if we sow seed, there will be a harvest. Many times when something happens to you and me, we do not understand why it happens, but if we have faith and patience, we will see the results from it. God wants to use us. The purpose of every Christian man and woman in this world is not just to stay here so many days and die; the fact is that we are in this world for a purpose—to win others for Christ. The Bible teaches us that this world is not our home. Wherever we work or whatever we do, there is a reason for our living. That is why we build churches, send out missionaries, print tracts, and so forth—to win others for Christ.

I always wanted to know why a man had become a success.

I read many books other than my Bible to gain all the knowledge I could, so as to be able to talk to all people in varied walks of life. I was eager to read about successful businessmen. It makes no difference what your talent is for making a living, you also have a talent to use for God.

When I left Paducah and came to Akron, I wondered why I felt the urge to come so definitely to Akron. But it did not take me very long to understand that God had a reason, and I felt the call of God in my heart and life. I came to Akron like many others, thinking that I would work in the factories perhaps all my life and make a living for me and the family I would have someday. This town and the work in it would make provisions for my marriage and our home. I soon found that I was in Akron for another purpose. God was preparing me for the ministry. The days spent in the rubber shop laid for me a good foundation for many wonderful friendships. I met men who later became deacons, trustees, officers, and members of my church, the Akron Baptist Temple.

I wonder, are you a Christian? You should be. Christ died to keep your soul out of Hell. Believe in Him and be saved.

7. Wedding Arrangements and Wedding

LOVE IS MENTIONED IN THE BIBLE MANY TIMES. IN JOHN 3:16 God so loved the world that He gave His only begotten Son, that whosoever would believe in Him would never perish but have everlasting life. We are told that God loved us. I am sure of one fact and great truth. The first time that I

met Nell Stokes, I loved her. In my heart and mind she was
different from all other girls. After several months of courtship and telling each other of our love, we began to make
plans for a wedding day. I had to make known to her parents
what my intentions were. So I visited her home and told her
parents of our plans. I asked her father and mother for permission to take their daughter's hand in wedlock. With her
parents' sanction, our real plans were begun. Some people
might take lightly this thing called marriage, but even the
birds build nests and the animals of the field prepare for
their families. I wanted something special for this girl whom
I loved and I was willing to leave her behind in order to go
ahead and get a start for us. Our letters bridged the longing
for each other.

In June, 1926, arrangements were made for a wedding in
the Emanuel Baptist Church in Paducah, Kentucky. We had
spent many happy hours together in this church. I wish that
in this hour in which we live there could be more people
having their courtship days in some good church with
Christian surroundings, rather than in the dance hall, bowling alley, skating rink, or swimming pool.

You will never find anything more closely woven together
than the weddings held at churches, where, with a minister
present, the Bible is read and prayer is offered. Those
weddings are interlocked with the church, which is always
called the bride and the Lord Jesus Christ the groom.

On the 14th day of June, Rev. Ellis met us at the church
altar. The Bible was read and prayer offered. My sister,
who had married Gobel Sullivan, stood with us as we took
our marriage vows. We joined right hands and promised God
in the presence of the minister to be no longer twain but one
in the sight of God. Thus began what has been a happy married life for me and my wife. We spent two weeks visiting
her folks and mine in West Kentucky, and then we returned
to Akron. Before leaving Akron, I had rented an apartment
which would be our first home. God had been good to me,

and I had saved a little money and had purchased a 1925 Ford car. I had carefully planned and saved for my wedding day and our future life together.

Almost from the beginning of our marriage, Nell and I began to talk of a church. We attended church most of the time at the Arlington Baptist Church in Akron. Days went by, and since I had been reared in a strict Methodist and Presbyterian home that believed in sprinkling, Nell and I began to talk also about Baptists, for Nell was Baptist by faith. Nell was saved when she was sixteen. She joined the church and was baptized. At this particular time I had not united with any church. Therefore, I had not been sprinkled or baptized. We slowly and carefully began to search the Bible to see what was found in the Scriptures. As we read and studied together we prayed, and I realized that all saved men and women should unite with some church. We found these words in Romans, the 6th chapter: "Therefore we are buried with him by baptism unto death." As Christ was raised up from the dead by the glory of the Father, even so we should walk in the newness of life. For if we have been planted together in the likeness of His death, we shall also be in the likeness of His resurrection. Thus it was not hard for me to make up my mind, through the Scriptures, that baptism represented a burial.

You might ask me if a young married couple can have happy hours together without worldly pleasures. We found that having each other, loving each other, and caring for each other was enough for us. It was always a happy time when my work hours were over and I went home. We had many enjoyable evenings attending revivals and visiting our Christian friends. We found that in order to grow in God's grace we had to continue to read our Bibles. When a baby is born into the world, it has to grow or something is wrong. Therefore, if we were to grow in God's grace we had to pray together, plan together. We began to own earthly possessions. We wanted to buy our own home.

One night as we sat and talked, I said to her, "Sweetheart, I am sure that I should be a member of some church and be baptized." However, as time went on I asked myself what church would I join. I studied the Bible to see what it taught. I wanted to know my future as a Christian. It was a joy to read the Bible, and since my conversion the months had seemed to fly by. The Bible gave to me a peace within my soul that I could not find anywhere else. I realized the contrast between what I liked now and what I had done when I was an unsaved boy at home. I found that the things I used to love I now despised. I did not care for church until I was converted. The revivals and the old hymns were now a real part of my life and a real part of our life together. As Nell and I studied and prayed together, we grew steadily in God's grace.

We began to invite people to attend church. We invited them to go with us to revival meetings. In our early married life we tried with all our hearts to live right and to do right. We tried to make every day count somehow, someway, to the Glory of God.

We found many people from the South who were not attending church. They had churches at home in the states from which they had come. They went to church at home regularly but, coming to Akron and away from the churches they were used to, they just did not attend anywhere. It was easy for them to drift from the teachings they had known back home. Our Bible taught us that if two would agree together, whatsoever they prayed for and asked, if it be the will of God or in the will of God, it would be granted. When we found people whom we hardly knew how to deal with, we would pray about it. We would visit them and insist that they get started to church.

The Bible teaches that all men need a helpmate, and the helpmate whom I had found had changed my whole life, being, and thinking. I am so glad that the Bible has so much to say about our companions. The Bible tells us that when you find a good woman, she is more precious than jewels, rubies, and gold.

From the day we were married, God has blessed and prospered our life together to give us enough of the financial blessings of this world and a great love for each other. I think the reason you find so many unhappy homes is that these people have never really loved one another the way God planned for a man and wife to love. The Bible says that a man should leave father and mother, houses and land, brother and sister, and cleave to his wife.

I can truthfully say that my marriage unto this day has been a happy one.

8. Birth of Our Son

IN 1927 WE WERE TOLD BY OUR GOOD DOCTOR THAT WE were to become the parents of our firstborn child. Somehow, it seemed from the beginning that I just made plans that the child would be a boy. We planned that if God should give us a son, we would name him Charles Franklin Billington. We called him Charles after Charles Spurgeon, a man about whom I had read much, and Franklin after his own father. Have you planned for a child to come into your home? If so, then you know of what I speak. Every father and mother who read this chapter, I hope, will receive a blessing to their hearts and souls.

As we waited for the child's arrival, we read books on how to care for its physical body, but we had already read the holy book, the Bible. We knew how to take care of a child spiritually. We found in the Book of God where it says to train up a child in the way he should go, and when he is old he will not depart from it. Baby clothes were purchased, and every preparation was made for that wonderful day when a precious child would be given to our home.

Around six o'clock one evening the doctor came and told me I was the father of a fine baby boy weighing almost nine pounds. Joy and peace came to our hearts to know that God had trusted us with a child. We thought of the poem which says that God is just lending us a child of His for just a little while. Here again was another extremely happy moment in our life.

We watched him day by day as he grew. Do you remember the first day your child ever sat alone? Do you remember the first time he pulled up to something and you could say, "Look, he is standing alone"? I remember coming home one night from the factory when the little fellow was old enough to sit all alone. He had grown tired sitting and had crawled underneath the dining-room table, where he had fallen fast asleep. We both looked at him as he lay there and made mention of how innocent and pure a little child is. We realized that day how great our responsibility was. Here he was big enough to sit alone, and later as we watched him make step by step, our hearts were thrilled. One day we heard him say, "Mommy, Daddy." We knew it would not be long until he could be taught words from our Bible. I know that some people say you can be too religious with children, but I have always doubted that. I, myself, was brought up in a strict Christian home, and sometimes I thought they were too strict; but nevertheless, I tried to think of many of those teachings in rearing our son.

As soon as he was old enough, we would have him say his little prayer. When he was eight months old, we made a trip to a Bible conference. We found there other children who were being taught things of the Lord as was ours. We took him to Sunday school when he was cradle-roll age and kept him there in Sunday school year after year, because we believed that if we ever hoped to have a boy of whom we could be proud, the more he knew about God, the more he would know about himself.

We never wanted him to be different from other children in regard to toys and other things in a normal childhood but just to be a regular boy, and yet one who loved God. We learned at a very early age with our baby how the human heart can grow jealous. We thought it was cute when we could teach him to come from one to the other. We would pretend we were arguing, and we would see him turn from one to the other. God has said that He loves us and is a jealous God.

After our son came to live with us, I began to read books, which other men who had sons had written, on the right way to rear a son. I remember that when Charles was about seven months old, a real estate man came by my home and asked us to buy a certain house. The man asked me if the child I had in my arms was my first baby. He said that he had three sons. One of them was in college, one was in business with him, and the other was in high school. He said that some people would tell me that I was giving him too much. Others would tell me that I didn't give him enough. "But," he said, "just be a real, real dad and do for him what you can, giving him if possible what other boys have; for I believe far more boys get into trouble for not having enough than having too much." This man is dead, but I never forgot what he told me.

I remember a story that was told about a man in Chicago who had been a bad drinker. I can thank the Lord I was never a drunkard. Each morning when this man got up, he would go straight to the saloon. He had a son who was four years old. Now, one morning as he went for his usual walk and drink, he heard something close behind him and, turning around, saw his own son following behind him. He said to his son to go back home. There had been a snow that night, and the little boy said, "No, Daddy, you keep on walking, I'm jumping right in your tracks." The man turned and picked up the child. He returned to his home with the child in his arms and worry written on his face.

When breakfast was ready and they sat down to eat, his wife noticed his expression and asked him what was troubling him. He shrugged off her question and left the house with that same worried look on his face. His expression had not changed that evening when he came home. He asked his wife where the child was. She told him the child had grown weary, and she had fed him and put him to bed.

The man looked at his wife and began to tell her what had happened that morning as he started for his morning drink. He told her how the child had said he was jumping in his tracks in the snow, but to the father he might have said in his tracks to the saloon. He vowed to his wife and to God never to drink again.

May I say this to every father who has a son, be he a son one year old, twenty, or thirty: if you have been the kind of a dad that God wanted you to be, your son thinks you are the best man living, the hero of his life. If you have been a pal to him, he would just as soon spend a day with you as with any-one on earth. My son, who is now past thirty, even though I was not a perfect father, would just as soon spend a day with me on a trip, in a hotel room, plane flight, Bible conference, or any place our work takes us, as he would with anyone on earth. I shall never forget the day when the doctor said, "You have a fine son."

We dedicated him to God. We gave him to the Lord and asked God to help us rear him in the right way. Until this hour, we have never seen the day when we were ashamed to say that he was our boy. We have never regretted that God gave us a son. We are deeply grateful and thankful —not boastful, but as the song says, "We're thankful, that's all"—for the boy known as Charles Franklin Billington, who was given to us through God's matchless grace.

9. Sick Baby

HAVE YOU EVER READ IN MATTHEW'S GOSPEL, CHAPTER 18, verses 1-3, where it says: "At the same time came the disciples unto Jesus, saying, Who is the greatest in the kingdom of heaven? And Jesus called a little child unto him, and set him in the midst of them, and said, Verily I say unto you, Except ye be converted, and become as little children, ye shall not enter into the kingdom of heaven."

Unless you have a baby and have had it at least one year, can you know how such a baby can steal your very heart away? It is true that we love our dear wives and husbands as the Bible teaches we should; however, this little one who puts his arms around your neck and tries so hard to talk to you with his eyes as well as his tongue, can fill your heart with an almost overwhelming love. One morning we found our boy was very sick. We immediately took our baby to one doctor who said he would probably be all right in a few days. However, he grew steadily worse. I began, as his father, to search my own heart; for I believed in chastisement and knew in my heart that I was out of the will of the Lord. From the time I had been converted, I knew God had called me to preach the gospel. I believe that God calls men to preach, just as surely as I believe I have a right arm.

I searched the Bible and found that sickness comes to all. I read in the Bible where people were sick and God used it for his glory. We prayed continually for our baby, and we had eight different doctors to check him. No one seemed to find the real answer. Finally one doctor told us that Charles had a serious glandular condition. His neck and underneath his chin were swollen until his neck was nearly as large as an adult's. The doctor recommended surgery. We never thought our boy would have to have surgery at such a young age. We decided to let the doctor operate at 3:00 P.M. that same day.

If ever a father and a mother prayed earnestly for a child, my wife and I did just that. We believed in doctors, for the Bible teaches it. God even tells us that He put the first man to sleep and operated on him while he was asleep. God put Adam to sleep and from his rib gave him his wife, Eve.

We were not religious fanatics or divine healers, but we did believe in Divine Healing. We believe God can and does heal if it is in His will. At three o'clock the nurse came and took our baby, and we watched her take him into surgery. This was his birthday—he was exactly one year old. He could say Mommy and Daddy and chatter a few words. We could hear him cry Mommy and Daddy as she took him down the corridor to the operating room.

While the operation was being done, I searched my own life. It had been quite some time since I was saved. I had searched the Bible and prayed, but I was always trying to find an excuse so that I would never have to preach. I had promised God everything else. I had promised greater offerings to the church. If God would let him live, I would train him in a godly way. All the time there was a sore spot, a bleeding spot, down in my heart. I knew what to do. I was trying to hold that final last thing from God. Beloved, who may read this book, you cannot hold out on God. The Lord Jesus Christ says that if you come to Him and you love father, mother, brother, sister, children, houses, lands, more than Him, then you are not worthy of Him. As I prayed, I knew well in my heart—a deep conviction came over my soul—that I was holding out. Then it was that I said, "Dear Lord, if you will let my dear baby, Chuckie, live, I promise you that, however I can or whenever I can or wherever I can, I'll do my best to preach the gospel of the Lord Jesus Christ." I promised God to tell others how He gave His Son to die on a cross, to be buried and rise again, that through His blood on the cross of Calvary I had been saved. I promised God I would do my best.

After a while the nurse came out and said the operation was a success. The doctor said it was just a matter of time before our baby would be well again. God never breaks a promise. It was almost an unbelievable story how quickly our son began to recover. He had been ill four months.

We asked my father and mother to visit us in Akron. We were glad to have them with us. My father and I spent several hours talking about how he reared me and my brothers and sisters. He told me of a brother, whose name was Charles, who had passed away at the age of eight months. When my father told of my brother dying when he was only eight months old, it seemed that the cold hands of death actually took hold of my heart.

My father told me that while this young child lay sick he had prayed to God that if this child could live and be a blessing to his parents and other brothers and sisters, if he could grow up to be the kind of man whom anyone would be proud of, then let him live. If not, Lord, thy will be done. My father said that he watched as the child's breath grew shorter. My father and mother had surrendered their will to God. Dad said that at first it was hard to understand. He said that before, when people talked to him about Heaven, he had thought of Heaven as being a million miles away. Now that his boy was gone and was buried in the old country graveyard, it seemed to him that Heaven moved in right next door. My father said that when he thought of Heaven, he thought of his parents, his baby, and most of all of Jesus, who made possible this meeting place for all those who believe.

I had made more than a promise to God, for sometimes a promise is broken. I had made a covenant. That was in the year 1928. I had studied before, but now I studied with a purpose. I made up my mind to study and prepare myself. My books were the King James Version of the Holy Bible, Webster's Dictionary, and the Cruden Concordance, and my study was the kitchen of our home. There in the kitchen I studied, planned, and prayed to prepare myself for the covenant that I had made. I never told my wife or my mother, but I feverishly studied to know more about the heart and mind of God, knowing that God would find a way when I was ready. You will see in the chapters to come how God led me a step at a time as I pondered and labored over His Word.

10. God Calls Preachers

ACCORDING TO THE BIBLE IN GALATIANS, CHAPTER 1, Paul was called of God to preach the gospel. In the Book of Exodus in the Old Testament, God called Moses to go back to his people and preach deliverance. I am sure that God called me to preach the gospel. I would like to read the account of Paul's call from the word of God. "Paul, an apostle, (not of men, neither by man, but by Jesus Christ, and God the Father, who raised him from the dead;) and all the brethren which are with me, unto the churches of Galatia: Grace be to you and peace from God the Father, and from our Lord Jesus Christ, who gave himself for our sins, that he might deliver us from this present evil world, according to the will of God and our Father: to whom be glory for ever and ever. Amen. I marvel that ye are so soon removed from him that called you into the grace of Christ unto another gospel: which is not another; but there be some that trouble you, and would pervert the gospel of Christ. But though we, or an angel from heaven, preach any other gospel unto you than that which we have preached unto you, let him be accursed. As we said before, so say I now again, If any man preach any other gospel unto you than that ye have received, let him be accursed. For do I now persuade men, or God? or do I seek to please men? for if I yet pleased men, I should not be the servant of Christ. But I certify you, brethren, that the gospel which was preached of me is not after man. For I neither received it of man, neither was I taught it, but by the revelation of Jesus Christ. For ye have heard of my conversation in time past in the Jews' religion, how that beyond measure I persecuted the church of God, and wasted it: and profited in the Jews' religion above many my equals in mine own nation, being more exceedingly zealous of the traditions of my fathers. But when it pleased God, who separated me from my mother's womb, and called me by his grace, to reveal his Son in me, that I might preach him among the heathen; immediately I conferred not with flesh and blood: neither went I up to Jerusalem to them which were apostles before me; but I went into Arabia, and returned again unto Damascus. Then after three years I went up to Jerusalem to see Peter, and abode with him fifteen days. But other of the apostles saw I none, save James the Lord's brother. Now the things which I write unto you, behold, before God, I lie not."

When I was called to preach the gospel, I did not confer with flesh and blood. I did not go to a Bible school or seminary or a place where men gather. This was not because I did not want to, or feel the need of it, or know the schools are necessary; circumstances did not permit me to do those things. I was married and had a son. Financially, I was unable to attend a school. I was compelled to study at home or not study at all. My second best was to borrow books which told me the life stories of great preachers such as John Wesley, Charles Spurgeon, and many others. Needless to say, reading about these great men of God and how they prayed and studied, I was encouraged and inspired.

There were no ministers in the city of Akron to whom I

was close enough to go and talk with. I began at the beginning of my Bible in Genesis and found God to be the fourth word. I had studied my Bible before but now with more zeal and purpose; and for the next two years I labored every available moment over the Word of God. There were Bible dictionaries, histories of both the Old and New Testaments, commentaries, and textbooks—all were my constant companions as I prepared myself for what God had planned for me.

By the end of the first year I was able to purchase a number of helpful books. The Bible says that Daniel learned from books. The prophets gave knowledge to Daniel. Like Daniel, I learned from my predecessors. I believe that if God calls a man to preach and if he will do two things—pray and put his trust in God and then study (for God tells us in II Timothy to study to show ourselves a workman approved unto God that needeth not to be ashamed, rightly dividing the word of truth)—then God will bless his efforts. What I learned, I learned by conferring with the Lord Jesus Christ. You might ask these questions: Can a man really know the Lord Jesus Christ? Can a man talk to Christ? Will Jesus answer you? To all of these questions I can say yes. Jesus said to His disciples that He was going away but He would not leave them comfortless; He would send the Holy Spirit into their lives to teach them all things. The Holy Spirit would guide them to all truth, whatsoever they might ask of Him. Another Scripture says that if any man lack wisdom, let him ask God, who giveth in abundance. Jesus will not answer your questions in an audible voice, but as you pray and are sincere, you can feel His presence; and the answer will be revealed to you in God's time.

The days ahead were Bible-searching days and searching days of my own soul. I asked myself what price would I be willing to pay for the gospel. Paul declared that when he was separated from his mother's womb and called to preach the gospel he conferred not with flesh and blood but went to the Arabian deserts. My study was my home, and it was not uncommon to find me all alone in the early hours of the morning studying the books of knowledge. While my dear wife and son slept, I studied and prayed. I cherish those moments, for I felt God's presence all around me, and His love filled my heart and thrilled my soul.

I promised myself that I would tell no one, not even my dear wife or mother, that I was going to preach. I wished to wait until I felt in my heart that when I preached my first sermon I would be sufficient in the Lord, not in man. I had no way of knowing who would hear me preach my first sermon, but I asked God that I would not have to take someone's pulpit to preach; that I would not have to ask another preacher to let me preach, for they would not know if I was qualified in the ministry. I promised God to study and trust in Him and get ready so that if the chance came, with God's help, I would do the very best I knew how.

My first work for the Lord began with a Sunday-school class of boys. I would go to the sandlot ball fields and invite boys into my class. The class had various ages. At the same time I was ushering at the Furnace Street Mission, where Rev. Bill Denton was the superintendent. When I was not at these duties, I prepared messages and prayed that I would see men changed and souls saved because of my messages. God calls men to preach for two reasons: God expects them to win the lost for Christ and to feed the sheep. There are many other duties which a pastor is expected to do, like visit the sick, bury the dead, perform marriages; but foremost and most important is winning the lost and keeping them in the fold.

Up until now I was content to study and prepare myself, but the time came when I longed for someone to let me preach. Even though I dreaded the first time, the urge was strong in my soul for my chance to tell of Christ. I wanted to tell others from a public platform what He had done for me and could do for them.

People used to think my wife and I were foolish not to attend the movie theaters, but God had told me to live a separated life and to come out from among the unsaved. God did not say not to associate with the unsaved, but when your companion wants to do a thing that you feel is unpleasing to God, simply say as a Christian, as kindly as you know how, I cannot do that. Whenever we were asked why we could not do certain things, we were given the best opportunity to witness for Christ.

God called me to preach the gospel, but God calls people to be Sunday-school teachers, choir members, for visitation work. Should God call you for these things, would you be willing to serve Him? Should God call you to the missionary field, would you go where God wants you to go? Would you do what God wants you to do?

11. My First Sermon

MY FIRST MESSAGE WAS PREACHED THE FIRST WEEK IN October, 1930, at a rescue mission known as the Furnace Street Mission. I was an usher at the mission, and on Sunday I taught a Sunday-school class at the Arlington Street Baptist Church. Rev. Bill Denton, who was in charge of the mission, told me one Wednesday night that I would have to preach that night.

Immediately I thought of my covenant with God. I had studied many sermons, and I tried to determine what would be best to use for my very first sermon. Rev. Denton had given me his Bible, and I went into his office and prayed. The mission was filled to its capacity, waiting to hear Rev.

Denton preach. Rev. Denton told the people that, since he was too hoarse to preach, he had asked one of the ushers of the mission to take his place.

I was introduced, and I realized this was different from standing before my class of boys on Sunday. I was very nervous and asked that we pray. I prayed my own prayer. It was not memorized or read from a paper but created in my heart. My Scripture was from the 15th chapter of Luke, beginning with the 11th verse: "And he said, A certain man had two sons: and the younger of them said to his father, Father, give me the portion of goods that falleth to me. And he divided unto them his living. And not many days after the younger son gathered all together, and took his journey into a far country, and there wasted his substance with riotous living."

I tried my best to talk as if I were talking to one man. Many newspapermen, preacher friends, scholars, theologians, and men from every walk of life have said to me that my ministry is different. That night I tried to point out what sin would do to a human life, what the results would be of a life that followed in sin. I used my own life, pointing out that I had left home when I was only seventeen. At least half of the crowd were men. They were gathered there from the southern states mostly; however, there were people there from all sections of the country, for the mission was city-wide.

They were told about the ninety-nine sheep that came home and the one that went astray. The shepherd left the ninety-nine to seek the one that was lost and, finding it, brought it home rejoicing. God likens you to a sheep. Sheep are easily led astray and are perhaps the most ignorant of all animals at finding their way home to the sheepfold at night.

In this same chapter, Jesus told of a man who had two sons. One was the sinful type, who simply said he would go his own way. But he found no joy in worldly pleasures and realized if he were ever to find peace, he would have to go home and seek forgiveness. This story tells us that all of us must of necessity turn our faces away from sin and return to God, if we ever expect to be saved.

That young man, filled with despair, turned and went to his father's house. He said to himself that he had wasted his father's goods and his own. He would say to his father that he had sinned against Heaven and before him, and was not worthy to be called his son but would ask to be one of the servants.

This story has a spiritual application, for you too need to turn and go home. You need to turn your face toward God and away from sin and by your own will go home. There is no way home except through repentance. The Bible teaches that all, everyone, has sinned and come short of the glory of God. There was only one ever born on this earth who had no sin, and that was our Lord Jesus Christ. There is only one who can forgive your sins. There is only one who can bring salvation, and that one is Jesus. Everyone who is born into this world and lives to be old enough to be convicted of their sins, has sinned. I believe that many fine boys and girls have been saved at a very early age because they were taught how to be saved, and knew well the power and penalty of sin, through reading and studying their Bibles. These boys and girls were reared under the constant influence of Christian teachings.

This being my first message, I was nervous for at least the first twelve minutes; and then a peace that only God can give came over my soul, and I actually felt that I was in the presence of God. I realized I was fulfilling a covenant that I had made with God. I had promised God that when the time came that I was asked to preach, I would, with His help, do my very best. That night as I preached I found the powers and blessings of the Holy Spirit. Looking into the sea of faces, I told them of a Saviour's love. My sermon told of the price of sin and the penalty of sin. God gave me the ability to reason, as I preached to the people, as if I had been preaching for many years. Scriptures came to my mind, and I quoted them like a seasoned veteran.

As I neared the end of my sermon, I began to ask them if they were prodigal sons or daughters. I asked them if they had left their spiritual home. I asked them if they were concerned about their souls. Were they away from God? Did they realize that one day everyone must meet God?

The hush of God came over the crowd, and the organist began playing, "I'm tired of sin and straying, Lord. Now I'm coming home. The path of sin too long I've trod, now I'm coming home." I wish I could instill in your mind the great peace and joy that can come to a soul who trusts in God. Especially after you are saved and know Jesus as a personal Saviour will you be aware of this wonderful peace.

When I asked the people gathered there to bow their heads, several people lifted their hands for prayer, knowing they were unsaved. Within four minutes after everyone stood and began singing, three fine men walked out into the aisle and came forward to accept Jesus as their Saviour. This was my first sermon and I was happy, for Heaven had smiled upon it. My soul was thrilled to know that God had used me to win these souls for Christ.

As you read this, you can know my Saviour just as they did. If you will only call upon His name, you shall be saved.

12. Back Home to Preach

I SAY WITH PAUL OF OLD, AS IN THE 9TH AND 10TH chapters of Romans: The truth is in Christ and I lie not, my conscience also bearing me witness in the Holy Ghost that

I have great heaviness and continuous sorrow in my heart. For I could wish myself accursed from Christ for my brethren, my kinsmen according to the flesh. Brethren, my heart's desire and prayer to God for Israel is that they might be saved, for I bear them record that they have a zeal of God, but not according to knowledge. For they, being ignorant of God's righteousness and going about to establish their own righteousness, have not submitted themselves unto the righteousness of God. For Christ is the end to the law of righteousness to everyone that believeth.

In the years before I became a Christian, while watching preachers and noticing other people and reading many books about heathen lands, I began to see that there is a difference between a religious person and a Christian. Religion is man's trying to do something for God which has been practiced by all nations, including the heathen in the jungle. Christianity is accepting the finished work of Calvary.

A rabbi on the road to Damascus was struck down, and our Bible tells us that he was also made blind. The rabbi cried for mercy and was told to go on into the city, where he would be told what to do. I have often wondered and wished that I might sit down at the feet of Jesus and ask Him why He did not tell Paul what to do then and there. Through the years I have answered this question, seeing that, though God could have given His own message, He would rather work through a willing servant. It is only logical that a doctor would have more opportunity to talk to doctors, since he is associated daily with men in his field; and the same is true of other professions. In other words, the people who know you are the ones whom you, more than likely, will be able to win for God.

I decided to go home to West Kentucky, but when I asked several preachers there for a church to preach in, they said they knew me only as the boy who had left there. They said they knew nothing of my ability as a preacher, and therefore I was denied a church. My two brothers-in-law, Roscoe

Towery and Herman Williams, said they would build a brush arbor where I could hold a service. I told them I would be glad to preach anywhere. On a sloping hillside a spot was cleared. It was perfect for people to be able to see over each other, since the spot was sloping. There was no piano or song leader. I only had seventy-five old songbooks. To my utter surprise—to the entire community's surprise—more than five hundred people attended on the first night. The people came in automobiles, wagons, buggies, and on horseback. Friends of my family heard that I was going to preach, and some of them came over a hundred miles to the service.

After I had led the song service, I laid down my songbook, picked up my Bible, and preached. Like Paul, I had a desire for my own people to know of my Saviour and His love. Many of my relatives and friends whom I had known as a young child came to that meeting.

I preached the first night on the subject, "What will you do with Jesus which is called Christ?" My message told them of my salvation. The second night the crowd was so large that the brush arbor had to be enlarged. They made more plank seats so that the ladies, at least, could all be seated. Before the meeting closed, the brush arbor had to be enlarged for the third time, and we found that we could not secure enough kerosene lanterns to light the area. Some of the ladies brought large lamps and lit them so that we would have light. Folks remarked about lamps burning through an entire service, with never a wind strong enough to blow out even one.

The first three people saved in that meeting were Stella Wilkinson, Ruth Wilkinson, and Lillie Compton. Until this day, I rejoice to tell you, they still are Christian ladies living for God. One of them is a Sunday-school teacher working in the church. They proved to be true and honest converts for Jesus Christ.

I had only a week off from my job at Goodyear Tire and Rubber Company, and I had to be back on the job. However, each time my shift was over at Goodyear, I would preach wherever and whenever I could. From 1930 to 1932 I traveled to Youngstown, about fifty miles from Akron, and to Dover, Canton, and Alliance, and did it not for material gain—for there was no pay—but because I loved to preach the gospel. In those two years, I believe I could be safe in saying, I preached about three hundred times for absolutely no pay or financial aid. We kept no record of the number of people who were saved, but the privilege was mine to see many souls won for Christ.

I had only one desire in life and that was to see people saved. I have been called a radical and overzealous in getting people to believe. Of course, the ministers who refused to let me preach in their pulpits had no way of knowing my heart, and I do not blame them for refusing me, for a pastor is a shepherd over his flock and must guard his sheep and those left in his trust. God had His hand in the brush arbor, and because of His blessings the meeting was a success. Herman Williams has gone to be with the Lord. He was saved and trusted the Lord; but when he died there was no time to prepare to meet God. That is why we try to warn you, for as he sat there in his chair, he suddenly dropped his head and was gone. Thanks to God, he was ready. Don't put off trusting in God. You may not have time. What a foolish thing to live all your life wasted! Perhaps you, like the thief on the cross, will accept just in time, but how empty your hands will be as you enter Heaven's gates. You might have had brothers or sisters, loved ones or friends, trust in Jesus because you showed them the way. By your careless life and saying "I will wait" you have robbed yourself of the greatest joy of winning someone for Christ and, what is even more heartbreaking, you might see this soul lost for all eternity.

It was a great privilege for me to go back home and have the opportunity to help others. It was a common thing to see people there going to an altar from the time they were young children until they were adults and hear them say they were still not saved. They were convicted of their sins, but no one seemed to be able to take the Word of God and show them how they could know they were saved. About seventy-five to eighty persons accepted Christ during my first revival meeting, and I dealt with them, eager that they would not doubt their salvation.

The people who were converted during that meeting joined churches throughout that area and were baptized in the big Tennessee River. Eight different ministers and deacon boards of that town came to me and asked if I could come to their churches and preach. During that meeting I learned that a Dr. T. J. Hensley, who had a great influence in the community, had paid me a great compliment: he had sent word far and wide for people to come hear the "Young Billy Sunday." Having read about Billy Sunday and how greatly God had used him, I was very happy and very humble.

You too can be saved like those who knelt in the old brush arbor. You too can get up with a smile on your face, with a peace in your heart that is past understanding. Your brush arbor can be in your living room, your bedroom—anywhere is all right with God as long as your heart is sincere. Believe in Christ, trust Him, and He will forgive your sins.

13. Judgment Seat Becomes Mercy Seat

PLACE: MURRAY COURTHOUSE, CALLOWAY COUNTY, MURRAY, KENTUCKY

"And Jesus stood before the governor: and the governor asked him, saying, Art thou the King of the Jews? And Jesus said unto him, Thou sayest. . . . When he was set down on the judgment seat, his wife sent unto him, saying, Have thou nothing to do with that just man: for I have suffered many things this day in a dream because of him. But the chief priests and elders persuaded the multitude that they should ask Barabbas, and destroy Jesus. The governor answered and said unto them, Whether of the twain will ye that I release unto you? They said, Barabbas. Pilate saith unto them, What shall I do then with Jesus which is called Christ? They all say unto him, Let him be crucified." Matthew 27: 11-23.

I went back to my home county and sat down to talk with the county court judge. I asked permission to use the court-house, which is called the court square, like many of the courthouses built through the Southland. The judge told me that, since he had known my father very well and since it was a public place, if I wished to use the courthouse to preach the gospel, he would grant my request. There was a time in August when there was no court in session. We installed speakers from the public-address system on all four sides of the courthouse. Mr. Ed Adams, a good friend of my family and me, who was with the State Police, arranged together with the city police that we might use the courthouse. After the stores closed that day, these men did not allow anyone to park in the court square unless they were coming to the church services. In this way they were able to handle the traffic more efficiently. The courtyard was completely filled.

I reasoned that night in the services with the people whom I loved on just who Pontius Pilate was. The Scriptures that I used were those that are written above. I pointed out that Pilate was the supreme governor over the area of Jerusalem. Herod was over the section of Galilee where Jesus preached and which was more home to Jesus, perhaps, than any other place. It had not dawned upon me that I was sitting at the seat of judgment where court convened and where, after the trials, judgment was declared.

People from at least five counties had come to hear my message. My message to them was on the mercy and love of Christ. However, I also told them that the wages of sin was death. Death, itself, had been pronounced upon all men, inasmuch as all men had sinned and come short of the glory of God. As I continued to reason with the people concerning the judgment to come without Christ, noticing their genuine interest as the Scriptures were read, I realized, as did they, that God had made the judgment and had pronounced it. God said in Romans 6:23 that the wages of sin is death, but the gift of God is eternal life through Jesus Christ our Lord.

I found out later that there were at least three men in the congregation who had been sentenced, from the very place where I preached, for taking someone's life. They had served time for their crime.

Jesus was brought before Pilate, and after examining him, Pilate said to the crowd, "I find no fault in him." However, the jealous crowd, namely, the chief priests and rabbis, demanded that Jesus be put to death and Barabbas, the sinner, go free. I told the people that Barabbas represented mankind, for we have sinned as had Barabbas. Barabbas was waiting in his cell for judgment. He was one of three noted criminals waiting for trial. The fourth man waiting for trial was the Son of God, Jesus Christ of Calvary. Jesus, branded as a criminal, had left Heaven's glory to die for Barabbas and all mankind that they might be set free. The Jewish boys and girls had seen the lambs brought and the blood of these lambs spread on the doorposts, making a perfect cross. Any Jewish child knew what was meant by the Lamb of God or anything connected with a sacrificial lamb. Jesus was brought early in the morning from the Garden of Gethsemane and had already had one unfair trial. The Romans were in charge of the civil courts and had all authority. Therefore, if Jesus was to be condemned to death, it must come from the Romans. Pilate, wishing to be rid of Jesus, since he could find no wrong in Him, sent Jesus to Herod, who was over the Jews.

Herod's soldiers took Jesus' seamless white robe from Him and put upon Him a scarlet robe. To further mock the Lord, a crown of thorns was placed cruelly upon His head. After they had had their sport, Jesus once again was sent before Pilate. Pilate had thought that when he sent Jesus away he was through with Him. Pilate tried to appease the wicked people and the high priest by reminding them of a custom whereby a prisoner was released each year to the Jews and set free to honor their Passover day. He told them of Barabbas and his wickedness and at the same time compared Jesus' apparent innocence to Barabbas' wickedness. Pilate thought surely they would see that Jesus deserved to be freed. When Pilate asked the angry mob whom they would have released, to his sorrow and disappointment, they cried, "Release Barabbas." Barabbas went free and Jesus took his place to die on the cross. As Barabbas went free because Christ died, you too can be set free. Anyone who accepts Jesus, admitting to his own sins, can be set free through Jesus Christ.

I asked the people who were there if they would put themselves in the place of Barabbas, deserving to die for his many sins. I told them that this court was the mercy seat of God and asked them to come forward and accept Jesus. One man came and said, "Everyone here knows that I am a murderer, for I was sentenced for that crime in this very court." He said that he wanted God's mercy. Because that man came, we saw many others accept the Lord. A great host of men and women were saved that night. Thus the judgment seat became a mercy seat.

14. A Car and a Boy

"AND HE SPAKE A PARABLE UNTO THEM TO THIS END, that men ought always to pray, and not to faint; saying, There was in a city a judge, which feared not God, neither regarded man: and there was a widow in that city; and she came unto him, saying, Avenge me of mine adversary. And he would not for a while: but afterward he said within himself, Though I fear not God, nor regard man; yet because this widow troubleth me, I will avenge her, lest by her continual coming she weary me. And the Lord said, Hear what the unjust judge saith. And shall not God avenge his own elect, which cry day and night unto him, though he bear long with them? I tell you that he will avenge them speedily. Nevertheless, when the Son of man cometh, shall he find faith on the earth?" Luke 18:1-8.

The Bible teaches us plainly that unsaved people do not understand the Scriptures, for they are spiritually discerned. If you can remember the days of the thirties, you will remember them as being hard times and depression days. I well remember that my work was very slow. Money was very scarce, and we carefully distributed the little money we had to make ends meet. It was amazing how far a dollar was expected to stretch and over how wide a variety of bills. Then it was that my son, nearly four years old, taught me the Scripture that men ought always to pray and not to faint.

It was nearing Christmastime. Following the custom of most people in our city, my wife and I took our son to the big toy department of one of the local stores. We came to a floor where they had little cars which were large enough for a child to get in and pedal around. One of the clerks whom we knew put our son in one of the little cars. I'll never forget my son's face as he took hold of the wheel and pushed the little horn button. He would turn the wheel and pretend he was going to speed. His joy was so great that when I removed him from the car he cried as if his heart would break. My wife and I thought if we could get his attention on other toys, he would soon forget. We began looking at the other toys and, turning around to call my son's attention to something I thought he would like, I found that he was not with us. The entire floor was being used to display toys for Christmas, and the crowd was tremendous. We realized our son was lost, and you cannot know the terror that gripped my heart unless you have had a small child lost.

We frantically searched about us, but we had to cover two more departments on that same floor. Suddenly, it came to me where our son could be. I told my wife we would return to the little car. When we reached the spot, we saw a small yellow-haired boy having the time of his life pedaling the car here and there. When he saw us, he began to plead with us not to take the car away from him. He asked me if he left it, would Santa bring him one just like it. My wife and I were embarrassed as we loosened his grip on the steering wheel and took him from the car. We just did not have the money for the car, and other people around us, probably sensing this, seemed to offer us sympathy through the looks on their faces.

Chuckie continued to plead as I carried him to our car. I learned from him what it meant to plead to God. The Scripture that told me not to faint but to pray became real to me then. I remembered the story of the widow who went back day after day begging. There was no agency, organization, or funds to aid this widowed lady, and poverty was great in the land.

I placed my son in the car with his mother and went back into the store. My pocket contained $1.19. I paid the one dollar down for the little car and made arrangements to pay so much for it each week. We needed that dollar for groceries and other things of far more value to our livelihood than the little car. I just simply bought this car for my son who pleaded for it. Out of a heart of love, I was willing to sacrifice the last dollar I had. It was not long until Christmas. On Christmas Eve my wife, son, and I read the Christmas story and had our prayer. When Chuckie prayed his prayer, he asked God for the car.

Like all parents who love their children, we were as anxious for the morning as was our son. Chuckie, in his pajamas, came bounding out of his bed and ran to the living room where the Christmas tree was. With a cry of delight, he climbed into the little car and began making the rounds of the living room with actual tears of joy streaming down his cheeks. Excitedly he pushed the little horn button; but after a while he stopped and came over to me and his mother. He put his arms around us and told us he had known we would get it for him. Our son's joy, delight, and thrill were no greater than ours. This must be the way Jesus feels when we pray, plead, and then, having our prayers answered, go to Him in thanksgiving.

Perhaps you have a problem in your heart that no one understands. You might have no one who cares enough for you to try to understand. Perhaps you are all alone with no one to share your burden. Will you learn to pray? Will you learn the power of prayer? Do like the little boy and faint not, but keep on pleading and going back to God for help. Never give up. Just be sure that what you ask for will glorify God. You will find that God is real. Christ was so real that He could fall asleep in a boat; so real that He could eat fish with His disciples, still the tempest; so real that the nails which were driven into His hands hurt Him until He cried out. Jesus wants to answer your prayer; all He asks is that you love Him, honor Him. I have found my God to be real through my many answered prayers. My prayer to God is that in reading this chapter you will find that God can be real.

15. House-to-House Visitation

WHILE SITTING AND STUDYING MY BIBLE ONE NIGHT, I read this verse of Scripture found in Acts 5:42: "And daily in the temple, and in every house, they ceased not to teach and preach Jesus Christ." I was still working at the rubber shop, and I had many friends who were not saved. It was easy for them to swear and take God's name in vain. They behaved in an ungodly way most of the time. I did not want to act as if I were better than they, for I was what I was only through the grace of God. One morning I said to my dear wife that I had decided to visit the homes of unsaved friends and invite them to church. If they would permit me, I would take my Bible and try to win them for Christ right in their own homes. My wife and I agreed that we would begin making home calls.

One Sunday morning I decided to go see a man whom I worked with daily. All the way over to his home, it seemed that all the powers of Hell were being let loose on me. The powers of Hell told me I was a fool, for this man was hard and tough, even feared by some. Few ever dared to talk to this man about anything he did, especially about his soul or his way of living.

It was early, and I wanted to get back home to take my family to Sunday school in time. I rang the doorbell; this man and his family were still in bed. I wanted to get him to go with me to the mission, where Jesus was lifted up and where the opportunity was always given for lost men to find God. Jake came to the door and expressed great surprise at finding me there at that hour. I told him that in reading my Bible the night before I had become impressed with the fact that as a Christian I should go from house to house seeking the lost for Christ. I told him I did not like to embarrass him in the shop, but because I loved his soul and wanted him saved I had come that morning to talk to him about Jesus. I stood there and watched the tears come to his eyes, and he invited me in and offered me a seat. Jake called to his wife, Jackie, and asked her to come and meet a friend of his. To my surprise and utter joy, he told his wife he wanted her to meet a Christian boy with whom he worked and a boy whom he loved. His wife seemed puzzled because I had come over to ask them to go to church. She asked me why, and I explained it to her this way: "If I were going on a wonderful trip with a friend and they had invited me with all expenses paid and had said that I might take as many friends with me as I liked; if I thought the trip was worth my while and a trip to be enjoyed, would I not be selfish if I did not take my friends? Your husband and I work at the same table, and he is my friend. I sincerely believe that one day when my life is over I shall take a trip to Heaven, and I want Jake to go with me." Then I saw the tears come into her eyes. She said that she and her husband had lived in Akron for many years, and I was the first person who had ever come to their home to invite them to church. She had gone to church back home in another state and had enjoyed it, but they began to associate with other people who did not attend church. She began to tell how they had spent their time with their friends, and after she had talked awhile, she called in Jake's sister, who was there with them.

As I talked to all three I began to notice Jake becoming concerned. Jake told me he wanted to be a Christian but he just did not understand what he must do. The Scriptures told him, I said, those that are burdened and heavily laden will find rest if they come to Jesus. Jesus said, Take my yoke upon you and learn of me; I am meek and lowly in heart and ye shall find rest unto your souls. My yoke is easy and my burden is light. Jake still did not understand. I turned in my Bible to Matthew 10:32, which says: "Whosoever therefore shall confess me before men, him will I confess also before my Father which is in heaven."

Jake told me he did not believe that he had to confess his sins to any man. I explained that the Scriptures meant that he must confess them to Christ and Him alone. I explained to him that if he went to church that morning and wished to be a Christian, he would go forward. In this way he would be making a public confession before men, not to men. He told me he did not even know how to pray. I told him I had to learn to pray; and, like a child that has to be taught to walk and talk, so must a child of God be helped by those who are older in Christ.

Before I left there that morning I had the promise of Jake, his wife, and sister to meet me in front of the mission. My heart sang with joy as I told my wife of the call. We had to hurry to get to church. I arrived before Jake and watched eagerly for his car to drive up, and finally it came, with all three coming to church as they had promised.

My wife and I met them, and all of us sat together. When the invitation was given, I told Jake that I would go with him to the altar if he would just go. Not only Jake but his wife and sister went too. They prayed the sinner's prayer: Lord, save me and forgive my sins. I dealt with Jake while my wife dealt with the wife and sister. We saw them stand to their feet with million-dollar smiles on their faces. They were saved for all eternity.

Jake became one of my most staunch helpers in the factory. In just a few weeks he was as brave as a lion for Christ's sake. The other men kidded him and tried to get him to curse. They tried to tell him smutty stories, but he would just walk away. His wife became a very loyal church worker, and his sister returned to her home in another state, where she began working for the Lord.

I spent the year 1931 going from house to house, visiting and asking people to come to church. Every available hour that I could find was spent in visitation. Whenever I got the opportunity to preach somewhere, my foreman, Thomas McBrayer, would make it possible for me to change shifts so that I might go. I even preached as far away as Parkersburg, West Virginia, driving three hours down and three hours back and still not being late for my shift of work. My foreman was a wonderful man, and because of him I was permitted to preach even more.

Won't you make a call for Jesus and go home rejoicing? If you make that home call, you may win a soul for Jesus. Won't you at least try?

16. Watch Jesus Win

IN FEBRUARY, 1932, WE HAD A BROADCASTING STATION in the city of Akron with the call letters WJW. I went to the president of the station and told him of my desire to have a broadcast time on his station to preach the gospel. The president asked me about myself and the church backing me. I told him that I was a Christian, and my desire in life was to point others to Christ. As far as a certain church backing me, I had none. He wanted to know how I expected to pay for the broadcasts. I told him that I worked at the Goodyear Tire and Rubber Company and would pay the fee from my own wages. He told me it was usually the policy to have backing, and a religious program, especially, should have a church back of it.

The president questioned me about my faith and asked me to tell him just what the nature of my programs would be. I took my Bible and began to tell him what Jesus meant to me and what He would do for others if they would only believe.

After the president was convinced of my sincerity and that the program would be acceptable, he told me I might have the time; but since I had no church to back me, each broadcast would have to be paid for in cash one week in advance. There was time available on Sunday at 5:00 P.M. Since there was no other religious program near that time, I felt it would be a good time. Perhaps more people would tune in to listen. As we talked, the president made the remark that I seemed to have a lot of confidence in my preaching. To this I said, "No, but I do have a lot of confidence in the Christ whom I serve, the Bible that I read, and the God in whom I believe."

A thirteen-week contract was given to me, and the cost was $7.50 per week. On the second Sunday in February was my first broadcast. A male quartet went on with me, and we had fifteen minutes. When I had been introduced that first time, I began by telling them they were listening to a station whose call letters, WJW, had a special meaning for me: WJW meant to me WATCH JESUS WIN. They introduced me as the Southern Evangelist, because I had no church. I remember that I used the first chapter of Revelation. This Scripture tells us to publish, study, and go out and tell others about Jesus. It also tells of the Blood of Christ saving us and of Christ's return. The quartet opened and closed the program. While the program was in session, the station received four phone calls inquiring about it.

Some of the Scriptures which I read were: "Blessed is he that readeth, and they that hear the words of this prophecy, and keep those things which are written therein: for the time is at hand. . . . And from Jesus Christ, who is the faithful witness, and the first begotten of the dead, and the prince of the kings of the earth. Unto him that loved us, and washed us from our sins in his own blood, and hath made us kings and priests unto God and his Father; to him be glory and dominion for ever and ever. . . . Behold, he cometh with clouds. . . ."

One of the calls was from an elderly Methodist preacher. He said that in the last twenty-five years he had not heard so plain a Bible message. He asked me to come and preach in his church, about twenty miles from Akron.

As always, in the message that night on the broadcast I told of a Saviour's love and how anyone could be saved. I warned those listening that, according to God's word, each living human being was responsible for his own sins. Each one of us would someday have to stand before God. I reasoned with them to believe on Christ and be saved. When I came to the thought, "Behold, he cometh with clouds," I told the people that Jesus would come back one day. Jesus had been to the cradle and to the cross, but He had said that He would come again. Not many people in those days preached the second coming of Jesus. Many were alarmed, and some laughed and mocked; but nevertheless, the following week we received mail from many asking that we pray for them. I told the people listening that I was working in a factory and attending a Baptist church, and also working in a rescue mission. Within that week I had more requests for calls than I could have made in a month as a pastor with no factory work to be done.

I pondered over the calls and tried to choose those which I thought were the most urgent. I sincerely believe the reason that so many churches do not grow today is that the pastor has become a playboy—sailing, golfing, bowling—instead of making calls on his flock concerning their souls.

There is never any reward offered for lost time, and every hour a pastor loses in winning the lost is gone forever. The Bible is true, and a Christian has no time to waste. The Bible teaches me that I travel this way just one time, and what I do for Christ is the only thing that counts or lasts.

The broadcast gave me the opportunity I desired to get into the homes with the Word of God and songs inspired of God. The quartet who sang for me worked at the factory, and they too expected no pay. The first week $4.00 were sent in;

however, we had not asked for any money to be sent. Weeks went by swiftly, and some weeks enough money came to completely pay for the broadcast.

Suddenly it became a great burden to me to realize that it was almost impossible for me to make all the calls that were sent to me. I asked Christians in the factory, men at the mission, and members at the church where I attended to help me make the calls. We all realized we were pleading with souls faced with eternity, facing God as their Saviour or judge. We pleaded that while they were in their right mind, in the capacity to think and reason, they make their decision for Christ.

When I found a man who was unsaved, I always thought of two certain chapters in the Bible as the greatest account of how to be saved: the 10th chapter of Romans and the 3rd chapter of John.

WJW (WATCH JESUS WIN) became a slogan in the city of Akron. There were very few church programs on the air in 1932, and ours became one of the leaders in popular programs. This proved to me once again that Jesus will always win. If you ask Jesus to save you, He will conquer Satan. If you ask that He forgive your sins, He will remove them and cleanse you through His precious blood. The Scriptures plainly say, "And from Jesus Christ, who is the faithful witness, and the first begotten of the dead, and the prince of the kings of the earth, Unto Him that loved us, and washed us from our sins in his own blood..." The blood of Jesus Christ, God's Son, will cleanse you from all your sin. Believe in Christ and be saved.

17. Out of Work

I WOULD LIKE TO READ FROM PSALM 37, WHERE IT SAYS: "The steps of a good man are ordered by the Lord: and he delighteth in his way. Though he fall, he shall not be utterly cast down: for the Lord upholdeth him with his hand. I have been young, and now am old; yet have I not seen the righteous forsaken, nor his seed begging bread. He is ever merciful, and lendeth; and his seed is blessed. Depart from evil, and do good; and dwell for evermore. For the Lord loveth judgment, and forsaketh not his saints; they are preserved for ever: but the seed of the wicked shall be cut off."

When I was laid off from my job at the factory, this meant several things. Many of my friends were laid off too, and some of them went to work on WPA jobs. However, many of my friends were completely out of work and had no way in which to live. To find consolation in the Lord, I read the Scriptures where David said, "I have been young, and now am old; yet have I not seen the righteous forsaken, nor his seed begging bread." We prayed that God would help us and our friends. Unsaved people may not understand, but Christians will, that one of our deepest concerns was what would happen to our broadcasts. Our broadcasts had been going on the air for a year now, and the time had come when I had in my possession only enough to pay for the next broadcast, leaving none for my family. My wife and I prayed about it and decided to use the last $7.50 we had to pay for the broadcast.

The following week I went to Mr. Townsend, the owner of the station, and told him that because of financial difficulties we would have to drop our broadcast. He was sitting in a swivel chair, and when I told him that I could no longer pay for the broadcast, he turned with his back towards me for about five minutes. Then he turned to me and said that he had decided to let me have the broadcast time, and if we were able to pay, all right; otherwise, we could have the time and they would wait for the pay. He asked us to continue with the broadcast until he should tell us to discontinue. There in the station office we had prayer to thank God for His goodness.

The Scripture tells us, "For what shall it profit a man if he shall gain the whole world, and lose his own soul?" Because I believed that, God gave me faith and courage to give the last dollar I had to keep a broadcast, that some soul might learn to know God.

A week passed and Sunday came, and it looked like the broadcast for the first time would go on unpaid for. Our doorbell rang early Sunday morning, and a man at the door said he wanted to see the Mr. Billington who was on the radio. This man's name was Ike Williams; he was a mechanic and a Christian man. He told us that he believed in tithing and had some of the Lord's money with him. He had been told that I was paying for the broadcast, and he gave me $8.10, which was his tithe, to pay for that Sunday's broadcast.

We always included in our prayers a prayer that God would give us money for the broadcast. The next two Sundays the station carried us. On another Sunday afternoon, at a neighbor's house, we met a widowed lady who was a businesswoman. She told us that she had received so many blessings from the broadcasts that she wanted us to have $5.00 for one. Our neighbor gave us the other needed $2.50.

Remember, I had no job, no income, and no one to turn to but the God of Heaven. But God said, "The gold is mine, the silver is mine, the cattle on a thousand hills is mine." We believed Him, and from here and there money would come in. They would say, here is money for groceries, broadcasts, rent, and so forth.

After I had had no work for forty-five days, a lady came one night representing a group that wanted me to hold a revival in Cleveland. (There was a friend in Akron who had promised to furnish gas for me to go anywhere to preach. Mr. John Haller had also promised gas for any home calls that I might make.) The group from Cleveland told me their people were laid off too, so they could not promise any love offering. The offerings which were taken were for the pastor and expenses of the church. However, in the rear of the church there was placed a little box in which the attenders could place any amount they could spare for the visiting preacher. Our bill at the radio station had gone up to $60.00 and my grocery bill to $24.00. When the meeting closed and the money was counted, there was enough for the station and grocery bills, with $4.14 left over. It pays to trust Jesus. It pays to pray and read your Bible.

The hard days were far from over. One morning I told my dear wife that I was going over to the factory to see if perhaps I might get my job back. I went into the foreman's office; he was sitting there reading the paper. He looked at me in surprise and asked me what I was doing in there. I told him that I had felt, although I did not know why, that if I came in today, he, Mr. Paul, would give me work. My wife, too, had felt that today our prayers would be answered. After a while my foreman took me up to the employment office and told them that he had the need of one man on a job which was just starting. He told them to get my card out and rehire me. If you ask me to explain this, I cannot. All I know is I kept clinging to God's promises. We were still on the broadcast, I had my job, and my faith was renewed. Jesus promised that they that put their trust in Him will not fail. If they fall, God will lift them up. He taught me to walk not by sight but by faith. God has promised never to leave me or forsake me. Won't you trust Him?

18. The Letter
Edged in Black

IN 1932 ON THE 6TH DAY OF MARCH, A COLD, SNOWY morning, when my family had just returned from church, we heard a rap at our door. When we opened the door we found a boy standing there, asking us to sign for a telegram which he had in his hand. With trembling hands I broke the seal and read these words: "Your father passed away this morning. Funeral will be Tuesday or Wednesday. signed Marvin."

There had not been a close death in my family. We had lost our grandparents, uncles and aunts, and now the death angel had visited our own immediate family circle. The Lord had said in Hebrews, it is appointed to men once to die. I hardly knew which way to turn. Nevertheless, I began to think of the brothers and sisters who perhaps had not read their Bible as much as I had, or even if they had, perhaps the Lord had not seen fit to make it as clear to them as I felt He had to me. I thought of my sweetheart mother, whose companion for many years was now gone. The death angel had separated them for the rest of her natural life, but because they both had trusted in God, the separation would be over someday.

The snow was so deep between Louisville and Paducah that it was utterly impossible to get there. The telephone wires were down and the planes were grounded. My father was buried in almost zero weather. Up until then, I had thought of Heaven and it had seemed far away, but when a real close loved one passes away, Heaven seems very near. My father had reared us in a godly manner and had taught each one of us the way of the Cross.

This was my first taste of death, and I knew I must prove

to my unsaved friends that death was not forever if you trusted in Jesus. Someone might ask me what happens to someone who dies. The real person whom you and I have loved moves out of the body. God has called this body a house and a temple, or a dwelling place and a tabernacle.

I went to hear a great Bible teacher from D. L. Moody's school teach on "After Death." I shall never forget that he said our eyelids were like window shades. After a person passes away, someone tenderly closes the lids of our eyes, for many times one does die with his eyes open. I have seen many people die with their eyes half open, as if they were gazing into space or into eternity. The Bible tells us of one man who, as he was dying, told them he could see Heaven and Jesus standing at the right hand of God. This story is found in the Book of Acts, the 7th chapter. We have no way of knowing what our friends or loved ones see when they are passing from time into eternity. Death is something that the little baby as it is born, drawing its first breath, is certain to experience.

My mind went back to the days that I spent at home as a boy. I remembered hearing my father talk about the things of Heaven. We lived in the country and only had church once a month. The nearest church which we attended was perhaps three miles away, and the other churches which we attended for revivals were even farther away.

The last time that I saw my father he was in good health. He owned and operated a large country store. My father was a very tenderhearted man, and the morning I left home he put his arm around me and said he would not forget to pray for me. The last thing I saw was a wave and a smile.

Time passes very rapidly, and according to nature I do not have many years left until perhaps I shall cross over. I shall find someone waiting for me inside the City of God, for the Bible teaches me that the soul of man never dies. When the inner beings of men, women, boys, or girls are saved, they are born into God's family. This gives them an inheritance to the City of God. Flesh and blood cannot *inherit* the kingdom of God. However, we know that flesh and blood can *enter*, for we know Jesus entered with a body after His resurrection. He had eaten and His body could be felt. He was a living, tangible body. Our bodies, however, came from dust and to dust they will return, while our souls live on forever. We also know and understand from the Scriptures that we will be like the Lord Jesus, for in I John:3 it says that it does not yet appear what I shall be like, but I shall be like Him when I see Him as He is. Some glad morning I shall behold the face of the Lord Jesus Christ and the faces of many friends and loved ones who are waiting for me. I shall see my grandparents, whom I loved so deeply and whose faces I still remember so vividly. My grandfather Kelly was of old Irish stock. His hair was white as snow and, being aged, his shoulders were stooped. He was a God-fearing, God-loving man who went through the Civil War riding on the same horse. He served for four years and came out without so much as a scratch, only hungry, tired, and cold from lack of clothing. I can remember him as well as if I had been a boy in his arms only yesterday, listening to his stories.

Sometime in your life, if it has not already happened, you will hear the telephone ring, or someone may ring your doorbell and hand you a letter edged in black with the message of death. I do not know how you will receive this message if you are not a Christian. If your dad died a saved man and you are not saved, then all you can say is good-bye, for the Bible teaches eternal separation at death for those who know God from those who know Him not.

I remember going to a home to arrange for a funeral. There was a daughter there past thirty-five years old, and she asked the rest of the family to leave the room that she might be alone for a few moments with her father and the minister. She told me after they had left that she was not a Christian, and as far as she knew there was nothing in her life to be ashamed of. But she knew she had never trusted Jesus and been saved. She had attended church and her heart had been touched, but she had refused to go to the altar. Her father was past seventy and had stayed with his children, being with one a few months and then staying with another. I showed her in that room God's plan of how the way of the Cross leads home. I showed her in my Bible the 14th chapter of John, where Jesus said He was the way, the truth, and the life. The Lord Jesus Christ is the only way to cross from earth to glory. She read Romans 10:10: "For with the heart man believeth unto righteousness; and with the mouth confession is made unto salvation." Then she read Romans 10:13: "For whosoever shall call upon the name of the Lord shall be saved." She opened the door of the room and put her arm around her brother who was waiting outside and said, "Now I am ready, the Lord Jesus has saved me. I know my father's Saviour, and now I won't dread so badly to see him buried. Someday we shall meet again, for God has promised a reunion in Glory."

What will you do when the message of death comes to you? Will you have Christ in your heart with the grace to stand the loss? Will there be a hope in your breast of seeing your loved one again?

19. The Need for a New Church in Akron

ONE NIGHT, AS MY WIFE AND I SAT TALKING, READING, praying, and trying to find the will of the Lord, we came to the Book of Nehemiah, and there we read the entire book.

I shall quote from chapter 1: "The words of Nehemiah the son of Hachaliah. And it came to pass in the month Chisleu, in the twentieth year, as I was in Shushan the palace, that Hanani, one of my brethren, came, he and certain men of Judah; and I asked them concerning the Jews that had escaped, which were left of the captivity, and concerning Jerusalem. And they said unto me, The remnant that are left of the captivity there in the province are in great affliction and reproach: the wall of Jerusalem also is broken down, and the gates thereof are burned with fire. And it came to pass, when I heard these words, that I sat down and wept, and mourned certain days, and fasted, and prayed before the God of heaven."

After I had read these words, I wondered if the people who had drifted here had gone so far astray that the old-time religion could not touch their hearts. There were people here from many states and many nationalities. Had they gone so far astray that the blessing of God was not upon churches as it should be? In the fifth verse Nehemiah said, "I beseech thee, O Lord God of heaven, the great and terrible God, that keepeth covenant and mercy for them that love him and observe his commandments." The more that I read this Book of Nehemiah, of what God called him to do, the more I felt burdened to build a church in the city of Akron.

I did not feel that I was the best preacher in the world; on the contrary, I felt very humble and dependent upon God; but I knew with all my heart that God was calling me to build a church. The more I searched the Scriptures, the more determined I became.

In the 2nd chapter, 11th verse in Nehemiah it reads: "So I came to Jerusalem, and was there three days. And I arose in the night, I and some few men with me; neither told I any man what my God had put in my heart to do at Jerusalem: neither was there any beast with me, save the beast that I rode upon."

I had begun to find out by this time that God had not sent me to the city of Akron to build tires; instead, He had sent me here to prepare me for the work He had in mind for me. God had sent Moses into the desert for forty years and He had sent Paul into the Arabian desert; He had sent them there for a purpose.

Akron was the rubber capital of the world, and people were coming here from far and wide. They were of many faiths, nationalities, and denominations. I heard many different preachers with faiths other than mine. I read periodicals written by all ministers in order to know what they taught and believed. In my own heart I believed that the walls—not the literal, but the spiritual walls—of the church were broken down in the city of Akron. People had left farms and come to the city, where they were making more money than they had ever made before; and they had forgotten God.

Nehemiah said that while he was in the palace some of his brethren came to him from Jerusalem, and he asked them about his kinfolk. They told him that the walls of Jerusalem were broken down and the Jewish people had been scattered here and there. You will recall that God had chosen the Jewish people and had blessed them. He had told them that if they would seek Him and His face and follow Him, He would be their God. He also told them that if they would forsake Him, He would permit them to be scattered abroad.

I love the Jewish people. I ought to, for the Old Testament was written by Jews. The prophets of old were Jews. Therefore, when I mention the persecution of the Jewish people I mention it humbly, reverently, toward their race.

The Bible teaches me plainly that all have sinned and come short of the glory of God. God has never brought any more condemnation to one race than He has to another. He has not persecuted one individual more than another. God will punish out of a heart of love. When a father punishes a child, if he is the kind of father he ought to be, he corrects the child out of love. God has said of the Jewish people that he that touches the Jews touches the apple of His eye.

Nehemiah, the cupbearer, was not the kind of cupbearer who sampled the king's food to see if it had been poisoned; instead, history teaches us that he was esteemed and an inner-cabinet member. He was aware of all the doings of the king. You might have called him the king's right-hand man. One day he came in to the king with a sad countenance, and the king asked him why he was sad. Nehemiah told him that he had had news of his kinsmen in Jerusalem and the walls of Jerusalem had been torn down. The city was in a terrible condition and was being pilfered by strangers. The king gave Nehemiah permission to go to Jerusalem to see what the city needed.

Nehemiah returned to Jerusalem and waited until darkness had covered the land and the heavens were crowned with a million stars, no one watching but God, no one to tell the story but the angels, who keep all secrets; then he slipped out while the watch on the wall was unawares. He looked at the walls broken down and the gates off their hinges. His city was an easy prey for anyone who wished to plunder. He called the elders together and showed them the letters which the king had given him to permit him to go to Jerusalem and learn of its condition. He declared unto them that they must rise and rebuild the walls.

I told my wife I believed that God would help me build a church. We decided on the name of Akron Baptist Temple. Akron was known worldwide because of the rubber industries there. We chose Baptist, for the Bible speaks of baptists. And we chose the word "temple," because the first building that was built for God was called a temple, not a church. Our body is called a temple wherein the soul and God live.

This was the year 1933 and money was still scarce, but always before me was the vision of the Akron Baptist

Temple. I nourished this vision with prayer, visiting, and preaching.

These years were hard years, and sometimes the bare necessities of life seemed out of reach. My wife and I bought groceries on credit until the bill grew to somewhere near $100.00. Our grocer was good to us but, wishing to pay him something, I went to a loan office to see if I could get a loan. The loan man asked me the usual questions of where did I work, what security could I offer, and how much did I want to borrow. When I told him I wanted to borrow $75.00, he asked me what I needed it for. He raised his eyebrows in surprise when I told him that first of all I would give $7.50 for a broadcast on Sunday. He asked me why a man in need of money would give it away to a broadcast. I explained that one tenth of all I possessed belonged to God. He said that at least I was truthful about it. Then he asked what I would do with the rest. I had an insurance policy that I would lose unless something was paid, and of course I would pay what was left on my grocery bill.

He told me that the furniture I had offered for collateral was not worth anything, but when I got up and started to leave, he pushed a button and asked a girl to bring in $75.00. This man was elderly and had silvery-gray hair. His countenance was kind—a face that anyone would find easy to love. He told me he knew no rule which enabled him to lend me the money in the regular way. He told me that he was going to lend me the money himself. He told me no one would come to look at my furniture, but if I ever could I should pay him back. He was amazed that I, needing money so badly, would give God one tenth of it. He said that many years ago, when he was just a young boy, he had trusted Jesus and had been saved. In the following years he had drifted far away from God. He reached me his hand and assured me that he would return to God. He promised to listen to the broadcast each Sunday, and if I was never able to pay the $75.00 back, I should consider it a gift from him.

20. Beginning of Akron Baptist Temple

"FOR THOUGH I PREACH THE GOSPEL, I HAVE NOTHING TO glory of: for necessity is laid upon me; yea, woe is unto me, if I preach not the gospel! For if I do this thing willingly, I have a reward: but if against my will, a dispensation of the gospel is committed unto me. What is my reward then? Verily that, when I preach the gospel, I may make the gospel of Christ without charge, that I abuse not my power in the gospel. For though I be free from all men, yet have I made myself servant unto all, that I might gain the more." I Corinthians 9:16-19.

My prayer is that those of you who read this Scripture may come to know there is a will of God in your lives. There is a plan in your lives, and if you fail that plan it is woe unto you. Heed the call that God gives you.

In June, 1934, a man by the name of Mr. Lee Dickens came to me and asked me to come to Rimer School on Manchester Road, where half a dozen families needed a preacher and a church. These families had been listening to the broadcast, and they wanted me to preach for them. Since I had no place to preach the next Sunday, I told him I would be glad to preach for them.

He told everyone he saw, and I did likewise. There was no chance to announce it on the broadcast, since this happened after the broadcast, and we would not be on again until after their services the next Sunday. However, we met that Sunday, and there were six men and six women present. We invited the building caretaker, a Mr. Longbottom, to come and sit with us. Kidding me about there being an unlucky number of thirteen, counting the preacher, he said he would make the fourteenth. Within a year's time we saw this man saved and baptized.

Thus, in the Rimer School building on the second Sunday in June, 1934, the Akron Baptist Temple had its humble beginning. The offering that Sunday was $1.18. God blessed and one lady came forward accepting Christ.

That night on the broadcast I made the announcement that I would be preaching at the Rimer School the next Sunday morning at ten. Our attendance more than doubled. There were thirty-nine adults and several children who had come with their parents. We met on the platform which was being used as the kitchen part of the school building.

The next week I went to Kentucky for a meeting that had been planned before, but I was anxious to return to Rimer School. I preached in the school until August, when my old home church, the Sugarcreek Baptist in Kentucky, called me to come home for ordination.

As the Scripture states, "For necessity is laid upon me; yea, woe is unto me, if I preach not the gospel." The same is true of any Christian. It was true of Jonah when he ran away and would not preach to the people of Nineveh. It is true of you if you have left a Sunday-school class, or if you have left your home and moved to another state, not only leaving home but leaving God there too. Woe be unto you if you fail in the plan God has for you.

There were two strong reasons why I decided to begin preaching. First of all, Jesus had saved my soul, and secondly, I loved Him and wanted to serve Him. I did not want to go to a church, but instead I wanted with all my heart to build a church. I wanted my church to have its plan and guidance solely from the Holy Bible. Even to this day, the Akron Baptist Temple and the two hundred churches which we have helped build use nothing but the King James Version of the Bible to teach and preach to the congregations who gather there.

From the beginning God blessed, with one adult being saved the first Sunday. Out of the thirty-nine adults who attended the second Sunday, seven came forward and were saved. Twenty-six years have come and gone, and I am happy to say that, in the history of the church, there has passed only one Sunday when no one was saved.

I had made some commitments to preach at other places; therefore, Mr. Dickens kept things going at Rimer School. I feel in my heart it was God's plan that I work with Mr. Dickens. We prayed and visited together. We opened a bank account at the bank, and we both had to sign the checks. From the day we started we kept Rimer School for seventeen years.

In October we had our first Sunday night service. Our broadcast was over two years old now, and we were told we had close to 100,000 listeners. We had announced the services for that night. The Board of Education allowed us to use 217 folding chairs. Thanks to God, every seat was taken and people had to stand.

My text that night was the story of Nicodemus, who was told he must be born again. We tried to explain to each one what "born again" meant. Forsaking sin was not enough, to reform was not enough; you had to believe in Christ to be saved, to be born again into God's family, having your sins forgiven. On the platform where we had begun the first Sunday were about twenty-five people whom we called our choir. The other people were seated on the playing floor of the gymnasium. Realizing that nothing but God's presence and His Holy Spirit could give us a good service, we prayed God's blessings be upon our service.

Giving God the glory, at the end of the message not one person sat in the group without tear-dimmed eyes. People from perhaps twenty-five different southern states were gathered there. When the message was finished, we stood and sang, "There is a fountain filled with blood drawn from Emanuel's vein, and sinners plunged beneath that flood lose all their guilt and shame." I asked them to come forward and kneel on the hard wooden floor and let someone show them the Scriptures in the Bible, which many times I called the road map from earth to Glory.

When I was a child, I was convicted of my sins, yet no one ever showed me the Scriptures. I felt that if we showed lost souls the very word of the Bible so that they might read it for themselves, they could see and believe. That night, Mr. Dickens and I were rewarded richly for our praying, preaching, and visiting; for we saw twenty-three souls accept Christ. We were watching the power of God work. I vividly remembered the Scripture which told Paul, Moses, and preacher boys like me: "Of necessity it is laid upon you to preach the gospel." Now I was reaping the blessings of obeying God.

I was beginning to walk with God and learning how to study His Bible in a more revealing way. God was teaching me how to present Christ and to introduce Him. That night shall remain in my memory always, as I joyously watched twenty-three kneel and take Jesus as their Saviour. Plans were rapidly taking shape for the dream, hope, and vision of the Akron Baptist Temple.

21. Ordained a Baptist Minister

ACCORDING TO THE AUTHORITY GIVEN TO PEOPLE IN THE Holy Bible, in August, 1934, on the tenth day, I was ordained at the Sugarcreek Baptist Church in West Kentucky. The church had called for my ordination, which is according to Scripture. I had moved my membership from the Arlington Street Baptist Church back to the Sugarcreek Church. Dr. Edward Skinner was my questioner. He asked me 212 questions pertaining to the Old and New Testaments. He asked me why I believed that I was called to preach, and then I was asked to preach. After this, Mr. Skinner recommended to the church that I be permitted to be ordained, for he felt me worthy and one called of God to preach. He recommended that I be given the full rights of a minister, not only in the United States but in every country under God's Heaven. I was accepted and ordained. Rev. Hal Thurman was the moderator and pastor of the Sugarcreek Baptist Church. Rev. Gregory, a man loved and respected in that community, gave me my charge. He said to me as he gave me the charge, "Dallas, beware; after you are ordained and are called a minister, your life will be as delicate as that of a sixteen-year-old girl. People will seek to find fault with you. They will do what they can to destroy you so that your ministry will not be effective." Rev. Ed Outland, another minister whom I loved, helped with my ordination.

On that day I was given my ordination papers, which were signed by four ministers of the Southern Baptist, giving me the right to preach and conduct services anywhere I was called upon to conduct. This gave me the right to conduct weddings, funerals, or any religious service which I might be asked to be a part of. I searched the Bible to see what God had to say about a man who has chosen to be a shepherd of a flock—a bishop, as the Scripture calls him.

I Timothy 3:1-6: "If a man desire the office of a bishop, he desireth a good work. A bishop then must be blameless, the husband of one wife, vigilant, sober, of good behaviour, given to hospitality, apt to teach; not given to wine, no striker, not greedy of filthy lucre; but patient, not a brawler, not covetous; one that ruleth well his own house, having his children in subjection with all gravity; (for if a man know not how to rule his own house, how shall he take care of the church of God?) not a novice, lest being lifted up with pride he fall into the condemnation of the devil. Moreover he must have a good report of them which are without; lest he fall into reproach and the snare of the devil." I Timothy 4:11-16: "These things command and teach. Let no man despise thy youth; but be thou an example of the believers, in word, in conversation, in charity, in spirit, in faith, in purity. Till I come, give attendance to reading, to exhortation, to doctrine. Neglect not the gift that is in thee, which was given thee by prophecy, with the laying on of the hands of the presbytery. Meditate upon these things; give thyself wholly to them; that thy profiting may appear to all. Take heed unto thyself, and unto the doctrine; continue in them: for in doing this thou shalt both save thyself, and them that hear thee."

I would like to clarify the truths which you have just read. These Scriptures do not mean that ministers can save people. When a judge is sworn into office, he swears that he will judge all human beings brought before him according to the evidence presented, judging which evidence is true and which is false. A judge listens to the case, and, finding the person guilty or innocent, he reads not from his law but from the statute law of the state. With the law as his measure, he passes judgment. A minister must study the law of God day and night. When a minister preaches the true word of God and has his message rejected, the one who rejects the message does not reject the minister but the law of God Himself. When you deny what the Bible says, you are not denying the preacher, you are denying God. The Bible teaches me plainly that God did not give any man the power to forgive sin. We use the written law of God as the judge uses the written law of the state over which he presides. The written law of the state sends a man to the electric chair. The judge, having had the case presented, will take a volume which has the murder laws written by his state. These laws have been passed by the House of Representatives and the Senate. Just as a judge knows where to turn in the lawbooks, a minister should know where to find the appropriate Scripture for a wedding, a funeral, sorrow, and so forth.

When a preacher says that you must be saved and turn

from your sinful ways or be lost and damned, he is not saying that he has the power to condemn you; instead, just as it is the duty of the judge who reads the law and sees the evidence, it is the duty of the preacher to pass judgment. It is not a pleasure to pass judgment, but a duty.

When I was ordained to be a full-fledged Baptist preacher, I was given the right by four aged ministers, and I deeply felt my responsibilities. I remember the seriousness of the silvery-haired minister who gave me my charge and the tears that came often to his eyes. Being past sixty years of age, Rev. Gregory told me of the many blessings which he had had in traveling this road for Christ, and of the many heartaches. There had been much sorrow, but with it a great joy.

By God's grace, from that day unto this, I have been permitted to conduct revival meetings in every state in the United States. I have visited the Holy Land. Therefore, I say to you, do not become offended at the minister when he warns you of judgment, for God speaks of judgment much more than He does of mercy. The law of God was written for the lawless, and everyone unsaved is lawless. The traffic light is hung in the street as a warning and is there for your safety. The Book of God is a book of warning, a book of judgment. The only true and living God is the God of judgment. Like the old balances which were used to weigh something, and had on one side something of a known weight which had to be equaled if it were to balance, so our lives are weighed and many found wanting. God condemns sin; but Jesus came and died that you and I, through the blood of Christ, would not be found wanting. Through His mercy and our trust in Him we can be saved.

Through the years as an ordained minister, I have tried my very best to preach the gospel without fear of any man, striving always to interpret the law of God to everyone I met. It is my earnest prayer that you will turn aside from the judgment of God and accept His mercy, by believing on the Lord Jesus Christ.

II
We Build God's House

22. Ordained, I Return to Akron

AFTER MY RETURN TO AKRON I FELT A DEEP RESPONSI-
bility bearing down upon my soul to do more in soul winning,
to go after each man and woman and win them for Christ.
I was more earnest than ever before to persuade those who
had no church home to come and be found in the house of
the Lord.

On the first Sunday night in November I read the following Scriptures to those attending church: "Then said he unto
him, A certain man made a great supper, and bade many:
and sent his servant at supper time to say to them that were
bidden, Come; for all things are now ready. And they all
with one consent began to make excuse. The first said unto
him, I have bought a piece of ground, and I must needs go
and see it: I pray thee have me excused. And another said,
I have bought five yoke of oxen, and I go to prove them: I
pray thee have me excused. And another said, I have married
a wife, and therefore I cannot come. So that servant came,
and shewed his lord these things. Then the master of the
house being angry said to his servant, Go out quickly into the
streets and lanes of the city, and bring in hither the poor, and
the maimed, and the halt, and the blind. And the servant
said, Lord, it is done as thou hast commanded, and yet there
is room. And the lord said unto the servant, Go out into the

highways and hedges, and compel them to come in, that my house may be filled. For I say unto you, That none of those men which were bidden shall taste of my supper." Luke 14:16-24.

I read this Scripture that I might persuade the people not to find excuses but rather to help me win the lost for Christ and fill the house of the Lord. I took each verse and tried to explain its full meaning. The highways and hedges mean roadhouses, beer gardens, dance halls, bowling alleys, pool tables, gambling houses—anything that keeps people away from the house of God.

I told them that night that I had come to Akron thinking I would obtain a job and spend my days there; however, God had other plans for me. Now I knew that God had called me to preach the gospel. In the congregation before me were nearly six hundred people from various states, of various denominations and nationalities. Our congregation was more or less a melting pot. I had never offended anyone for their speech or their religion. I just simply preached Christ in the only way I knew—from the Bible; I read that Jesus is the way, the truth, and the life, that no one cometh to the Father except through Christ. My ministry has been known for presenting the gospel in a down-to-earth manner, using everyday language, referring to everyday life.

It was and is my honest opinion that many ministers are more interested in becoming great theologians, using expressions known only to the very learned, than in winning the lost, using language that even a child can understand. Even learned doctors and lawyers, not knowing the theologian's terms, will go home not understanding. Such ministers are more interested in their reputations as Bible students than in making sure the true message is given as God wishes. To me, a student of the Scripture is one whom God has called to preach the Bible, and whenever he reads a chapter he tries to reveal its meaning clearly to all people.

A minister who impressed me perhaps more than any other

minister whose life I've read was one of the greatest scholars of all times—Dr. H. B. Riley. Dr. Riley would smile and say that he was not too much interested in making the college professor understand; he wished the eighth grader to understand, and then he was sure all would get the point he wished to make. This remark has remained with me through the years. I have kept it in mind as I studied and preached to win souls for Jesus Christ.

The parable which you read at the beginning of this chapter mentions a certain man who had prepared a great supper. The man is God; the supper or feast will be in Glory; and that which we feast upon is the Word of God. The home that is spoken of is Heaven. Thus, God told His servant to go out and bid many to come. We find a similar parable in Matthew's Gospel, which mentions perhaps a few things not mentioned in Luke's Gospel; however, from both parables we definitely get the message. It matters not what your profession or work or education is, you should be able to understand.

The one sad Scripture we find here, representing a great truth, is the excuse: I have married a wife, and therefore I cannot come. I find this everywhere I go. There are so many mixed marriages. The husband and wife each have a different faith; and since they cannot agree on one, they go to no church at all. They do not consult a minister or a priest before their marriage, and often are not even married in church. They begin their marriage out of church and continue that way. I meet them at court, in jail, at the detention home with their children, sometimes in death row. They begin their life together without Christ; they rear their children the same way. Pleasures of this life are enjoyed. Much time is spent in laying up treasures upon this earth and no time taken to prepare for eternity. Radio and television, for the most part, furnish food for the man, the woman, the child of flesh, while they starve for spiritual food. The Bible teaches us that man cannot live by bread alone. The Word of God is a necessity.

Today there are many things taught and practiced which will never bring one to the City of God. In the Old Testament there are accounts of children actually sacrificed to some idol in the name of religion. There is a vast difference between religion and Christianity.

The servant came back to the lord and said he had done what the lord had wished him to do and yet there was still room at the table. There is room in Glory for you, and please do not be the foolish one to say that Heaven will be a small place. The lord asked the servant, which is you and I, to go everywhere and compel them to come in, that his house would be filled.

If you and I are going to compel people to come to the house of the Lord, our lives should be such that the ones we ask will have respect for the way we live. If a Christian visited your home and told off-color stories, had a social glass, or used language not becoming a Christian, you would not trust your loved ones to his group or church. On the other hand, if the same man came with the Word of God on his lips and sat down reverently, behaving as a man of God should, you couldn't help but feel God's goodness and the man's sincerity. You would consider his words and his church. This man has kindly refused the glass of wine, the cigar, the game of poker. He is different, not a religious fanatic, not "holier than thou" or pious, but just "Christian." Tell me, which of these men could persuade you to the house of God?

A Christian is not discouraged by the first unkept promise of a friend to visit church, but instead, will return again and again to compel him to the house of the Lord. The spirit of God will enter into the hearts of those with excuses, and one day you will find them in church. They will say to you one day that their consciences bothered them and, while in church, they wanted to cry. Now the animals, the birds, and the fish never feel this way. God has given us an immortal soul, a God-created eternal being, and our destiny is either Heaven or Hell. This feeling that they have is Jesus, the Christ of Calvary, knocking at their heart's door. Then it is, working through a servant, that God quickens through the Holy Spirit and they are compelled to come. The invitation is given to come forward and publicly accept Christ, and the excuses are forgotten.

It is my heart's desire that, as you read this in your home or wherever you are, you will bow your head and accept Christ.

23. Church Is Organized

THE MORE I STUDIED MY BIBLE, THE MORE I KNEW THAT God had intended something more in Jesus' coming than people merely being saved and then turned free to return to the places of sin. I knew that Christ had died for the church. I found in the Scriptures where Christ was the head of the church. Realizing that God was blessing our services, for the six hundred folding chairs which we had purchased were nearly filled and at every service souls were being saved, I knew in my heart something had to be done towards organizing a church. On Easter Sunday, 1935, we organized what is now known as the Akron Baptist Temple.

The following Scripture was read on that day to the church: "When Jesus came into the coasts of Caesarea Philippi, he asked his disciples, saying, Whom do men say that I the Son of man am? And they said, Some say that thou art John the Baptist: some, Elias; and others, Jeremias, or one of the prophets. He saith unto them, But whom say ye that I am? And Simon Peter answered and said, Thou art the Christ, the Son of the living God. And Jesus answered and said unto him, Blessed art thou, Simon Bar-jona: for flesh and blood hath not revealed it unto thee, but my Father which is in heaven. And I say also unto thee, That thou art Peter, and upon this rock I will build my church; and the gates of hell shall not prevail against it." Matthew 16:13-18.

During that service we asked those who would like to form and help organize what would thereafter be known as an organized missionary Baptist church to come forward and stand with us at the front of the congregation. Exactly eighty-one persons came forward to unite as a church. We clasped each other's hands, forming a circle; and I stepped in the center of that circle and read the above Scripture. I explained that we were binding ourselves together as one man to purchase property to build our church, to send missionaries to foreign fields, to help the poor and needy, and to perform every duty that God had planned for us as Christians. From that time forward we would be an organized group of which the Lord Jesus Christ was the Head. Our church was not being built upon Peter or any of the disciples, for when Jesus said "upon this rock" He referred to Himself. Our church was to be built upon this Jesus who laid aside royal robes to take a robe of flesh. He was, is, and always will be the Son of God. Jesus was, is, and will be forever more.

I said to this same group that we, as Christians, would become stones in the spiritual church. Peter, like us, is a stone, a part of the Eternal Temple or Church. God is no respecter of persons: Peter was no different from any man who had believed in Christ. Christ told Peter that his knowledge that Jesus was the Son of the living God was revealed to him by a spiritual discernment. A minister can only read to you and reason with you with words; it is the Holy Spirit who reveals the truth unto you. If through your own will the Holy Spirit never reveals this to you, you are lost when you die. We mean when we say "lost" that you are separated from God and Heaven and all Christian loved ones who have gone before you.

Our church had its organized beginning on that day with eighty-one members. We were recognized for the first time as a church. Our real work had begun. First of all, we had the task of proving to the city of Akron that we were real Christians. We had to walk where Christians walked, behave as Christians wherever our duties or work called us. We would not wear banners or dress in an unusual way, but our lives were to be the proof Akron must see. Our conversations, activities, and motives would be analyzed. We, as a church, had to pray and believe, and trust that God would reveal to our enemies, to public officials, and to people of the city that He was with us. We had to live so that God would bless our church and its endeavors. There was nothing so small that prayer was not needed. Whatever we did, we tried first of all to please God and prayed we would not offend those we would win for God. It was hard to establish ourselves, but we had set our faces toward Calvary and had chosen for our purpose: "Upon this rock I will build my church; and the gates of hell shall not prevail against it." If you drive by the front of our church and look up, you will find a large engraved open Bible facing the east, upon which these words are inscribed.

You might say to yourself that you would be afraid to be a Christian, for you could not live it. You cannot live a Christian life by yourself, but Jesus will live it for you. Jesus dwells in you when you become a Christian, and "the gates of hell shall not prevail" against you.

Our building began with a cornerstone, and other stones were placed upon it. Jesus said that He was the chief cornerstone. You and I who believe in Him are added to that cornerstone. When the church is completed and Jesus returns for the church, He will also become the Head of the church. We can ask you, "Are you a stone in Christ? Have you been converted?" You can say, as millions have, that Jesus is the Son of God and put your trust in Christ, who shed His blood that you might be saved.

You will find that the happiest life is a Christian life. When you become a Christian you will find the burdens lift and the road seem easy through faith in Jesus. Christ will give you grace to bear the sorrows and faith for the tests. If you are tired and weary of a sinful life, perhaps with a broken home, there is a way of hope for you. If you will sincerely, with all your heart, believe in the Lord Jesus Christ—even though you are not in church, because it makes no difference where you are—you shall, not maybe, but you *shall* be saved. Some of the most wonderful converts whom I have ever known were saved in a hospital or at their homes.

I remember well a Jewish girl who is now the wife of a Baptist minister. She was saved at home one Wednesday night while I was visiting there on my way to our prayer meeting services. She had attended a Sunday service and had heard about Jesus. She wanted to know who He was. I went to her home and with the Word of God explained Jesus. She accepted Christ and has been a devout soul winner for Christ ever since. She is the wife of a beloved minister friend of mine, Elijah Benningfield.

You can be saved anywhere; salvation is in your heart whenever you trust Jesus. Will you trust Him today?

24. Christ Lifted Up

I WOULD LIKE TO HAVE YOU READ A FEW VERSES FOUND in John's Gospel: "Father, glorify thy name. Then came there a voice from heaven, saying, I have both glorified it, and will glorify it again. The people therefore, that stood by, and heard it, said that it thundered: others said, An angel spake to him. Jesus answered and said, This voice came not because of me, but for your sakes. Now is the judgment of this world: now shall the prince of this world be cast out. And I, if I be lifted up from the earth, will draw all men unto me. This he said, signifying what death he should die."

Sometimes, even now, I look upon the early days at Rimer School, immediately after the organizing of the church, when it was my privilege to see doctors, lawyers, and men and women of every walk of life, coming from every section of the country, sit down and bear with me as I told them of my Christ. The church grew so rapidly that we hardly knew what to do next. When I think of the miraculous way God blessed, it still makes me tremble.

It was necessary for us to think about buying property and building a church. Just across the street from us were two large lots. We found the owner of the lots and purchased them. Immediately, we sought an architect to draw up plans for the church. The architect told us that if we built on this property, the building would only hold between five hundred and six hundred people on one floor. Our congregation was well over that number now. Therefore, the lots were inadequate and would have to be disposed of. We were not discouraged, for we knew God was with us: we saw the evidence Sunday after Sunday, when countless numbers crowded our school building and many, many were saved.

I do not care what your profession may be. The hour will come when you need Jesus. You may go through half of your life and say that you have gotten along fine. You may say that you have not needed Christ. However, storms one day will break at your house and heavy clouds (and I do not mean the clouds from which rain comes, but sorrowing clouds), and things which will cause you to stop and think will become a vivid reality to you. Jesus said, "And I, if I be lifted up from the earth, will draw all men unto me." Not all doctors, not all lawyers, but, as Jesus plainly teaches, some from *all* walks of life will be drawn unto Him.

Moses, the greatest scholar of all times, believed and turned his back upon the worldly pleasures of Egypt and her people. He gladly gave up prestige, wealth, and power that he might know God and walk in His ways. Paul, the great writer of the New Testament, turned from a place of popularity, power, and notoriety—for he could have been the chief rabbi of his day—to become a humble servant for Jesus. Jesus asked Paul why he persecuted Him. To this Paul answered, "Lord, what wilt thou have me to do?"

Preaching Christ was my one aim in life. My messages began and ended with holding up Jesus to the world. We warn you to turn away from sin in your early days. Seek God and read your Bible daily and learn to pray. I know many fine surgeons in the city of Akron who pray each time before going into the operating room. We have a great number of nurses, members of the Akron Baptist Temple, who pray for their patients. Beneath that uniform beats a Christian heart which gives comfort that medicine cannot give. We have had persons who, having recovered from an illness, come to church testifying that the first person ever to tell them of Christ was a nurse, and because of her they want to know Jesus.

I well recall a story concerning Dr. C. F. Wharton, who was a Christian and a member of our church. A man and his wife came into the doctor's office, and it was easy to see from the man's bleary, red eyes that he was an alcoholic. The man said he needed help. He asked for medicine, drugs, or anything which would help him overcome this awful sickness. After the doctor had talked to him for some time, he finally looked at the man and said, "I have a preacher friend who can help you." The doctor told him that the preacher had helped him. He was never a drunkard, but he had talked to him and had helped his attitude toward living. Of course, the doctor gave him medicine; but before the man left the office, the doctor had his promise that he would visit the church on Manchester Road.

I did not know of this man but God did, and that Sunday I preached on the wondrous power of Jesus. I told of His power to cleanse the lepers, open the blind eyes, unstop the deaf ears, and raise the dead. That Sunday, this man trusted in Jesus and turned away from alcohol. The seed had been planted by the medical doctor, who was not ashamed of Jesus and His love; and again the Scriptures were proved, for Jesus was lifted up and this man was drawn to Him. The difference in his life was made when the Holy Spirit revealed to him the truth.

It is up to you what you do with the Holy Spirit. When you feel that it is no longer the word which you have read but the very God of Heaven speaking to you, then while Jesus stands knocking at your heart, yield to Him and accept Him as your Saviour.

The lots which had been bought were of no use to us and needed to be sold. A meeting of the church officers was called to plan to buy property elsewhere. We had seen the hand of God upon our ministry, and we had a vision of what God might do for us if we remained godly and humble. We knew our people witnessed in the factory, over the fence at home, and in the classrooms, showing a deep concern for everyone they met. They were walking advertisements for our church. They asked everyone they met to come to church. They had a testimony that only God can give. They were unafraid and unashamed to work for Christ. They asked the people to come to a church where one sang "Amazing Grace," where the story of Jesus was told—of His wonderful love and sacrifice on Calvary—where anyone who would believe could find salvation and peace. Because of the enthusiasm of these God-fearing people and their own stories of freedom from sin, the crowds came looking for the peace which they were told would come through Christ. You can imagine what a stir it caused in our city. Within two miles of the church a man who was selling liquor said, "So many men who used to buy my liquor have been saved out at the Baptist Temple that I've just had to quit selling it, for I have no customers for it." The men who had bought his drink began to talk to him about his soul, and they convinced him that they would no longer buy alcoholic beverages. His brother-in-law persuaded him to come just one Sunday to see for himself. After listening to the message and hearing the old gospel songs, he was spoken to by the Holy Spirit and was saved.

Unless you are a Christian, it will be hard for you to imagine how fast our church was growing. We were not putting on any fancy show. There was no expensive advertising being done. We were just telling people about a Wonderful Saviour. We had lifted Him up as the Prince of Peace. He was the sacrificial Lamb of God. We had told everyone we had seen—the professional man, the tire builder, the housewife—that Jesus saves. Now something had to be done about our building, for the plans and the lots across the street were too small. Can you wonder why I believe in God so strongly? You may ask me how I know my God is real. I know, because He lives within my heart.

25. Our Building Difficulties

IN THE BOOK OF HAGGAI WE READ THE FOLLOWING verses: "Thus speaketh the Lord of hosts, saying, This people say, The time is not come, the time that the Lord's house should be built. Then came the word of the Lord by Haggai the prophet, saying, Is it time for you, O ye, to dwell in your cieled houses, and this house lie waste? Now therefore thus saith the Lord of hosts; Consider your ways. Ye have sown much, and bring in little; ye eat, but ye have not enough; ye drink, but ye are not filled with drink; ye clothe you, but there is none warm; and he that earneth wages earneth wages to put it into a bag with holes. Thus saith the Lord of hosts; Consider your ways. Go up to the mountain, and bring wood, and build the house; and I will take pleasure in it, and I will be glorified, saith the Lord. Ye looked for much, and, lo, it came to little; and when ye brought it home, I did blow upon it. Why? saith the Lord of hosts. Because of mine house that is waste, and ye run every man unto his own house. Therefore the heaven over you is stayed from dew, and the earth is stayed from her fruit. And I called for a drought upon the land, and upon the mountains, and upon the corn, and upon the new wine, and upon the oil, and upon that which the ground bringeth forth, and upon men, and upon cattle, and upon all the labour of the hands."

We began our building in the month of August in the year 1937. There was a man at the head of a large industry in Akron who had helped others in church work. Our friends told us that this man might consider helping us with our building. Three of the trustees and I obtained an appointment to talk with the secretary of this industrial head and wealthy businessman. It was learned that it was this man's custom to give up to $10,000 to new churches in the area. The secretary recommended that we see the boss, for, considering how rapidly we had grown, it might be possible for us to get even more than $10,000. However, before we could see this man, he passed away, and our church never received money from any of the rubber industries in Akron. It was a disappointment, but we realize now why it happened. Had we received a large sum from any industry or any individual, our church would have been referred to as "the large church that So-and-so built." The church was built from combined small earnings. Many of our people worked on WPA. We sought aid from banks, not only in Akron but in other states. We went everywhere we could think of to get aid.

I well remember going to one man and asking for help. He refused to give us a loan, and I seriously told him that by God's grace we would build without his help. God would answer our prayers, and someday we would have our building. He could not understand my faith and said I could die of a heart attack, my boy could be kicked out of school, and my wife could be driven insane if I persisted with this plan.

I prayed like Daniel—morning, noon, and night. I had promised my people at Rimer School that with God's help and theirs I would build a church in Akron. Over our radio station I repeatedly said, "God will build a church for us." I pleaded with the people, using the Scripture from the Book of Haggai. Pointing out that they had homes, I asked them, Should there not be a house built for the Lord? I knew these were hard days and money was hard to obtain, but I knew the only way we could build was for me to convince the people of their obligation to God.

Close to Christmas, we had the roof on the building. There were no windows or doors and no money. A man from the Loomis Company offered to let us have everything we needed and said that we could pay them when we were able to. They let us have the cement to put in our concrete floors. However, we now owed several thousand dollars. We had just $3.00 in our account. Other companies had given us credit, and they were asking that we pay something on the material used. About the middle of December, a group of men and myself stood in the unfinished building and reluctantly told our contractor, Mr. McCoy, there would be no material or work for him the following day. There would be no work in the temple; the hammers would not be ringing. Then we made up our minds that, since there would be no work the following day, we would meet that day for a prayer meeting. After the workers had gone and I had gone home for my supper, darkness covered the land. I looked outside and saw the heavens crowned with millions of stars. I made up my mind to go that night to see if there was someone who would lend us enough money to finish our church. I got in my car and drove back to the church. I stood outside looking at the church with no windows, doors, or heat. We had no collateral to obtain a loan. We had started with $1,600, which had fast disappeared. As I stood there I realized that I had come to the end of my journey. There in the stillness of the night I talked with God. Like a child, I cried saying, "Lord, I have told people in the city of Akron that with God's help I would build a church for the Glory of God. By God's grace I told them we would have a church. Lord, if this building is not finished, then who am I? I am just a boy from the foothills of West Kentucky who walked away with just an eighth-grade education. I am what I am today by your grace and guidance. I've studied your word and have believed. You have brought us safely this far, and I pray it is your will that we go on." I reasoned with God as I would have with my own earthly father.

It was cold, and I shivered as I stood there pondering over the things that had happened. I remembered the disappointment when the industrialist had died and we were denied help. All hope had seemingly gone. Every avenue of help seemed to be closed to us. Christmas would soon be here, and there was little money in Akron for toys, let alone money for half-finished churches. Men working on WPA were fortunate if they had money for candy for their children. I knew people were saying our church would never be finished. They said it would stand there to mock a young preacher boy who had had a vision. Needless to say, I slept very little that night. The next morning came, and once again I felt drawn to the cold, barren, half-finished building. I don't know how many times I prayed that day, but my mind was ever on the fact that I had persuaded people to give their money to build a church which was at a standstill, only half done. I remembered the Scripture where Jesus had said for us to count the cost before we start the building. Perhaps the work would go unfinished and the building become a mockery of me. I remembered the man who had implied that my dream was too much and that I would die of a broken heart. He had said I was overly enthusiastic and not practical. I remembered what he had said of the unfavorable future for my son and wife. He had said depression days were not the time to build a church.

The contractor had told us that he needed only $5,000 to finish the building. That figure was firmly fixed in my mind, and on Sunday, when close to 1,600 people gathered, I told my adult class that we must pray for $5,000. Now, $5,000 in those days was far harder to raise than $100,000 is today. Today, not boasting, giving God the glory, our church can raise a million dollars by using the telephone. God has really blessed us.

On our broadcast that night I read John 14:14, "If ye shall ask any thing in my name, I will do it," and I prayed that God would give us the $5,000 we needed. I pleaded with every Christian who knew how to pray to ask God that this be granted.

After the broadcast we hurried to church. Every Sunday before the services it was our policy to hold a prayer service, the men meeting in one place and the women in another. I told my wife to ask the women in her group to pray earnestly for $5,000 and I would ask the men in our prayer group to do the same. The prayer rooms were darkened and no one could see the tears on another's face, but one could hear weeping. The unsaved went into the prayer rooms, and that night nine men and three women were saved there. The church was more than two years old. The auditorium was filled and overflowing into the boiler room of the school. We asked everyone there who knew Christ to pray for the $5,000.

The following morning I went to the hospital, where a man's wife was having an operation. I stayed with the man until about eleven o'clock and then went home. My wife told me an elderly lady had been trying to reach me. She had called several times, and one could tell from her voice that she was very old. She called again and asked that I come to her home. I told her that I had a funeral and would come later. She said I would have time to come now, for she would not keep me long. We had helped many elderly persons, and I thought perhaps this was another in need; so I took the address and hurried to her home.

I drove up in front of a beautiful home. I was startled and checked to see if this could be the right address. I went up on the porch and rang the doorbell. Never in all my lifetime will I be able to explain in words what I beheld. There before me was a sweetheart grandmother. Her hair was as white as snow, a silvery-white. Questioning her, I knew that I was at the right home. She said that she knew who I was, for she had heard our broadcast, and that was why she had sent for me. Having asked me to be seated, she left me, going through a dining room into the kitchen. She returned after a few minutes and put before me a shoe box tied with calico strings. The box was so old it had begun to change color.

Amazed, I listened as she said, "Brother Billington, in this shoe box is $5,500. I heard your prayer for $5,000 to finish your building. Here is the money and $500 more. This is not a loan, but a gift. I used to keep boarders when I was young and lived in the mining regions of West Virginia. When I came to Akron I kept boarders and saved my money. I have two brothers who are wealthy and will never need my money. I still have money to take care of me, so accept this gift to use in the Lord's work on Manchester Road."

I was not ashamed of the tears that filled my eyes. She asked me and my church to pray for her in her lonely hours, and before I left she kissed me on the forehead as if I had been her own baby boy. I left her home with the old shoe

box tied with calico strings under my arm. I went to the
church grounds, where I found Mr. Mark Starnes, chairman
of the board of trustees, and many other men who were there
with the material which Sunday's offering had purchased.

I had not untied the box when I walked up to Mr. Starnes
and told him I had $5,500. I handed him the box and told
him to keep it, for I had to hurry to the funeral. While we
were still talking, a man in a trench coat, looking like a
businessman, walked in and asked for the pastor of the
church. He handed me a large brown envelope and told me
there was $1,000 inside and also his name and address. If
someday the church could pay him back, fine; if not, he
was willing to donate it to the church work. He was a
Christian man who had listened to our broadcast. When the
sun went down on Monday night, after our weekend of
prayers and pleading, we had $8,200. How can you ask me
if God is real? Do you believe He controls the money strings?
Do you believe He rules in the hearts of men? Do you believe
that riches are controlled by God and He gives it to whom
He will? Perhaps the reason you have never had anything is
that God could not trust you.

You talk about shouts of joy, about the bells of Heaven
ringing in men's and women's souls, about doubt and fear
fading away, about knowing God lives—these things had
become a reality for me and my people.

I was asked to write this story in my own way, in order that
your faith might be strengthened, not for building a church,
but for creating a little castle, a dwelling place, in which to
rear your family. Therefore, God will do for you, a father
and mother, what He did for us, a church, that you may rear
your children in a godly manner. When your teen-age daughter does not come home at midnight, you will need Jesus.
God will be just as close to you as you yourself permit. God
will be just as real as you will let Him. Read the Bible and its
promises of prayer. Claim the promises of prayer. As Paul

said, the story which you have read happened not in a far-away land or to some prophet of old but happened in this day in which you and I live. The church is still standing; many of the people in the story are still living. We have the name in our church records of the dear lady who helped us. She has since passed away but will never be forgotten in my heart. It was her request that her name never be published or made known. When I had her funeral services many years after our church was completed, people wondered about the preacher who wept, but I looked upon her then as my second mother, since my own mother was gone by that time and could not help me.

Read the Bible, pray, have faith and believe in God. You will find He is very real!

26. Dedication of the Church

"AND THE LORD APPEARED TO SOLOMON BY NIGHT, AND said unto him, I have heard thy prayer, and have chosen this place to myself for an house of sacrifice. If I shut up heaven that there be no rain, or if I command the locusts to devour the land, or if I send pestilence among my people; if my people, which are called by my name, shall humble themselves, and pray, and seek my face, and turn from their wicked ways; then will I hear from heaven, and will forgive their sin, and will heal their land. Now mine eyes shall be open, and mine ears attent unto the prayer that is made in this place. . . . But if ye turn away, and forsake my statutes and my commandments, which I have set before you, and shall go and serve other gods, and worship them; then will

I pluck them up by the roots out of my land which I have given them; and this house, which I have sanctified for my name, will I cast out of my sight, and will make it to be a proverb and a byword among all nations. And this house, which is high shall be an astonishment to everyone that passeth by it; so that he shall say, Why hath the Lord done thus unto this land, and unto this house? And it shall be answered, Because they forsook the Lord God of their fathers, which brought them forth out of the land of Egypt, and laid hold on other gods, and worshipped them, and served them: therefore hath he brought all this evil upon them." II Chronicles 7.

Our Bible plainly teaches that we must serve God and worship Him. On the day of the dedication, April 17, 1938, the above Scripture was read to the congregation. Dedicatory prayers were offered. Needless to say, the papers carried the story. Our crowd surpassed our greatest expectations. Some said the crowd outside, not able to get into the church, was greater than the crowd inside. Our own Akron *Beacon Journal* had given us valuable publicity. Mr. Knight and his editors had given us fine coverage on our services.

On the first day that our church was opened we saw sixty people saved. After that Easter Sunday, we held a week's revival. During that week of revival we saw two hundred people saved and join our church. Most of the two hundred converts were adults; however, some were teen-agers. God has never broken a covenant. It is we, the human race, who break covenants. God has continued to bless from the day we began as a church at Rimer School unto this day.

It should be interesting to you to know that the bills or money taken from the shoe box, which enabled us to complete our church for dedication, were so old that they were much larger in size than those we have now and had been done away with by the government. This dear old lady had kept them so long that the bills were actually stuck together. Mr. Leonard of the Firestone Bank got them okayed in

Washington and even had to pull them apart to send them to Washington. They were accepted by the government, and we received credit for the money.

We were in our church and it had been dedicated; however, it was far from being free of debt. Our task was before us. Statements began pouring in which had to be met. We preached tithing to our people. The Bible teaches us that one tenth of our money belongs to God.

It is the custom of the Akron Baptist Temple to assemble all of the adults or married couples into one Bible class, which the pastor teaches each Sunday morning at ten o'clock. I know of one church which has fourteen different adult Bible classes. Some of those classes have less than twelve people in them. I am questioned many times concerning this. I simply tell them I teach the Bible, book by book, and in the ten-o'clock hour an invitation is always given. We mean by "invitation" that the opportunity is given to all adults there to receive Christ in their hearts. We ask them to come forward to accept Christ as their own personal Saviour. At the close of our adult Bible class on Sunday, souls are asked to accept Christ. We like to think of it as being like a Billy Sunday meeting. We have an altar at our church where people can come and kneel. Testaments are found at intervals across the platform, which is about eighty feet long, and when men and women come seeking Christ, a personal worker can take the Testament and show them what God says about salvation. We always refer to God's Bible as the road map from earth to Glory.

The year 1938 became a memorial year for me in the ministry. God was so good to me. My mind wanders back many times, and, as if it were yesterday, I remember the almost unbelievable way in which God undertook to help me and my people. I rejoice, looking back over my life, at the great things God made possible for us.

I believe with all my heart that God had planned to place this dear lady in our pathway, that a way of victory might be had for those who trusted and believed in a living God. She was part of a plan for a church which was to become known the world over for God's glory.

Dr. Tom Carter, a man who was saved in prison and who had been pardoned and paroled, was sent to us for the purpose of holding the first revival in our church. Dr. Carter told our people that Paul had said he was a prisoner for Christ, but he, Dr. Carter, had been a prisoner because of his guilt. His mother had given him to God from his birth to become a preacher, and his sinful ways had caused people to laugh at the mother who still hoped one day to see him working for Christ. Even after he was arrested and given the death sentence, she continued to pray and believe that someday her son would preach the gospel.

In this one short week of revival, we saw people from practically every walk of life come in to the services. We saw men and women come from every factory in Akron, and we saw them walk up the aisle and kneel, accepting Christ. We have always referred to this week as the dedication week.

Our church has never condoned screaming, rolling in the aisles, or any kind of radical exhibition; but, rather, we encourage a quiet, reverent, serious, holy, and rational confession of sin and salvation of the soul. The Bible tells us that Jesus wept, and that is the way the people came to Christ, with their eyes dimmed by tears. They were tears of sorrow turned into joy and peace that only God can give. We saw them come to the altar weeping over their sins, and then we saw them stand to their feet fully satisfied in Jesus.

When they came to the altar, we showed them that they were sinners, for in Isaiah it tells us that all have sinned and come short of the glory of God. They were shown the Scriptures that they might read for themselves. Romans 10:13 promised them that whosoever would call upon the name of the Lord would be saved.

The dedication week of the first church building on Manchester Road, where our church had had such a humble beginning, saw evidence that God was smiling upon us and pouring blessings upon us. We had been blessed with His Holy Spirit in our midst, and our church was being noticed.

Humbly we say this and not to boast: it has been our privilege to have judges of the city in our congregation. The mayor of the city has sat upon our platform. From the beginning, we in our church have tried to live and so conduct ourselves that we might never be called a radical people. Jesus went about his work in a quiet, determined way, with a purpose in his heart. We too have a purpose— to win all we can for Christ.

If you come to Akron and attend one of our services, you will find that we are old-fashioned, as far as believing every word of the Bible. You will find us God-fearing as well as God-loving people, like the prophets of old. We still believe the Bible in its literal meaning, unless it indicates a spiritual application. Jesus used parables that the unsaved would see the truth more clearly. Always when Jesus talked to farmers, He talked to them in a language which they understood. When He talked to those who worked in the vineyard, He talked in their language. He talked to the physician and the statesman in like manner. Jesus was and is our example. Jesus was and is our sin-bearer, dying on a cross in our place, to pay for our sins, giving us a home in Heaven.

This dedication was the beginning of other dedications: since that day we have seen dedicated four other large buildings. Our church has been blessed so greatly that God has permitted us to start over two hundred Baptist churches in this land of ours and in many foreign countries. Jesus said to go into all the world and preach His gospel to every creature. This we as a church are trying our best to do.

27. Preacher Arrested

AFTER WE DEDICATED OUR FIRST BUILDING IN 1938, OUR crowds were still so large that a great number of people were turned away. It was apparent that something had to be done with the people who stood outside. The city of Akron had an ordinance forbidding a loudspeaker outside of a building. I was unaware of this ordinance. We went out to the airport, borrowed some bleachers, and brought them back to our church grounds. On days that weather permitted, people would sit on the bleachers and in their cars, listening to the message broadcast over a loudspeaker from our pulpit. When the invitation was given, it was a very common thing for many of these people to make their way into the building to the altar and there accept Christ.

The building was always filled inside, and the crowd outside grew rapidly. On one Sunday morning, during the ten-o'clock hour, someone said to me there were police officers outside who wished to see me. I finished my message and went outside. The police had been sent to tell us to turn off the loudspeakers. I learned then about the ordinance. I realized all these people sitting here had come to hear the message, and I did not intend for them to be turned away. I tried not to seem disrespectful toward the law, but when I asked if they had a warrant for my arrest and found that they did not, I asked them either to come in and worship with us or get off the property. I made it plain that I was not going to turn off the speakers.

A neighbor who lived in the church community did sign an arrest warrant, and the next day the chief of police, Ray Williams, called and told me he had a warrant for my arrest. He wanted me to come down to the police station to sign my bond until the day of trial.

I walked into the police station, where I knew many of the fine policemen. I saw one detective shake his head and say that with all the sin in our city, why should a preacher be brought in for preaching the gospel to an overflow crowd. After a while the sergeant at the desk called me over and read the charge of disturbing the peace of the community. Up until that hour I had never been arrested for one thing. By God's grace and mother's prayers, I had never been brought before a judge, accused of a crime.

The day was set for the trial, and I had several lawyer friends who offered to take my case free of charge. Attorney Daniel Faulkner was a good friend and a member of our church. He and a friend of his, Mr. Myers, were selected to represent me and the church.

I had all respect for the judges of the city, but I felt in my heart it would be better to have the decision of twelve people than the decision of one. They arranged for me to have a jury trial. I had read in an old English lawbook where it said that if the defendant should show just cause why he should be tried at night or have a continued trial until the finish, he could request it; and if the court wanted to, it could grant the request. The trial was set for Monday, and I was supposed to be at a revival meeting in Chattanooga, Tennessee, on Tuesday. My plane was to leave around noon Tuesday. Therefore, I made the request through my attorney that the trial continue all day and through the night, if necessary, so that I could keep my revival engagement.

When it came to the selection of the jury, I shall never forget that the prosecutor objected to the jurors' being Baptist. Others were called, and when some Catholic people were selected, I told them I had no objection to the religion or race of anyone sitting on my jury. It was almost noon before the jury were selected. Judge Kelly asked the city council to dismiss or move to another location, so that there would be more room for those attending the trial. Someone made the remark that this should not be done. To this the judge answered, "This is my court, and I can hold it out in the open air if I so desire." The change was made, and the fine city councilmen graciously gave up the city council's chambers, that there might be more room for the trial's spectators.

"And they that had laid hold on Jesus led him away to Caiaphas the high priest, where the scribes and the elders were assembled. But Peter followed him afar off unto the high priest's palace, and went in, and sat with the servants, to see the end. Now the chief priests, and elders, and all the council, sought false witness against Jesus to put him to death; but found none: yea, though many false witnesses came, yet found they none. At the last came two false witnesses, and said, This fellow said, I am able to destroy the temple of God, and to build it in three days." Matthew 26:57-61.

Around sixteen or eighteen witnesses were brought in who lived in the neighborhood and community of the church. Some said the speakers were so loud that they could not hear their own radio. One woman said the speakers were too loud and bothered her. However, her husband, who came in right after her, said that he had never heard them. The testimonies were conflicting, and all kinds of stories were offered; but, as when Jesus was on trial, no two witnesses agreed.

Court was dismissed for lunch but was resumed again soon after, and the examining and cross-examining began. The day wore on, and a reporter from the Akron *Beacon Journal* came over to me and asked if I objected to having my picture taken. The story was run on the front page of the city's newspaper. I had asked my wife not to go to the trial, and when the paper came out that evening, it was my son who carried the paper slowly in to his mother. Like all boys who love their dads, he was angered at the injustice being done to his. He told his mother that he wished he were a lawyer who could get even with those who had arrested his daddy. It was not easy for him at school. It hurt me more to see my wife and son hurt than anything anyone might say or do to me.

After supper the trial was resumed, until there remained only one witness. The very man whom I had told either to go into the church and worship or get off the property was called as the last witness. He had also been prosecutor for the case and had turned over the questioning to his assistant, so that he might be a witness.

Then they asked me to take the stand, and I was sworn in. They asked me to tell the court and the judge what had happened. I turned to the jury and said that I was guilty of preaching to an overflow crowd. I told them I had read of the persecution of churches in faraway lands and even of people losing their lives. The prosecutor objected often as I talked, but I continued to give my honest opinions. The prosecutor asked me about the speakers and why I had them, even though the city ordinance forbade it. He prosecuted me as if I had been guilty of the most vicious crime ever committed, judging from the things he said about me as a Baptist preacher. I tried to take it all with a smile, yet deep within me my heart was bleeding. Mr. Faulkner and Mr. Myers asked me questions concerning my childhood, parents, reasons for coming to Akron, and my church.

Finally the case had been presented by both sides, and the judge gave his charge. He told the jury that in his opinion Dallas Billington had no intention or thought of breaking the law, as his reputation proved; however, he charged them to bring a verdict according to their own honest opinion.

I was told later that, as the bailiff took the jurors to the room and they began to discuss the trial, one woman juror told them she would stay there ninety-nine years before she would say that the preacher was guilty. They decided to take a vote, for it was about 11:00 p.m. On the first vote, eleven voted not guilty and one, guilty. The foreman asked the one that had voted guilty to state his or her reasons. A woman spoke up and said that she had voted guilty because she thought I should be made to take down the speakers. The foreman explained to her that was not what they were in there to decide. The next vote gave me an acquittal.

The decision was reached in about nine minutes, and the jurors were returned to the courtroom. The foreman gave the bailiff a folded piece of paper, which, in turn, was given to the judge. We were told there were from 3,000 to 5,000 people outside waiting for the verdict. The judge congratulated me and thanked the jury for their verdict. Then the judge turned to me and said, "This concludes the trial; however, would you like to say something before we adjourn?" I saw my choir leader and many of my people in the room. I asked that they sing, "There Is Power in the Blood," and then I would close with prayer. We sang, and before I prayed I thanked the judge and the jurors for their consideration. We bowed our heads, and I could hear people weeping all around me.

Before I left that night I shook hands with each juror and both prosecutors. I told them they had their job to do and I held no malice in my heart for them. I thanked my lawyers. But that was not the end of the effect it had on the city of Akron. The man who was mayor at the time ran a year later and was beaten badly, and the following year he ran for sheriff and was beaten again. People seemed to think that, had he wanted it so, the case would never have been brought to trial.

However, I can say now that I am thankful it happened, for as the song writer asks, "Should Jesus bear the cross alone and all the world go free? No, there is a cross for everyone and there's a cross for me." The *Beacon Journal* stood by me with fiery editorials. Had they wanted to they could have hurt me badly, but they were very fair with me. They simply ran the news as it happened. Up to that time that was the only night trial ever held in the state of Ohio. That which had started to wreck my ministry and tear down the cause of Christ in the city of Akron, brought glory to

God. When I read of Jesus' false witnesses I can look back and in a small measure understand a great deal more what Jesus suffered. There were no stripes put on me, and I was not put in prison. No one mocked me or spit upon me. Jesus was found innocent and yet condemned to die, while I was let go free. Jesus could, had He wished, have gone free; but He paid the price that you and I might be free.

I thought I loved Jesus all I could, but I found that I could love Him even more. I am thankful for the power of God. What He has done for others He can do for you, if you will only believe and trust Him. It is no secret what God can do, just ask anyone who knows Him as their Saviour.

I would like, in this book, to thank the Honorable Judge Kelly and the jurors still living for the way they allowed God to use them.

28. Second Building

EARLY IN 1939 OUR CHURCH OFFICERS AND I MET WITH the members of our church in order to plan to build another building, which was to be behind the building we were now holding services in. Our Sunday school had grown so rapidly that we were running between 1,600 and 2,000 every Sunday.

We had organized our church in 1935, and at that time Mr. Stanley Bond, a marvelous Christian man, took on the duties of Sunday-school superintendent. One year later he told me that when it came time to elect church officers, he would be glad to step aside and let someone else take his job for the next year. He said the job had a great burden and a cross to bear, but with it was a great honor; and, while he loved the work, he was humble enough to give it up in order to share the honor with some worthy man.

I asked this man of God to pray with me. We knelt on the platform at Rimer School. I decided, then and there, this was the man God wanted to head our Sunday school. I told him that if he would work, pray, and stay with me, going two and two, God would give us the world's largest Sunday school. I honestly believed God would do this for us if we remained true to God's Word and earnest in His work. Years ago, when I had my first Sunday-school class, I purposed in my heart never to stop working until I had the largest class in the world worshiping Christ. I had a vision in my heart that one day I could say I was preaching to the greatest Sunday school in the United States, for the glory of God.

Perhaps you might say I was egotistical, but I read in the Bible where Jesus had the men sit down and there fed 5,000 men, women, and children. The Bible said that if I would lift up Jesus, all men would be drawn to Him.

We had the plans drawn for a building 80 feet by 80 feet with two floors. As the first building was 80 feet wide, we would be able to attach the second building directly to the back of it. This annex was to be our Sunday-school plant. The center of the building was to be made into auditoriums, while classrooms were to be built around the sides. Since then, the same pattern has been used in other church buildings all over the United States. We have had men from Texas and Kentucky and men of other denominations come to see how we arranged our building.

When we began to build, lumber was so high that it almost seemed an impossible as well as an impractical time to build. I found that lumber was being sold to contractors for building small homes at a price much cheaper than that which had been quoted to me. I met with the lumbermen and insisted that they give me a better price. They refused.

I had been in the state of Alabama to hold a revival. While

there, I met two fine Christian men, Mr. Moore and Mr.
Jackson, who were owners and operators of one of the largest
lumber companies in the South. They had the finest in every
kind of lumber. When I told the lumbermen in Akron that I
intended to order lumber from the South, they looked at me
as if to say, "What do you know about lumber?" They had
no way of knowing that, as a boy, I had gone to the woods
with a staff of men who knew lumber and had helped bring
it to the sawmill which my father operated. I had worn the
buckskin gloves and carried slabs from the old mill, as the
saw ripped the logs apart. Little did I realize, when I worked
as a lumberjack, that God was preparing me for His job
later. By God's guidance, I knew the timber business backwards and forwards. I could look at a tree and measure
around it and guess to the first limb within fifty feet how
much lumber could be got out of that tree.

Even though the lumbermen did not take me seriously, I
told Mr. McCoy, who had built our first building, to figure
out what amount of lumber we would need for our new
building. I asked him for the exact sizes and amounts of
each kind that he would need. When Mr. McCoy came in
the next morning to the church office, he told me we would
need lumber enough to fill six cars. I could count on this
man to have figured in every little detail where lumber was
needed.

I took the sheet which he had prepared for me to order
from and called Cullman, Alabama, asking for either Mr.
Jackson or Mr. Moore. I informed the operator that the call
might take an hour and perhaps she should notify the operators on the circuit, so that we would not be interrupted or
cut off.

First of all, I told Mr. Jackson that I had an order that
would amount to six cars of lumber and I wanted to know if
he would send the lumber and follow with his statement, or
did he want a check in advance before shipping. He told me
he would send me all the lumber we wanted and we could

have as long as twelve months to pay for it. After the order was given, Mr. Jackson said he would give us special consideration, to enable us to have the lumber in four days.

The Akron *Beacon Journal* carried the story. Several lumbermen in Akron were surprised to see six cars of lumber arrive from Cullman, Alabama. We had our own trucks, and we broke the seals and loaded the lumber onto the trucks. I was determined to get as much for God's money as I could. I had soon found that preaching was only part of the duties of a minister. I had one office girl, Miss Lucille Stamps, who did the office work and answered the telephone; however, the finances of the church were my burden.

After many hours of work and still more hours of prayer, the building was finished, and we moved into it in October of that year. Our complete Sunday-school staff of teachers, Stanley Bond, and I met and prayed God would fill the building for us. By the end of the winter and the beginning of spring, we were having 2,000 in Sunday school. Now these two floors were packed and filled. We were getting letters from people in Akron desiring a bus that they might attend our Sunday school. We had buses running through the areas where there were no churches. Some of our members would go up and down those streets and tell the people what time the bus would be there. The driver was instructed to stop at any corner or even in the middle of the block; all that was necessary for the people to do was to flag the bus. This was God's plan, going from house to house. Thus, God continued to bless, and souls were being saved. It was not uncommon to see as many as twenty-five taxicabs pull up in front of the church, bringing people to our Sunday school.

We were given good publicity from our own Akron newspaper, and *Look* magazine ran a story about us. The staff from *Look* came into the classes and actually counted the children. They had heard about our offerings, that there were no pledges but that tithing alone was taught. We told them we did not care if they counted our offering in order to see for themselves. The *Look* man called his office from my office in the church and told them he needed more help if he were to cover this church. There were too many classes, too many activities, and too many stories for the men who had been sent to cover the church.

We were thankful for this publicity in a national magazine about what God had done for us. Little did we dream that from such a small group so large a group could grow. The Bible speaks of small things, such as the size of the first cloud Elijah saw when he prayed for rain being the size of a man's hand. The cloud grew and God blessed the earth with life-giving rain. He had permitted our little group to grow, and blessings were continually falling.

We had watched our church grow from an unorganized group in 1934 to a church so large that, in the fall of 1939, we moved into a second building. We had no problem financing our second building. God had given us collateral, giving us a name and at the same time glorifying His Name. God had made a covenant with me, a preacher boy. He had promised that He would never leave me or forsake me, and He proved Himself over and over to me and to the members of my church, as well as to the city of Akron.

29. Serious Heart Attack

ON JUNE 12, 1941, EARLY IN THE MORNING, I WAS STRUCK with a coronary heart attack. This was graduation day for my son, Charles, from grade school. My condition was serious and this meant, of course, that my wife would remain with me, and my son would have neither father nor mother at his graduation. Douglas McClure, about six or eight years older than my son, who was and still is a dear friend of his, came by and took Charles to school. He remained with him all day and was there when he received his diploma.

No one but God realized how very sick I was. Dr. C. L. Beatty, our fine family doctor, was summoned at four in the morning. He told my wife that my condition was so serious that I might not make it. The doctor did not want me moved, but he returned several times that day and night to check on me. The doctor felt that it would be fatal even to move me to the hospital, but that if they could keep me quiet and alive for forty-eight hours, there was a chance that I might live. I was in a delirious condition for many days, hardly knowing my family or when the doctor came and left. Nurses were hired to care for me and stay with my wife.

On the first Sunday after my heart attack, the church was told of my condition. I was told that over a thousand people remained after the morning services and did not go home for Sunday dinner, but were found in Sunday-school rooms or any place where they could petition God that if it were His will, their pastor's life might be spared and restored to health.

The years had not been easy. The strain had finally caught up with my heart. In my eagerness to prepare myself for the ministry I studied long hours, never missing a shift of work; and perhaps I got much less rest than was required. I was a young man, but the financial worries had taken their toll of sleepless nights. With God as my witness, I made calls when I myself should have been resting. God forbid that I tell you this to suggest that I should be given the credit. I knew from where my strength came, and I knew in whom I believed. I did not know why I lay stricken; but I knew God did not make mistakes and somehow everything would be all right.

Days passed and weeks into months, and it looked as if there were no improvement. I would have sweating seizures and have to be rolled in blankets to keep from having pneumonia fever. A sign was placed on our door—No Visitors Allowed—for I was too weak to talk. A little bell was placed on my bed so that when I needed help, I could summon someone with a shake of the bell.

When I was conscious, I would pray and read my Bible. I resigned myself and my life into the hands of the good Lord. I lost count of time. One day, knowing I was growing steadily weaker, I asked everyone to leave except my wife. I told her I did not want to frighten her or make her cry, but if a change did not come very soon, I knew this was the end of my life. We had never discussed death. Did you ever try to talk to a loved one about her passing or yours? It is a very difficult thing to do, but for her sake and my son's, it was only fair that we understand each other. We chose the undertaker, and said they could choose the pallbearers, for there were too many men in the church whom I loved for me to choose between them. Nell left the room and sent my son in at my request. I told him that it looked like Dad might have to leave him and Mother, and if so, there were some things I would request of him. My son had become a Christian when he was nine years old, so I was not concerned with his soul; however, I did ask him always to live for God. I asked him to be good to his mother and to care for her. Everything that I had made in the past years had been put in my church. We did not have any money saved.

I told him that the church would be good to him and Mother. The church had just purchased a new large car for me, and I suggested to Charles that the church trade it in on a smaller model for them. God had always taken care of us, and I was sure God would look after my son and wife, should He desire my life.

Charles listened very attentively and then, like a soldier of thirty, stood up by my bed and took my hand in his. With a trembling voice he said, "Dad, you are discouraged; Mother needs you and I need you. Won't you fight for me and get well? Won't you try your best for the thousands of people praying for you at church? Just pray, Daddy. I'm praying and Mother is praying. Don't give up, Dad, please don't. Remember, Dad, I need you!"

It broke my heart to hear him plead. I wished I could honestly say that I had finished my work; but I felt like there was so much yet to be done. If it was God's will, I was willing to bow to it. I was receiving shots every four hours to relieve me of the severe pain around my heart. When the nurse came in that midnight to give me my shot, I asked her to let me try to go through the night without a shot. I wanted to spend the entire night as rational as I could be. I asked her to sit in the hallway so that I might be all alone in my room. She was reluctant to leave me, but I told her she could hear the bell. To please me, the nurse took her chair and, leaving the door open, went out into the hall. This nurse was like our own family. She came early and stayed late, taking her meals with my family. She was a great source of comfort to my family during my illness.

While the nurse read in the hall, I talked with Jesus. It seems to me that I told the Lord I was ready to leave that night. I prayed that this would be the night I might fall asleep without the hypo, without the pain, and wake up somewhere on Heaven's shore, where there is no sorrow, pain, or tears. I would rest awhile, and then I would pray again. If you had been close by, you would have thought I was talking to someone in the room. Jesus, who had said He would never leave me, was there with me that night. You would not have seen Him with your visible eye; you would not have touched Him with your hands; but He was there. It seemed to me that a sweet, peaceful sleep came over my mind and body, and for the first time in many nights I slept without the aid of medicine.

I awakened the next morning with the sun streaming in the two large windows before me. I could see the green leaves of the two large elm trees as they glistened from the dew. There was not a cloud in the sky, and the world looked beautiful to me. It was summertime, and the day had come alive in all its radiance. I tapped the bell, and instantly my nurse was by my side. I smiled at her and said, "Thanks to the Lord I've had a good night's rest."

The doctor came that morning and said my pulse was stronger and I definitely had taken a turn for the better. He told my wife he believed I would make it.

"According to my earnest expectation and my hope, that in nothing I shall be ashamed, but that with all boldness, as always, so now also Christ shall be magnified in my body, whether it be by life, or by death. For to me to live is Christ, and to die is gain. But if I live in the flesh, this is the fruit of my labour: yet what I shall choose I wot not. For I am in a strait betwixt two, having a desire to depart, and to be with Christ; which is far better: nevertheless to abide in the flesh is more needful for you. And having this confidence, I know that I shall abide and continue with you all for your furtherance and joy of faith; that your rejoicing may be more abundant in Jesus Christ for me by my coming to you again." Philippians 1:20-26.

I sent for my secretary and asked her to take a little note to my church. In the note I told my people that God had answered our prayers: whatever my illness had been planned to accomplish was done, and I would be back. God had given me many precious hours to think and pray. There are lessons to be learned in sickness which have never been written in books. There are experiences which only suffering can give you. No mortal man can write with pen and ink how a man can feel so very close to God.

I began to recover rapidly, and the nurses were told they need not come back. One day I was told I could go downstairs. No one ever appreciates his health until it is gone. I could not hide the tears when I saw our living room again. Each day I felt my strength returning. Paul has said in his writings, the sufferings of this world cannot be compared with the glory that shall be revealed in Him.

The day came when my doctor said that I might go back to church for just a little while. He instructed me to go into services after they began and to leave before they were over; for he knew my dear people would want to see me and perhaps shake hands, and I was not strong enough for that yet.

I called to my memory where it said in the Bible that Paul and Silas were sent to the Macedonians, who had asked for help. These were men who had hazarded their lives for the sake of Christ. I can say with Paul that I gloried in my infirmities. I was drawn much closer to God, and I knew that I would make a better preacher. Perhaps I understood more about the sufferings of Christ. My Bible tells me that if we suffer with Christ we shall reign with Him. God was molding me for still a greater work. I was not afraid, for I knew God loved me and was too wise to make a mistake and too kind to be untrue. In the last few years, being so eager to build and being involved with problems of finance and construction, I had not read my Bible so diligently as I once had. But during these days of sickness, with four walls for company, I had plenty of time to read and think. They would not let me preach or go to the hospital and make calls. For these days, I had but one thing to think of, and that was the glory of God. I read about the things that came to pass for those who loved God. Day after day I read my Bible. I found in the Book of Hebrews where it said that God chastens every son whom He loves. I had been interested in doing the things of the Lord, and I was a builder. I had never asked one member, officer, or trustee to raise a dollar. I though I had to do it all myself. Then I found myself unable to do one thing for God, except sit and read His word.

I am sure my illness was for me. God caused me to stop and think. My illness gave me untold faith. My illness made me very humble. I realized I could do nothing without God. My sickness was over, and the pain was over, and gradually God was restoring me. I was rich in God's love and mercy.

The first place where I was permitted to speak after my illness was Rimer School, where we were still keeping our boys and girls of high school age. I told them of the trials and tribulations of Joseph and Daniel. God had used my sickness for His Glory. Things do happen to us for the furtherance of the gospel. I was only permitted to speak twelve minutes, and when that time was up I closed my sermon, telling them how much I loved them. Someday, perhaps, when they were older—perhaps before the open casket or on a battlefield in a foxhole—they would find a time when all was done for them that could be done, when they ought to be able to say with the psalmist David, "Yea, though I walk through the valley of the shadow of death, I will fear no evil for thou art with me." The invitation was given and forty-nine high school boys and girls trusted Jesus as their Saviour.

Then I remembered what Jesus had said: except a corn of wheat die it abideth alone. My illness and absence from my young people had taught them my love for them. I can say with Paul that for any Christian to die is to gain. But God willed for me to stay with my family and preach, winning all I could for Christ.

30. War 1861—War 1941

HERE IS A PROMISE OF GOD: "HE THAT DWELLETH IN THE secret place of the most High shall abide under the shadow of the Almighty. . . . A thousand shall fall at thy side, and ten

thousand at thy right hand; but it shall not come nigh thee."
I remember, as a boy, sitting at the feet of my grandfather
Billington and hearing him tell how he took his horse and
joined the group fighting for what he thought was right.
He served for four years and came home on the same horse
on which he had ridden away. Night after night he would lie
and pray, oftentimes with his clothes wringing wet. He carried a small Bible with him and never once lost it, but
brought it through the war and back home. Grandfather
would take this Bible and read the above Scripture to as
many men as would listen.

The hardships were many. Their corn bread was kept so
long that it would mold from the dampness and heat. Grandfather often told me a man really gets to know God when he
is put to a severe test. He and a good friend were instructed
to scout ahead and see if they could spot the enemy. However, both of them were captured far into enemy territory.
They were imprisoned in a log cabin in a wooded area.
Since they were captured in the act of spying, there could
be no other fate for them except death. The two were
escorted into the cabin where the officer in charge and his
aide were sitting.

They were left alone with the officer. He told them he
had always wondered what he would do when faced with
having to order a man shot. Grandfather told me that with
lips closed, he prayed for himself and his wife back home. He
knew that his buddy was also a devout Christian. Grandfather finally spoke to the captain and asked him if he were
a Christian. The captain sat for some time with his head
down; then he slowly lifted his head and said, "Yes, I am a
Christian." Grandfather told him that he knew the captain
had his duties to perform, and he wanted him to know that
he would not blame him, because he, like Grandfather, was
fighting for what he thought was right. They could never be
enemies, since they were both fighting for the same wonderful country. The captain called for their horses, and they

were brought. The aide was put in front, and the captain followed behind Grandfather and his friend. They were led down a dark hidden path. The Yankee officer stopped them when they reached a clearing and gave them their freedom, saying, "Men, if this is ever discovered, I shall be shot by a firing squad." My grandfather and his friend rode to safety, hardly daring to believe it could be true. They had been given their freedom, because two men became brothers through the Cross of Calvary.

Grandfather Billington would tell his grandchildren this story, and his chin would quiver and his eyes would fill with tears, as if he were reliving those uneasy, yet thankful, moments so long ago. He used to tell me, "When it seems that every star in your heaven has gone out and even though the sun has gone down, remember God still lives."

Samuel Kelly, also my grandfather, was in the same war. He too, was God-loving and God-fearing. He, too, spent those years in the war and returned unharmed. You might ask the question, Why were they returned when many Christian men died? I do not know what God had in mind. Perhaps He planned for us to hear these stories to strengthen our faith for the coming years.

I remember well, in 1917, when my family drove my older brother, Henry Billington, to Murray, Kentucky, to see him off to the army. As the weeks passed, our family would gather around the table and read the letters which he wrote to us. As a family, we would pray for him. There are promises in the Bible for you in wartimes as well as promises when all is well. There is a secret hiding place in the heart of God for those who are in trouble. There are many today who have sons, daughters, brothers, sisters, husbands, left on the battle-fields of Flanders. Don't ask me why, I do not know. This one thing I do know, that whether it is on the sea, or in the air, or on the ground, God is real. God says all power is given to Him.

As I grew older, I read the history books which contained

my great heritage. I read the stories of other wars, where George Washington and his men crossed the Delaware River, leaving bloody footprints upon the ice. I read in my history book where they prayed.

I believe with all my heart that the greatest learning a boy can have is at the feet of his father and grandfather, who have been God-fearing and God-loving men, listening to their experiences and profiting from them.

When the day comes when other men try to tear from the heart of a boy the faith instilled in him by godly forefathers, that boy will remain unmoved in his belief that God is real. If he has been taught the love of God from the cradle and reared with Christ before him, the worlds may fall apart around him, but his faith will last. There are not enough people on earth to laugh, mock, or ridicule the Holy Word to keep that boy from clinging to its promises.

A Jewish boy told me he had always been taught that God had all power; and the Jews all learn some trade, so that when they are chased from their land or homes they might still earn a living. He smiled, and with tears, he told me they could not take material things with them, but that which was within their hearts and minds no one could take from them. A man can be carried a million miles from his home, but the love of God is close by and very real when He lives in that man's heart. You never find out how real God is until you need Him.

After the attack on Pearl Harbor in December, 1941, around June, 1942, the government in Washington declared there could be no more chartered buses for any purpose whatever. This was done to save tires and gasoline, which were vital to our war effort. Our church at that time was using twenty-one chartered buses from the city. We had definite routes over which the buses ran each Sunday morning, picking up many people all over Akron, bringing them to our services. Many children who had no means of getting to church were riding these buses. We were averaging about fifty children per bus. We were notified by letter that the city buses could not be chartered any more. We were told that in two weeks the buses would stop, and they sent us a copy of the declaration which had caused this. Nevertheless, I had learned when trouble came, to pray.

I called my church together, and we read this Scripture: "And whatsoever ye shall ask in my name that will I do, that the Father may be glorified in the Son. If you love me, keep my commandments." This is God's Word and He has promised to do anything we ask if it is in His name. Whatever you ask, let it be glory to God. I asked my people to pray night and day, anytime, anywhere. I asked all the children large enough to understand the word to pray in their Sunday-school rooms. The Sunday-school superintendents told the children that I wanted them to pray, for our buses were going to be stopped unless God intervened. They knew they would have no way to come to church, and the teachers had taught them that God hears the prayers of a little child. The children remembered how God was with Samuel and Daniel when they were very young, and they believed in their little hearts that if God ruled, then Washington would change.

It seemed almost foolish for a preacher to have the nerve to ask a congregation to pray about a thing which Washington had decreed. We were at war, and all over the United States people were abiding by this declaration. High schools could not take their teams anywhere for games. The rule was observed from coast to coast. If my son, Charles, were to ask me for something, I would first judge whether it was necessary. I would not embarrass my son, but if it was worthy to be granted, then I would grant it. This I was asking my Heavenly Father to do. I was asking Him to judge whether it was worthy of being granted. I was not afraid to ask God. There had been many storms in my life already. I had already seen things happen which, if I had been faint in heart, I would never have seen. A Sunday passed, and we just kept on praying. Finally the letter came telling us there would be no more buses. I called one of Akron's lawyers and asked him to call our congressman. He was my congressman and I had voted for him; but if I were a man who was easily discouraged, I would have given up after he spoke of his amazement at my wanting to change a law of Washington. He asked me who did I think I was to ask him to embarrass himself by going to the powers that be to ask that buses for a church be allowed to run.

I told him that if it would embarrass him to ask the transportation authorities to let us have our buses, he need not do it. He told me he had no intention of doing it. I thanked him and hung up the telephone.

I watched trucks loaded with beer leave Akron. When they got out on the highway, I would stop them and ask what they were carrying. They freely told me it was beer. They did not know who I was, nor did they care. I counted the number of tires which each truck used. I did this several times, writing down all the information.

Using as much good sense as I could, so that people would not think me an agitator or anti-American, I said on our radio broadcast how unjust it was to take our buses from us. Was it so wrong of me to want buses to bring people to church when trucks were being permitted to use gasoline and tires to haul beer? In my opinion, the trucks hauled that which damns and dooms the souls of men and women, while our buses hauled men, women, and children to the house of God. When our buses were stopped, there were over a thousand people who could not come to church. I vowed to preach against this until the day I died. Then, if the time came when I might be imprisoned for declaring this injustice, I would preach to those within the prison walls, saying that my government, the United States of America, with its flag of stars and stripes, was not true to all its citizens, for it had taken away church buses and granted beer trucks the right to roll the streets.

I went to the Akron *Beacon Journal* and asked for someone who might help me in my fight. An attorney, Blake McDowell, Sr., was referred to me. I knew this man and went to his office. I had learned from the newspaper that he was going to Washington. He listened to my story, and I gave him a copy of what I had said on the broadcast. This man went to Washington and represented our church. He told Washington how our church had worked and grown. Washington issued a new proclamation saying that all churches which had been running buses to bring people to church prior to the Pearl Harbor attack could continue those buses until further notice.

The transportation company here in Akron found this hard to believe. We were told that over 2,800 newspapers carried the story all over America. It was easy for me to see why it happened. Daniel had prayed in the lion's den, and the next morning he was found safe and unharmed. God has said if we ask anything in His name, that will He do.

Let me reason with you. Are you weary, heavyhearted? Just tell it to Jesus. Is there something in your home or life that is almost too much to bear? Is there no way to turn? Have you been forsaken by friends and loved ones? Will you then apply this Scripture to your lives?

God forbid that I should try to give myself the credit, for what I am and what I have done have been because of God. However, God has let me be instrumental in turning men's thoughts to God, and many through the broadcasts have found Christ. The very purpose and aim in God's calling a preacher is not necessarily to help just the preacher himself, for many times I have been made a laughingstock, but always to keep Christ before men, that they might see God and love Him.

Matthew's Gospel tells us that if two or three meet in God's name, He will be in their midst to bless. Our church knows no other way out of trouble except to pray. It has been tried many times and has never been found wanting. When our problems get too big for us and we, as individuals, meet with obstacles that no one understands, we just pray.

If you are not a Christian, pray the sinner's prayer: God be merciful to me a sinner. After you are saved and become a child of God, there is no prayer you can pray which God will not hear, if it glorifies Him.

We as a church did not defy the United States government; but we as a church went to the throne of grace, and God changed their minds.

31. Eight Men in Prison

DURING THE YEARS OF WORLD WAR II, THERE WAS LABOR trouble in the city of Akron. In a parking lot at one of the large rubber factories there was a fight one night. Several people were involved, and eight men were arrested and brought to trial. They received $1,000 fines and six months in the county jail. All eight of these men worked in the heavy truck-tire department in the factory. At the same time that they were sent to jail, the cry was coming from the battle-fields for more tires for the trucks. Pleas of every kind were made to the judge who had sentenced these men, and finally it was suggested that a plea be made to the governor. All agreed that there was no way to get these men released. They had been sentenced to six months and a day, and all judges agreed that what one had passed the others would stand behind.

I was holding a meeting in Texas at that time, and my associate pastor, Rev. James Moore, called to tell me of the eight men in the county jail. I knew the story, but Rev. Moore had been asked to tell me the eight men wanted to see me. When I got home, I went to the Akron *Beacon Journal* and

asked them to put my story on their front page. I told them
that I did not deserve the recognition, but that I was going
to get these eight men out of jail. I shall never forget the
newspaperman who listened and then laughed. He said that
I had often said the good Lord used me to do things for
Him, but if Moses himself were living he could not get these
men out of jail.

The labor leaders had tried, the judge had said he could
not take back the sentence. The newspaperman asked me
what I proposed to do. I asked him for a secretary to take
a statement for the paper. In this statement I said that I
did not intend to be a legal adviser for the eight men now in
the county jail, nor was I going to represent them in any
legal capacity, but our church had been praying that they be
released for two reasons: (1) all eight of these men were
home owners, living close to twenty years in Akron without
ever having been in trouble before; (2) two men were
members of our church, two others belonged to another
church here in Akron, and I was acquainted with the other
four men. I did not want the city of Akron to look upon me
as trying to settle a labor strife or to dictate policies to our
honorable judges or to belittle the prosecution office. However, I did propose to get these men out of jail.

The newspapermen asked me how I intended to get them
out of jail, and I told them that was my secret. They said if
I wanted to stand the embarrassment, they would run the
story. The story appeared just as I had dictated it.

I asked the prosecutor, who had done his job well and was
merely performing his duty as a public servant, if he would
become offended if I got these men out of jail. The prosecutor told me not to make him laugh and said I had his
permission, good wishes, and God's blessings to go on, but
his manner assured me that he felt it was pure foolishness.

Next I went to the judge's courtroom and found him taking a fifteen-minute rest period. I asked him if I could talk
with him about the eight men in the county jail. He had been

hounded because of those eight men, and he asked me why I too had come to him. I asked him would I offend him, one of our honorable judges, if I were to get these eight men released. The judge looked at me and said, "Dallas, don't be so full of ego that it mars your reasoning." The judge did not know that I had studied law. He reached me his hand and gave me his word of honor that if I could get them out, I would have his blessing.

I had a good friend, who has since gone to Glory, who was sheriff at the county jail—Walter O'Neil. I went to see him next. He was sitting on his porch reading the paper. I told him I was there on a mission, and he invited me to sit down and talk awhile. I told him that I had had a meeting with my board of trustees, and the church had been holding prayer meetings concerning the release of these eight men. I told him that I proposed to post $20,000 bond for each of the eight men. They were to be freed each morning to go to the plant and work to build the tires. They would return each night to the jail. I told him that I had read in an old lawbook that after a man has been tried and sentenced, he becomes a jailer's prisoner. The jailer is responsible for that man. I had talked with the eight men, and on their knees they had sworn to God they would not betray the church's trust in them if I could get them released to go to work.

The sheriff went with me to see the eight men again. He asked them if he and the preacher worked out something so that they could get out and go to their work, would they promise not to betray their trust and be back at the jail one hour after quitting time at their job. He asked them as one man to another to give him their word. They all vowed they would keep their promise. I shall never forget the tears I saw in the sheriff's eyes as he turned from them and said we would work out something.

He told me then that it would seem as if he were afraid of his job if he had to ask a church to put up bond, so if he let the men out, he would do so on his own. I assured him that the judge and the prosecutor had promised they would not criticize him if the men were released. The papers had always been fair and would not be unkind in any way.

I called the paper and told them the men would go to work in the morning and they should call the sheriff to get the story. Friends from the rubber shop met these eight men each morning and drove them to the shop where they worked; then within one hour after quitting time each night they were back at the jail. This continued for four weeks. One of the wives called me and said that she had a little girl who cried continually for her daddy. She wanted to know why her daddy didn't come home to take them to church. She had kept the fact from her child that her daddy was in jail. She said she knew that a lot had been done and she was so grateful, but was there any chance that these men could be permitted to go to church on Sunday and then go back to jail. I told this mother there was a good chance, for Walter O'Neil had a heart as big as all out of doors and as pure as gold. It would be up to him, but I felt in my heart that he would take this responsibility too.

On Saturday I went to see the sheriff, and he asked me what brought me there. I told him I hated to take advantage of his good nature, but the men whom he had released had lived up to their bargain and had never been even so much as a minute late, and now I had one more request to make. I told him about the wife who had called, and then we read a chapter from the Bible where a church prayed for a man in prison who was released by the angel of the Lord. It caused my heart to rejoice that I could sit down and talk with a man like Mr. O'Neil. This man understood my intentions—that I did not want to go against the law but was just doing what I thought a Christian should do.

I told him that in the 12th chapter of Acts it reads: "Peter therefore was kept in prison: but prayer was made without ceasing of the church unto God for him. And when Herod would have brought him forth, the same night Peter was sleeping between two soldiers, bound with two chains: and the keepers before the door kept the prison. And, behold, the angel of the Lord came upon him, and a light shined in the prison: and he smote Peter on the side, and raised him up, saying, Arise up quickly. And his chains fell off from his hands." To anyone who had visited Peter in prison it certainly looked as if it was impossible for him to be released. James had already been slain, and the king was very pleased to have Peter in prison, so that he might have Peter's life also. However, man's extremities make God's opportunities.

I asked the sheriff then if he could make it possible for these men to attend church at ten o'clock. The complete morning services would be over and they could have dinner with their families, if the sheriff would permit, and be back at the jail by 1:30 P.M. The families would pick the men up by 9:00 A.M. and see that they were back on time. If it was not permissible for them to have dinner with their families, they could at least go to church and be back at whatever hour he would designate. I looked at the sheriff, and he let the tears fall down his cheeks unashamed and said to me, "If I were in prison, you would let me out. If any one of the people involved in this case were in prison, you would let them out, wouldn't you?" Of course I agreed with him. I told him I did not believe the paper would criticize him for doing this.

That evening after the men had returned from their work, the sheriff and I met with them to tell them of the plans for them to attend church. Their families were to pick them up in front of a church across the street from the jail. The smaller children need not know where their dad had been. The sheriff allowed them to stay with their families until 2:00 P.M. We had prayer with the eight men, and the next morning, cars from all the families were there to pick up the men to take them to church.

Our church had prayed, and we had found many friends

willing to help us who were not members of our church. The Akron *Beacon Journal* and Mr. Walter O'Neil, along with the honorable judge and the prosecutor, proved to be friends in the cause of Christ. We had only hoped to get these men released to go to work, but God gave us more than that and permitted them to go to church. You cannot read this story and doubt that God is real. You will never know how real He can be unless you let Him dwell in your heart.

My reason for telling you this story is that you know and I know many men in your town and mine who are in greater prisons than those with iron bars. It could be a drunkard's prison, a gambler's prison, a persecution complex prison, or bound with the fetters of sin, with the chain of the devil and his crowd. This one would give all he owns if he could break from the crowd and go back home to his wife and children. That one got into gambling circles and is afraid to quit, for fear he will be harmed.

Read the entire 12th chapter of Acts. You will find that Peter followed the angel first one way and then another until the angel had led him home. Those who were praying for him at a certain house were astonished and could not believe it was Peter knocking at the gate. Someone said it must be Peter's spirit, for no one could escape a Roman prison. However, Peter kept knocking, and finally they opened the gate. Peter told them how he had been asleep and someone touched him. The chains fell from him and he walked out of prison. There is no problem too big for God. It was not easy for a young preacher to go into a newspaper office or into the chambers of an honorable judge to plead his case. I prayed all night before I faced the prosecutor, for I wanted words which would not offend any of them. I had a great respect for the law and these men. I was asking for mercy for eight men who were right or wrong—only God knew their true hearts.

Would you like to be free from drink, to go home and spend the whole day with your family a sober, happy man?

Would you like to be free from the harlot who is destroying the home you once cherished and loved? You are bound by her power as surely as if there were chains. She threatens to tell the truth to those you love, and the chain tightens. Would you like not to be afraid to go home once again?

Remember this: Almost all of us, with very few exceptions, have had a problem which seemed impossible to solve. We felt in our hearts there was no one to whom we could go for help. We lacked the courage to share our problem. Perhaps all the time there were those who could have helped us, but we were ashamed and frightened. When you become a Christian, God gives you courage which we call Grace. God gives us a new supply each time we need it. Grace is like a bank account. Your bank account may be limited, but you may have a relative who has an unlimited amount, as far as the needs you would ever have are concerned. However, you hate to turn to that relative. In the Bible Jesus is referred to us as our sin-bearer or substitute; however, He is also our Brother. Yet, we seem to be afraid to ask Him for help, to come to Him in a time of sorrow. God's grace is unlimited. You may draw from it sufficient amounts to cover your needs. When I realized that I must go to these different men if my mission for the eight men were to be accomplished, I searched my heart for the courage and found deep in my breast God's grace. If you are not a Christian and know not my Jesus, then the prison which holds you will one day damn your soul for an endless eternity. There is no friend powerful enough to break the chains that bind you. The chains of sin and crime separate you from God. God can break those chains, but He will not break them against your will. There is one called Jesus who can visit your prison, as the angel did Peter, and set you free; but you must accept Him as your Saviour.

Perhaps you have a daughter gone from home, and you would give all you had to see her again. God may not return your daughter, but God can give you grace to bear the sorrow and lighten your burdens and cares. He can take away from you the thing which imprisons you. Why won't you just try Jesus? God understands when no one else does. God made you; you are twice His: once because He created you and twice because He bought you with the precious blood of his Son. God knows your tears and your joys.

When you get tired of straying on the paths of sin and mean it in your heart, then God will release you. God can bring a peace to your soul as He did for Peter. You can see God work through men, as He did in this story, that men can find peace and encouragement through their times of trial.

32. Gas Rationing

"BE NOT AFRAID OF THEIR FACES: FOR I AM WITH THEE to deliver thee, saith the Lord." Thus reads Jeremiah 1:8. During the war days gasoline was rationed, which was necessary for the war effort. However, down through the Bible days, the days of Moses and the Law, through all the poetic books of the Bible, with the minor and major prophets, and into the New Testament days and into this day in which we live, war days have been days of trouble. I don't believe any man of God has any intention of breaking a civil law, but our Bible teaches us that we are to obey God rather than man. Jeremiah was placed in prison, where his hands and feet were put into stocks, because he kept warning his nation of the things to come. Of course, when gas rationing was put into effect, each preacher was given the same allowance for gas. I am sure the board were honest in their hearts, but they just did not understand the whole truth. During the war days, our church had about nine thousand members. Rev. James Moore, our associate pastor, and I were in charge of serving these people. It was no time until both of us were out of gas. We were driving close to a thousand miles per week. One time when we had a funeral and had no gas, we called the rationing board and they allowed us more stamps. Friends and members of the church rode the buses to work and gave us their gas rations, so that we could make the calls for the church.

I was on my way home from a meeting when somewhere between Ashland and Mansfield, Ohio, I got behind a string of four trucks. I pulled out, increasing my speed too much, so that the State Police, who had seen me pull around the trucks, motioned me over to the side and gave me a ticket. One paper came out with the headline: "Baptist Preacher Drives Winged Chariot." The article appeared in many newspapers and even got into the army and navy papers. Naturally I was called before the board and was told it was wrong to be fifty or sixty miles from Akron when gas was scarce. Yet, as I've mentioned, beer trucks were hauling beer to Cincinnati and far and wide. Many uses were being made of gas that could by no stretch of the imagination be called godly. My mission was solely a mission for God, for I had been in a revival, winning souls for Christ.

When the Akron *Beacon Journal* found out that I was to appear before my rationing board, they asked if they could have a reporter listen. The board read the charge against me and asked me if I was not aware that I was not to be out of the city. I told them, according to their law the answer was yes; however, God had said I must go. I knew from the language and actions used that some of the men there were not Christians. I told them that if I had it to do over again, I would be compelled of God to do so. The blessings I enjoyed while in the revival meeting would be worth all the ridicule and trouble it would cause me. In the eyes of man I was guilty, but in the eyes of God I was innocent.

My car and gas were taken away from me for thirty days.

I went down and rented a car and used the gas allotted to it to make calls. But the day came when I was stranded again without gas.

A week had passed, and one day my phone rang. A woman, weeping, said that she was a secretary at one of the rubber shops, and she had a husband who was a very sick heart patient. Every day at noon she would go home to see if he was all right. She would always pull the door behind her to lock it as she went out, and her husband would always let her in at noon. This day, she had gone home and could not raise him. When she looked in the window, she could see her husband lying there. She had gone to the telephone to call me, for she feared he was dead. I told her that I would try to get to her house.

I called the *Beacon Journal* and told them my story. They promised to send me a car and to send an ambulance to meet me at the home. There at her house I broke a window, climbed through and opened the door. It did not take a doctor to tell us that he was dead.

The next morning the newspaper carried the story of how a pastor was left stranded while his people needed him. They compared the number of people which our church had with the number at smaller churches where the pastors had the same gas rationing as we did. On the strength of this article, the ration board gave me back my gas, and from that day until the end of the war and rationing, I was given sufficient gas to take care of my people.

Jeremiah was told to speak out and be bold. There have been times in my ministry when even my best friends did not understand me and it appeared to them that I was intentionally trying to be contrary. However, the Bible tells me to live by faith, and I went on my faith. And God glorified His name through gas rationing.

I did not feel it was wrong to use other people's stamps. The gas was given to them for their benefit, and if it benefited them more to aid the cause of Christ, then who can say it was wrong! The Bible says that all things that happen to us, if we serve Him, happen so that God will receive the glory.

Many of the newspapers carried stories on how God had delivered His preacher. God had said for me to go when the law forbade that I go. God had delivered me as He had before. One Texas paper said, "If God be for you, who can be against you?" The papers stated that a man of God had to obey God rather than man. All of this had happened for God's glory and for the furthering of Christ's gospel. Because our country was at war was no reason for the gospel of Christ to be stopped. The papers said that all ministers should have enough gas to perform their duties. To stop the work of Christ in war days would be the worst thing that could happen to America. If you will put God first, you will find how very real He can be.

33. Lunch with Governor John Bricker

WHILE THE HON. JOHN BRICKER WAS GOVERNOR OF THE state of Ohio, he learned about our church through the many write-ups appearing in papers throughout the state. Mr. Russell Pfister, who was working for the Akron *Beacon Journal,* was in Columbus, talking to a Mr. Young, either publisher or editor of the Columbus *Dispatch.* Mr. Young asked Mr. Pfister to bring me to Columbus to see him.

In the meantime, arrangements were made for me to have lunch with the governor. I was surprised to find a statesman so great a believer of the Word of God. He told me of his experiences in the army, where he had served as chaplain. I found that his faith was as old-fashioned as mine. It was a most enjoyable three and a half hours that Mr. Pfister and I spent with the governor. He had heard that I had once nourished the desire to study and prepare myself to be governor of Kentucky. It seemed a long time ago, but I was still much interested in civil government and loved the books that I had read concerning law and the history of our great country. The way our country grew and developed never ceases to interest me. The desire that I had as a boy to learn stayed with me; but after I became a Christian, my desire became entirely the will of God. I read countless biographies and autobiographies of many great men in all fields and enjoyed them; but there has been no book that has come near the precious Word of God. God always used a man to point men to God.

That same day Mr. Pfister and I went to Mr. Young's office. Mr. Young misunderstood the introductions and was not aware that I was Rev. Billington. I knew this, for he asked questions about the preacher in Akron, about whom so much had been written. He was sarcastic and even used swear words. I knew then that he had assumed I was just another newspaperman like Mr. Pfister. I shall never forget the look on his face when Mr. Pfister made him realize that I was the man he had been talking about, and he had enough breeding to know that his conduct could not have been pleasing to a man of God. He stood to his feet and said that he was sorry for the remarks he had made, especially the profanity. He wanted me to forgive him. I told him that he had not offended me. Mr. Young said he was a good citizen but not a Christian or a godly man. After he had talked a little while and asked me about my life and my work, he finally said, "What do you mean by 'being saved'?" My heart sang when I heard him ask that. I pulled out a little Testament from my coat pocket and told him he was not the first man who had asked that. In the 16th chapter of the Book of Acts, Paul and Silas, two of the prophets of God, were arrested, beaten, and put in prison for preaching the gospel. At midnight these two sang praises unto God. They were not crying, looking for sympathy, or feeling sorry for themselves. Instead, they sang, because they could be persecuted for the cause of Christ. While they sang and prayed, God shook the prison and the doors were opened. The jailer who was responsible for each prisoner started to kill himself, because he thought the prisoners had escaped. Paul told him to do himself no harm, for none had left the prison; and that jailer asked Paul and Silas, "What must I do to be saved?" Paul told him to believe on the Lord Jesus Christ, and be saved, and likewise, his household.

Although Mr. Young must have been close to sixty-five and had obtained wealth and prestige, he had no knowledge of Jesus as a Saviour. Slowly and carefully I showed the great newspaperman how to be saved. He read Romans 10:13, "For whosoever shall call upon the name of the Lord shall be saved," and John 5:24, "Verily, verily, I say unto you, he that heareth my word, and believeth upon him that sent me, hath everlasting life, and shall not come into condemnation; but is passed from death unto life."

I asked him if when he was alone somewhere, that night before he slept, he would ask God to save him and forgive his sins. He promised me that he would.

When I had been home a few days, a letter came from Mr. Young. He had opened the letter by writing "Paul-D. F. Billington (God's Man)." In the letter he thanked me and Mr. Pfister for coming. He also assured me he would never be the same again.

I have had many other letters from Mr. Young. He has since passed away. He has a residence in Glory. It was a wonderful trip, for I learned that even though most people think that wealthy, professional men are too busy to be approached about their souls, they are just like you and me. They need the Lord just as much as the bum in the street does, but oftentimes their prestige makes it hard to talk to them. God is just as necessary to a rich man as He is to a poor man, and He can be as real. That day was a profitable one for the opportunities God gave me to talk with the governor and the newspapermen. I was privileged to meet many of the governor's staff. I did not walk in as a pious somebody; I just walked by and handed them a small tract. There was one tract I carried on sickness. It says in it, you don't need oil on your head, you need Christ in your heart.

There will come a day in your life, as it did to the newspaperman, when you realize that you are not a child of God. You must take Christ in simple, childlike faith and believe in Him who died that you might have eternal life.

I look back upon that trip, and I am humbly aware that God has allowed a man, whose education came from his own desire for learning, to talk with high government officials for whom he has great respect. It seems almost fictional, but God has said, Seek you first the kingdom of God and his righteousness, and all things will be added unto you.

It was an extreme pleasure and great honor for me to have lunch with the governor of Ohio, and God has given me the privilege of meeting twelve other governors and also diplomats of foreign countries. I am thankful today that before these great and influential men I was not ashamed to claim Jesus. Are you ashamed of Jesus?

34. Mother Goes Home

IN THE YEAR OF 1945, IN APRIL, MY SWEETHEART mother fell and broke her hip and never seemed to have much fight in her to get well. She just wasted away. Each month I went home to see her, and my church and I prayed earnestly for her to get well if it would be the will of God.

In November of the same year, Mother had my oldest sister send me a telegram which read, "Do not pray for Mother to get well, but pray God's will be done." I read this message on our Sunday morning broadcast, and the next morning the word came that she had gone home to be with the Lord.

Proverbs 31:10,11,28,29: "Who can find a virtuous woman? for her price is far above rubies. The heart of her husband doth safely trust in her, so that she shall have no need of spoil. . . . Her children arise up, and call her blessed; her husband also, and he praiseth her. Many daughters have done virtuously, but thou excellest them all."

All of the old-time preachers used to say the woman or the female can have more to say about changing lives and attitudes of nations toward God than anyone else. The mother has the children in their tender years, when the father is away earning their livelihood. A Sunday-school teacher can only have them twenty-five or thirty minutes each week, while the mother is given hours of each day. The public school teacher was not given the responsibility of teaching Christ—only the fundamentals of reading, writing, and arithmetic. I hear people talk about religion being forced on the schools. I don't know the answer to this; however, I would not want someone who was not a Christian and did not know Christ to read the precious Word and pray in mockery in front of my children. The teacher's life and disposition are seen by the student and perhaps would discourage him, become a stumbling block in his life.

I had other brothers and sisters living here in Akron, and we made our plans to drive to Kentucky. We arrived at the funeral home where Mother was lying in state. I had preached many funerals, but I kept wondering how I would feel when I looked into the face of my own dear mother, whose face was white in death. Mother was saved when she was about thirteen years old, and I believe, as one who lived with her and watched her, that she lived her life true to God. The song writer penned these words, "What Is a

Home without a Mother?" You will never understand the
meaning of those words until you go home and your mother
is not there. I loved my father very dearly; but the mother,
if she is a good mother, has a place in the home that no one
else can fill. No father or man can ever fulfill the place God
intended a mother to have. I still have brothers and sisters
back in Kentucky, and they treat me like a royal king when
I go home. They are so good to me that it embarrasses me,
but still, they cannot take the emptiness from my heart as
I long for my mother.

You may not understand it, but God plans to break family
circles, and we know not the time or day when our beloved
mothers will be called home. When I was a boy, and even
later in life, I heard preachers talk about people getting
ready to die and saying peculiar things. I thought it strange
that persons would say things at a time like this which
seemed to be inspired, or almost as if they were peeking into
Heaven's shores. On the morning that my mother passed
away, she called for my father, who had passed away in
1932, and said, "Daddy, I am ready." About two hours before
her death, she called again and said, "Come on, Daddy, I am
ready, let us go."

You might ask if I really thought that she had seen my
daddy. I would have to say yes, for in the Scriptures it tells
us that Stephen saw Heaven open and Jesus standing at the
right hand of God. It is true that, while Stephen did not call
a loved one's name, he did see Heaven and the Lamb of
God. There is a record in one of our hospitals here in Akron
of a minister's wife's death. At death she said to her husband
that she had her baby. The baby had passed away several
months previously. She further said to her husband that she
wished he would come and go with her, for this place was
so beautiful. The nurses left the room with tear-dimmed eyes,
knowing from her pulse that she was dying. It was more than
they could bear to hear her talk with her husband the wonderful way in which she did before death came.

Funeral arrangements had to be made, and we got Mother's old pastor, who had been good to all of us. We drove from the funeral home in Murray about eight miles to the church where I had been ordained—the Sugarcreek Baptist Church. The ambulance drove so slowly that it made me think of the song, "Undertaker, undertaker, please drive slow, for this body that you are taking how we hate to see it go." We watched as Mother's casket was taken through the doors of the church and placed in front of the altar. Hymns were sung about mother and home and Heaven. Dr. Hamilton, the preacher whom Mother loved for being always faithful to the church and Christ, assured us from the Scriptures, let not our hearts be troubled, if we believed in God. He looked at us and realized that from Woodrow, my baby brother, to Connie, the oldest, all were saved.

The dreaded moment came when the last remarks had been made and the morticians with tender hands slowly tucked the cover around Mother's shoulders. I remember looking into her pale, peaked little face as they slowly lowered the lid. To all unsaved it meant good-by forever, but thanks to the God of Heaven all her children were saved and one day they would meet again. We could kiss the little pale face of one who had never ceased to pray for us, who had loved us and cared for us, and know that this was only good-by for a while. She had stood by the wooden cradle when we were sick, while everyone else was asleep. She seemed to get her strength from an unknown source, always rising to any situation with renewed courage and hope.

Now Heaven is much closer, for Mother and Daddy are there. Other loved ones are there. I have a brother who was born before I was but lived only eight months. His name was Charles, my own son's name. Some glad morning Jesus will say to me, "Come on, Dallas, let's go home; your work on earth is finished and your race is run." I shall go home to see my precious Saviour, who loves me, who died for me. I shall see my mother and father smiling and waiting for me in the

City of God. How about you? The only way to see your loved ones who have reached the City of God is to become a child of God. You must trust Jesus and ask Him to save you.

35. A Sermon in the Congressional Record

OFTEN, I CAN FIND THE HEADLINES OF TOMORROW'S paper in God's Bible. God is still using men to proclaim His unsearchable truths and to warn any man in authority, no matter how high his office or how low.

Some years ago, when we were just coming out from the horrors of the war, I had the experience of finding some of my remarks, based on this belief, quoted in the Congressional Record.

One day, I received the following letter and enclosure:

Reverend Dallas F. Billington
2312 Manchester Road
Akron 14, Ohio

Dear Friend:

I am sending you herewith a copy of the Congressional Record of November 6, on page A-5096 of which you will find some remarks I made in reference to your warning to government officials which I inserted in the Record.

I thought you might like to know of the extensive circulation your statement will receive, and I sincerely hope it will have some beneficial effects.

Very truly yours,
Henry Dworshak

Below is a copy of the remarks which were printed in the Congressional Record. Mr. Dworshak presented this to Congress in the House of Representatives on Monday, November 5, 1945, as follows:

Mr. Speaker, under leave to extend my remarks in the Appendix, I am inserting a warning to Government officials made by the Reverend Dallas F. Billington, of Akron, Ohio, in the Washington Star. Will this warning be heeded?

II Kings 20:12-18, "At that time Berodach-baladan, the son of Baladan, king of Babylon, sent letters and a present unto Hezekiah: for he had heard that Hezekiah had been sick.

"And Hezekiah hearkened unto them, and shewed them all the house of his precious things, the silver, and the gold, and the spices, and the precious ointment, and all the house of his armour, and all that was found in his treasures: there was nothing in his house, nor in all his dominion, that Hezekiah shewed them not.

"Then came Isaiah the prophet unto King Hezekiah, and said unto him, 'What have they seen in thine house?" And Hezekiah answered, 'All the things that are in mine house have they seen: there is nothing among my treasures that I have not shewed them.'

"And Isaiah said unto Hezekiah, 'Hear the word of the Lord. Behold the days come, that all that is in thine house, and that which thy fathers have laid up in store unto this day, shall be carried into Babylon: nothing shall be left, saith the Lord.

"'And of thy sons that shall issue from thee, which thou shalt beget, shall they take away; and they shall be eunuchs in the palace of the king of Babylon.'"

Mr. President, Senate, and the House of Representatives, how many of you in some lodge or church have said your faith was in God?

This being true and your faith being well founded, how can you as leaders of America deny all the teachings of God?

Are you now willing to do as the foolish king did, show the atomic bomb and its secrets, the bomb sight, our poison gas, and all that God has permitted the wise men of our country to find out? These have been given to us for our protection.

Now shall we be as foolish as some ancient king and call in all the foreign countries and show them our secret weapons, our treasures, the way we operate our factories, and the way we do things?

Are you aware of the fact that God said in the Bible all these things were written for our learning?

I repeat, Mr. President, Senate, the House of Representatives, take warning for God's sake, don't sell our country, permit our boys to be carried off to a foreign country, by revealing to them all the treasures and secrets of the United States and the Stars and Stripes.

If God used prophets in days of old, why not let our own Nation come back and listen a little more to some of the ministers of the gospel rather than listen all the time to the college professors and many others who deny the teachings of Almighty God?

I beg you in the name of the Lord Jesus Christ, please take warning and save our Nation from having the foreign countries come in to take away our treasures and our sons and daughters.

The part that you have read was the remarks presented that day in Congress; however, that was not all of the sermon. The Scripture was as follows: "And when he had opened the second seal, I heard the second beast say, Come and see. And there went out another horse that was red: and power was given to him that sat thereon to take peace from the earth, and that they should kill one another: and there was given unto him a great sword."

On a Sunday night prior to the publishing of part of my sermon in the Congressional Record, I had warned the world of Russia, its red horse and its rider. When the Book of Revelation was written, the fastest means of moving was on a horse. The fastest thing in the air was the eagle. I told my people of what the prophets of old had to say. I also warned them that in ten years' time it would be interesting to see what would happen. The Bible plainly tells what will happen. God warned me in His Word, and I in turn warned my government about Russia. Years have passed and you can see that God's Word is true.

When a preacher picks up his Bible and warns from the Word concerning what happened to other nations that turned from God, most of the time the example he uses is the nation Israel. God had chosen Israel, a small nation, to prove to the world that His power was not in the number of men: it depended upon whose side God was on. I believe with all my heart that the wealth and good things which America enjoys today exist because of Christian men and women praying for God to protect our country. Our forefathers came here looking for a place where they might worship in freedom. Therefore, the Bible tells us first to seek the kingdom of Heaven and all things will be added.

All of the things that I said to warn our statesmen and lawmakers about the red horse and its rider and the many times I begged and pleaded with them to stay close by their Bibles and watch are now seen to have been justified.

God told the prophet Ezekiel to take heed to the warnings: "Again the word of the Lord came unto me, saying, Son of man, speak to the children of thy people, and say unto them, When I bring the sword upon a land, if the people of the land take a man of their coasts, and set him for their watchman: if when he seeth the sword come upon the land, he blow the trumpet, and warn the people; then whosoever heareth the sound of the trumpet, and taketh not warning; if the sword come, and take him away, his blood shall be upon his own head. He heard the sound of the trumpet, and took not warning; his blood shall be upon him. But he that taketh warning shall deliver his soul." Ezekiel 33:1-5.

God warned the leaders of the cities and the watchmen on the wall who, while walking the walls, kept watch over the cities while the people slept. The watchman watches the horizon for the weather or to spot an enemy approaching. He notifies every minister whom God has called to preach the gospel to warn everyone, including the President of the

United States, concerning men of other countries who would harm this country we all love. It is my duty to use the newspapers, television, literature, or any means to warn our country of an enemy. God has commanded that I do so. There were men in the Bible who were kings, and because they were so ungodly, God permitted many things to happen to them and the people. God would call someone else to take such a king's place, and God blessed those who harkened to Him. These men listened to God's prophets and went to God in prayer, so that their decisions would be in the will of God. In 1945 I was trying to warn as best as I knew how and I shall not stop, for I feel a deep calling to warn people of judgment. Often I have said things which other preachers would not say, and I am still saying what God lays on my heart. I feel that it is God's will, and my heart would see no peace if I did not speak as God directs. Some have told me that I am just a rabble-rouser because I am so earnest in my believing that every word of the Bible was written for our learning.

Right now our nation is in trouble; even the high school boys and girls know this. The office and factory workers are aware of this. The businessmen and clergy will agree to this. Our people, great and small, learned and unlearned, rich and poor, are perplexed and worried. Even our scientists are warning us through the newspapers. I often bring a newspaper to the pulpit with me to prove the things which I read to my people from the Bible.

Our Bible told us of the atomic bomb and the secrets which have now been found. I have dared to be a Daniel. God has let me live and see many things which I warned the people about come to pass.

As Saul of Tarsus said about his conversion, "It happened in no secret corner." We have the published facts which should impress upon you: Prepare to meet thy God.

36. Akron Chamber of Commerce

WE HAVE TRIED TO LIVE BEFORE THE CITY OFFICIALS AND everyone in the city of Akron, including every boy and girl, in such a way that we might convince them that God is real. Matthew 21:22 says, "And all things, whatsoever ye shall ask in prayer, believing, ye shall receive." I went to the Akron *Beacon Journal* and talked with someone there about hanging banners in the streets to get people to go to church. I also went to the Akron Chamber of Commerce to see if they would grant me permission. I was assured that the newspaper and the Chamber of Commerce would work with me. The banners would be hung across Main Street, with these words inscribed: "Ten thousand in Sunday school—Will you be one?"

I had seen different banners hung across Main Street, at one time or another, to advertise many different affairs or coming events. I had prayed about the banners and wished only that God would be glorified. The Chamber of Commerce had the banners painted free of charge. The banners were about 42 feet in length and about 40 inches wide and could be read from both sides. They were hung at two different places on Main Street.

The electric company hung the signs, and people noticed them and talked about them all over town. Those were war days, and people all over the world were in trouble. I asked the Akron *Beacon Journal* to help me get out a full page which would help get people into church. The goal was set for Easter Sunday. The editorial department helped arrange the page, and one of their artists drew a picture which I shall always remember. The page was to come out on the Saturday before Easter Sunday. The picture showed a man with a haggard face, which clearly showed he had spent much time in trouble and sorrow. He wore a uniform bearing many service stripes. One of his hands was lying across a piece of paper, on which he had written, "Dear Mom and Dad, I am in an old barn somewhere in Germany. If I were back at home, I am sure I would go to church at the Baptist Temple on Sunday. They are expecting 10,000. Will you be one? I will picture in my mind a vision of you, Mom and Dad, and Sis being in church Sunday," signed Bill. If you looked at the right hand closely, you would find that two of Bill's fingers were missing.

When that Sunday came, we had 10,123 people who signed cards at our ten o'clock service. God did answer our prayer. Some people wondered why we went perhaps to the extreme in advertising, and yet Jesus told us to go into the highways, the byways, and the hedges to win the lost.

When we asked how many had seen the picture in the paper and how many had noticed the banners, it seemed as if all 10,123 hands went up. I believe with all my heart that Jesus expects us to use every means available to tell the story of Christ. From the beginning, when he read the Scripture and claimed its promise, God seemed to go ahead of us to prepare the hearts of the men whose cooperation we had to have to go ahead with the project.

We took the cards, which were turned in with the individual names and addresses, and began a house-to-house campaign on those who were looking for a church home, or were interested in our church. From the one-page ad and with valuable assistance from the Chamber of Commerce, many people came to church that day for the first time. Since then, they have come regularly. There are many members in our church today who could tell you that is the reason they came that Sunday. Over eighty people were converted that Easter Sunday. It was a rare thing to find a person who was not affected by the separation from some loved one, and tear sheets from the ad were sent to many of our boys overseas. We received comments and letters from servicemen all over the world.

I am telling you this story that you might understand why I keep saying God is real, that He loves us. He demands and expects us to worship Him. All that God requires of us is that we love Him. He asks that we put no other God before Him. It was more than my heart had ever expected, that I would find favor among men. I knew God and knew He loved me, but God had given me even more by blessing me with many men's friendships, which I shall always cherish. I found men in the city of Akron who were just as willing to help me as my own father would have been, had he been living.

America is a place which has freedom of speech and freedom of religion, and where your fellow man will try to help you. You have to convince your fellow man that you are sincere. Our Bible tells us that there are too many people who are insincere and not to be trusted, who are not willing to worship God in spirit and in truth.

Perhaps you are a newspaperman or a member of your town's chamber of commerce and, heretofore, have never helped the cause of Christ in your city. You can see by this true story how valuable your assistance can be. It is the newspapers of America that can swing an election. Think what it would mean if every newspaper in America would give ten to fifty inches each week on their front page to God. I don't mean to give it to the Catholic, Jew, or Baptist, but just to glorify God with the printed page. It would be a tribute to the living God, who controls the stars, clouds, sunshine, rain, and the storms. Someone asked Billy Graham what he attributed his success to, and he told them to Christ first and to his friends in the advertising business second. No one would have known about Billy Sunday if the papers had not carried his story. How else would we know of Charles Spurgeon of London, if the London papers had not carried the account of his ministry? The papers told of John Wesley and his brother.

It is my prayer that someday, before Christ returns, our newspapers, coast-to-coast television, worldwide radio, and every possible means of communication will be given over for perhaps a week or a month to presenting Christ to the whole world. It could be done if enough Christian God-fearing men would bind themselves and their influence to a common cause for the glory of God. They could select a minister to head their town or state on the basis of his record. They could choose the minister with the largest church, but that might not be the right choice. Sometimes the smaller church is where God is blessing. I grant you it would take much planning, but we put on big doings for sports, politics, and man's accomplishments. Why not have a spectacular for the glory of God?

37. Vice-President Alben W. Barkley

VICE-PRESIDENT BARKLEY AND I GREW UP IN THE SAME town, Paducah, Kentucky. I had moved to Paducah at the age of seventeen from my birthplace above Paducah on the Tennessee River. My people were staunch Democrats. Mr. Barkley was a personal friend of mine. He wrote me a letter and told me he admired the work that I and my church were doing. He invited me to Washington for a visit and instructed me to come straight to his office and simply ask for Alben W. Barkley. I shall never forget the look on the office girl's face when I did exactly what he had told me. One girl asked me if I were related to the Vice-President.

As a young boy, it was always my dream to visit Washington and see the important buildings and the White House. When Christ was a boy, in Bible times, Rome was the city which was talked about. Perhaps the young boys back then dreamed of going to Rome just as I had dreamed of going to Washington. I could not help but remember Paul and his visit to Rome. How different was my visit to Washington, for I was greeted with friendship and kindness.

Now I had actually been invited to come to Washington for no particular business or reason except friendship. I had lunch with some senators and representatives and was asked to have prayer for that group. Our Bible tells me that the heart of the king is in the hand of the Lord, and I kept remembering this as I ate with the Vice-President that day. I believe too there is nothing impossible with God. The spider is in the king's palace because he chooses to be there. There is not a marble wall tight enough to keep the spider out. You can close the doors, and yet in time you will see the spider's webs. I had nourished the dream of going to Washington and, in my busy days, had stored it carefully away in my heart. Now, by God's grace, my dream as a boy was fulfilled. The Vice-President gave me a special pass which enabled me to visit several meetings. There was a trial going on concerning the president of Montgomery Ward Company. I was in Washington at the time General MacArthur made his famous speech there, in which he said, "Old soldiers never die; they just fade away."

I am trying to get you to see that if God be for you, who can be against you. God can bring the impossible to pass. That which is utterly impossible and beyond human reasoning is possible if you believe. God controls the heavens, the earth, the nation, and the hearts and minds of men. God says, Only believe. Believe that what you pray for, God will do under one condition, that it will glorify God.

Everywhere I go or anything I do, I believe God has planned it that way. God made my reservation. I am here today because God made the arrangements. If you are not a Christian, you will not believe this. When Jesus comes to live in your heart, then will you believe that God has made all things possible. Without God I can do nothing.

I am planning to go to a place far greater than Washington. It is called a place of rest, or Heaven. Life is a very short journey for everyone. God is no respecter of persons, and what He has done for others He can do for you. God loves you just as He loved Paul. Paul's prayer was answered when he prayed to go to Rome, but Paul arrived there as a prisoner because he had preached the same gospel that I preach. In those days they did not have the freedom of speech which we have in America. Many foreign countries even now do not have our privileges.

Paul was brought before a man by the name of Felix, who was a high-ranking officer of the Roman government. Paul told Felix and his wife what God had done for him, in order to convince them that God was real. Paul had been a persecutor of Christ, and he told them how God had struck him down and made him blind. He cried out to God for help, and God sent him into the city, where someone would help him. So in earnest was Paul, in telling what God had done for him, that Felix said Paul was beside himself, or like a madman. Then Paul came before King Agrippa, chained, with shackles on his hands. Paul then said to King Agrippa, "King Agrippa, believest thou the prophets? I know that thou believest." Then Agrippa said unto Paul, "Almost thou persuadest me to be a Christian." And Paul said, "I would to God that not only thou, but also all that hear me this day, were both almost, and altogether such as I am, except these bonds."

I am praying that you, my reader, will not just be almost persuaded to become a Christian but will be persuaded all the way. I am hoping that you will get your Bible and search for its whole truth. Somewhere, before you die, God will use some written word, message, or song to convince you of your need for Christ. You will come face to face with the reality that you are lost. God's Holy Spirit will quicken your reasoning until you know without a shadow of a doubt that you need Jesus. You will be warned of a coming judgment without God. Will you be almost persuaded but lost?

God will not always give you the wealth of this earth, which might ruin and wreck your life, even though you have prayed for it; for the things which you pray for must glorify God. When this is true, you may be sure God will bring it to pass.

The important thing is this: Are you persuaded to become a Christian? God has only promised us seventy years, and when those years come to an end, you can look back and see God's handiwork in your life. God planned that I would go to Washington, not to glorify Dallas Billington, but to glorify God. I talked to the Vice-President about a better world, and we had prayer together. We prayed for the people of our country—that God would bless this land of ours. Jesus was the gateway from his heart to mine.

38. Class of Silent People

ABOUT FIFTEEN YEARS AGO I RECEIVED A CALL FROM one of the local funeral homes asking me to conduct a funeral for a two-year-old baby. Both of its parents were silent people. They could neither speak nor hear. The parents were well educated—I believe both of them were college graduates. I asked the funeral director how it would be possible for me to conduct a service without using the sign language. The director told me that there were interpreters working at the Goodyear Tire and Rubber Company who might, if asked, help in the service. I decided to call to see what might be done. The Goodyear office gave me two names and recommended Virginia Quinn as the most rapid interpreter.

When I asked her to help me with the baby's funeral, she was quick to say she had never done anything like that. She was used in hiring, for picnics—for anything that might arise in the general run of a factory. Her own mother had been a silent person, and because of this she had learned to use her hands well. Even though at first she hesitated to help me, she finally agreed to do what she could.

I took her to the funeral home, where about a hundred silent people had assembled. Our first job was to become acquainted with the bereaved family. I learned that it was the father's wish that the body of the baby be cremated. Arrangements had already been made for the baby to be taken after the funeral to Cleveland, Ohio, for cremation. Some of the baby's loved ones, who attended our church, had been responsible for calling me as the minister for the funeral. These loved ones had told the mother that Rev. Billington would make arrangements for the baby to be buried and not cremated.

I had been preaching for many years and had many unusual experiences, but this was one that I shall never, as long as I live, forget. I took the Scriptures and began to reason with the father that the Lord had said, "Dust thou art, and unto dust shalt thou return," while the soul would go back to God who gave it. We were able to persuade him to cancel the arrangements for cremation.

Miss Virginia Quinn did not claim to be a Christian. It was her nature to use slang and even profanity while working in the shop. While I pleaded with the father not to burn the baby's body and had him read the Scripture, I thought the mother, by using her hands, was trying to tell me that she would not be able to fix the little crib any more. I looked at Virginia Quinn, and she had begun to cry until she was overcome with weeping. The silent people watched her, and finally, when she regained her composure, I asked her what had happened. I asked her if I had said something wrong. To which she exclaimed, "Oh, Lord, no! What this mother has said is to thank you for putting out the fire, so they won't burn her baby."

Virginia wept again and went out into the washroom to bathe her eyes. In my whole life I have never had an experience like that. I felt so very close to God. I felt how neglected these silent people had been. We were told that nearly 1,500 silent people lived in Akron, and no one had a church for them. Their lack of Christian teachers made them seem like the forgotten crowd.

Of course, there was no singing at the funeral; however, I got a hymnal and read to them "Safe in the Arms of Jesus" and a verse of "Gathering Buds." My interpreter was so disturbed that even during the interpretation of the songs she broke down and wept aloud. I read to that group the wonderful Scripture found in Isaiah, where it says: "Strengthen ye the weak hands, and confirm the feeble knees. Say to them that are of a fearful heart, Be strong, fear not: behold, your God will come with vengeance, even God with a recompence; he will come and save you. Then the eyes of the blind shall be opened, and the ears of the deaf shall be unstopped. Then shall the lame man leap as an hart and the tongue of the dumb sing; for in the wilderness shall waters break out, and streams in the desert." These people began to ask me questions through the interpreter. The mother asked me about her baby being saved, since it was not baptized. I read to them Matthew 18:1-3: "At the same time came the disciples unto Jesus, saying, Who is the greatest in the kingdom of heaven? And Jesus called a little child unto him, and set him in the midst of them, and said, Verily I say unto you, Except ye be converted, and become as little children, ye shall not enter into the kingdom of heaven." I explained that Jesus died for sinners. This baby was innocent, holy, and perfect. It had never known sin—had never committed a sinful deed. Jesus has told us that this little child and children like it were the greatest in the City of God. This child was like Jesus to this extent: neither had ever spoken a guileful word or committed a sin.

Someone then asked if the sin of Adam and Eve would not be on every baby. I assured him that sin came and passed upon all men, not babies; the baby had not sinned. So sincere and genuine were the questions of these silent people that the funeral lasted much longer than we had expected. However, I closed the service with John 3:16 and told them this Scripture was for each of them. They seemed to understand and nodded their heads.

We lifted the little casket and drove out to the hillside cemetery, where a grave had been opened. We gathered around the grave, placing the flowers around the casket. I read the Scriptures where Jesus told them He was the resurrection and the life. We were placing the little body in the earth, but the soul had slipped away to be with Jesus. The mother asked me again if her baby was in Heaven, and I assured her from the Word of God that it was at home with Jesus.

When the service was over the mother of the baby thanked me and asked if there was anything she could do to pay me for having had the service. I told her just to pray for me. She told me that she could not pray, for she could not talk. I let her read in my Bible, Romans 10:10: "For with the heart man believeth unto righteousness; with the mouth confession is made unto salvation." Belief comes with the heart. I turned to John 1:12: "But as many as received him, to them gave he power to become the sons of God, even to them that believe on his name." I asked her if, right there by the open grave of her baby, she would receive the Lord Jesus in her heart as Saviour. She answered with a nod, saying yes.

The services were over, and Miss Quinn and I rode back to the factory. I asked her if she would help me to start a Bible class in our church for the silent people. She told me no. I then asked her if she thought it was right that they had no church and that no one cared about their having a church.

She began to weep and told me she was not fit to stand before a class. I told her she would not be the teacher; God would use her hands to interpret his message. In this way the silent people could be helped spiritually. In Matthew's Gospel it tells us to go into all the world and preach the gospel to every creature. Surely this included the silent people. We had several blind people who were attending regularly at our church, and their loved ones or friends brought them in their cars; but they could hear the Word.

Before she left the car she promised that she would try it for one Sunday. She would tell all the silent people about the service and ask them to tell others. I told her I would announce this on the broadcast and ask those who knew any silent people to tell them of the service where an interpreter would give them the message. We agreed that they should be seated in a special section where they could easily see the interpreter. Of course, we realized the other people would be a little curious at first; but that would all pass, no harm would come to the message, and God would bless. Our church had a large platform, and Miss Quinn was to sit in a chair on the left side, in front of the section reserved for the silent people.

The first Sunday morning, the Lord blessed us with eighty silent people. When the songs were sung, Virginia interpreted them and they followed her in the song with motions. Our lesson that morning was in the Book of Revelation. God told them that blessed are they that read this word and keep it and the sayings written therein, and also it was written there that the blood of Jesus Christ would save us. Jesus wrote there that, "I am he that liveth, and was dead; and, behold, I am alive for evermore."

We made it very plain in our message that it made no difference that their tongues were silent; belief in Christ came from within the heart. When we stood to our feet and sang the first invitation song, the first to come to the altar of God was the mother of the baby whom I had buried. I took my Bible and showed her verse by verse how God said in Matthew 10:32, "Whosoever therefore shall confess me before men, him will I confess also before my Father which is in heaven." Miss Quinn worked with me at the altar with all the silent people who came to the altar. When the service was over, five of their number had trusted Jesus as their own personal Saviour.

The next Sunday came, and God blessed again; but at the close of the service I noticed that Miss Quinn was almost running to get away from the front of the church and was heading for the church's office. My wife and I went into my study to find Miss Quinn there, weeping her heart out. She told me she could not stand any more. She said her heart was grieving; she wanted to be a Christian, but she did not know what to do. She went over to my wife and asked her to please help her. This girl had a Christian mother who had passed on, and we knew this mother's prayers had followed this girl, for we saw her bow her head, asking forgiveness and accepting Christ as her Saviour.

More than fifteen years have passed since then, and our interpreter is now an invalid, having been ill for many years. We now have Mrs. Waddell as our interpreter, who was recommended to us by Miss Quinn. We have never since that day been without a class for the silent people. When our revivals are on, we have the interpreter come out and sit on the platform, that they may get the message also.

Thus, a little child, barely two years old, who had been born into this world to stay such a short time, had fulfilled a mission for God. Many came to know Christ because this child had been taken. The silent people could have said, like David, that refuge had failed them and no one seemed to care for their souls. However, God sent a little child into their midst and then permitted this preacher, with the help of Miss Quinn, to point their hearts toward God. In one short month God had given us twenty-five conversions in our silent class. The first year gave us over a hundred such converts. Our Bible teaches us that God does His work in marvelous ways His mysteries to perform.

Up to that time there were no churches in Akron for the silent people; however, now there are other churches which do have classes for them. At the present time we have a television show. Every Thursday night we bring our interpreter to the station, and we give that night to our silent people. Our interpreter has them get their Bibles and read along as I teach and she interprets. This is the only television program for the silent people in our area. God has richly blessed our efforts. By the grace of God, there is no means which we have overlooked whereby we might send out the gospel and win the lost. Our church was the first to start a class for the silent people; we have purchased Braille Bibles and books for the blind. We are helping to finance 160 different missionaries, besides some full-time missionaries whom our church alone finances in foreign countries. We have a German boy, captured during the war, who was brought to the States and educated. He was returned to Germany, where he is preaching Christ to his people. We are supporting many missionaries in Japan. Our newspaper ads, along with radio and television and gospel tracts, are spreading the gospel. We have purchased two airplanes, which carry the missionaries with the gospel to the heathen.

It has been my wonderful privilege to go into the offices of many men who were very influential, even as I mentioned, to the office of the Vice-President of the United States, and there talk about Jesus and His wonderful, matchless Love.

Will you come some Sunday and see how God has blessed us? There will be five uniformed men handling the traffic, and more than twenty men with white coats on parking the cars and helping people get located. It takes a staff of 800 to operate our Sunday school, including teachers and assistants, superintendents, song leaders, pianists, ushers, choir members, a full-time staff of five secretaries, four custodians, and two men who operate our up-to-date print shop.

III

Our Trip to the Holy Land

39. My Trip to the Holy Land

"BUT CONTINUE THOU IN THE THINGS WHICH THOU hast learned and hast been assured of, knowing of whom thou hast learned them; and that from a child thou hast known the holy scriptures, which are able to make thee wise unto salvation through faith which is in Christ Jesus. All scripture is given by inspiration of God, and is profitable for doctrine, for reproof, for correction, for instruction in righteousness: that the man of God may be perfect, throughly furnished unto all good works." II Timothy 3:14-17.

As a child I was told of a place called the Holy Land. I thought of the Holy Land as a place second only to Heaven, because they told me that Jesus was born there, lived there, and had His unfair trials and was crucified there. Next only to wishing to go to Heaven, I wished to go one day to the Holy Land. Little did I dream as a youngster growing up, having the Bible read to me and hearing about Jesus, that I would ever be permitted to see the hill where the old rugged cross stood. It never even entered my mind that one day I would have the great privilege of walking the same streets where Jesus walked. Nevertheless, when I became a minister I began to plan in my mind the places and things which I would be sure to see if ever I got the chance to visit the Bible land.

A member of our church said that he had always wanted to go to the Holy Land but time did not permit him to go, so he gave the church a $5,000 check which was to pay for my trip to Jerusalem and the countries I would go through. Since he could not go, he wished me to take pictures and bring back to the congregation my own thoughts concerning the Bible land. The church voted that I go, and because of this generous member my trip was endowed with sufficient funds.

Our plane took off from Idlewild, New York, with our party, numbering thirty-two, aboard. The plane circled the field and then pointed its nose, with all four of its motors humming, toward Shannon, Ireland. We landed in Ireland, the birthplace and home country of my grandparents, the Kellys. We spent about four hours eating and resting before we boarded another plane for London, England. Within a few hours' flying time our plane set down in England. There were so many things there which I had read about and longed to see. I had heard the slogan "Over the river, Charlie," which was a common phrase back in the days of Charles Spurgeon. Our group got into taxis the next morning and drove out to the old Spurgeon tabernacle, which was bombed during the war. Not very much of the building remained; however, worship was being conducted in some of the basement rooms in the rear.

I remembered the many stories I had read about this great man: of his faith in God, his speaking ability, and his writing ability. As far as I know, all ministers of the Protestant faiths have books written by Charles Spurgeon at their disposal for reading and learning. Even though Mr. Spurgeon died while a young man, he left a treasure of experiences and ideas which should be profitable for every young minister or layman to read. Perhaps not since the Apostle Paul, who wrote fourteen epistles in the New Testament, has there been anyone whose life has been read about more than Charles Spurgeon.

The Scripture used at the beginning of this account speaks of remembering many of the stories which one had heard about and read about as a child. We walked around the Spurgeon tabernacle, which seemed almost like hallowed ground to us. We then made our way across town to the church of John Wesley, who was known as the Methodist "war-horse" for God. Before we left London we visited the graves of the missionaries who had given their lives in the field and whose bodies had been returned to England.

In this city of London, with its more than eight million people, there is more to see than you can ever imagine. It is there you will find the place known as Madame Tussaud's Wax Works, where the wax likenesses of human beings seem so real that you cannot tell them from the living. There are two windows at which you can get tickets to go inside the museum. At one window a live girl is sitting; at the other window sits her image in wax. You cannot tell one from the other. It made me think of so many persons we meet who say they are Christians. We can see only their outward appearance and from this we cannot tell the difference. But unless Jesus lives in their hearts, they are just as dead as the wax likeness. One is dead unto sin, while the other has life through Jesus Christ. We are dead in our trespasses and sin and must be made alive through the blood of Christ.

As we traveled, I kept in mind what would profit my people and readers in a spiritual way, hoping sincerely, as I viewed these things and prayed, that God would give me a greater power to serve Him as a minister and soul winner. I wanted this trip to make of me a stronger Christian, a better man, a better leader of my church, and a light to strangers whom I might meet on life's journey.

I would like to make this trip so plain to you that you would feel as though you were walking with me. We visited the old London Tower, where the cells told the stories. We saw the crown jewels which had been worn by the different monarchs of England. The richness and beauty of the jewels were in sharp contrast to the slum areas which we drove through in that great city. It was enough to make you weep as you looked at the hungry people along the dirty streets. I realized this was true all over the world. Jesus had said we would have the poor with us always. I thought, as I looked at the elaborate jewels profiting no one and behind the secured protection of guns and bayonets, what good was this beauty to anyone.

Travelers far and wide come to see the changing of the guard at Buckingham Palace. You cannot view this awesome palace without thinking how great the undertaking had been to build such a beautiful place. It would be hard to imagine how many men, how much brick, stone, and tile, had been used in erecting even the bell towers of the palace. No words can describe the extravagant beauty of the gardens, landscaped with flowers of every species. There were pools and fountains of water, which seemed to give the place a feeling of Utopia or the very place in which nature had combined its efforts with man to make the most beautiful on earth.

Dr. B. R. Lakin, a friend of thirty years, two other ministers, and I left the other members of our party and took a taxi through London, so that we could talk with the people there. I had letters introducing me to newspapermen and dignitaries of London. I found the men of prestige, with money and pomp, to be no different in England from those at home. The middle-class workingman or -woman had the same joys and heartaches as our people. We tried our best to be a witness everywhere we went, and by asking questions and answering them we found out a great deal more than we would have had we remained on the regular tour routine. To the average citizen of London, walking its streets every day, the city held no particular splendor. But to me, having a great love of history, it was as if I had turned back the pages of time and were living again in the country which had given birth to my own great country. Its history had been courageous and its ideals lasting. I kept wondering how much these streets would tell if they could speak. I shall never forget my trip through this great, aged city where people used to say, The sun never sets on our territory.

Our plane took off, and we knew our next stop would be Paris, France. I consulted my notes and recalled that this is the city where fashion has its beginning. This is the place where millionaires' families come to buy the latest creations. Someone had said this is the home of the most beautiful women. My brother had fought in the war in 1918 and had told me many stories of his stay in France. I remembered wanting to see the statues of Napoleon. We visited from place to place, eager not to miss one historical relic. Our group stayed in one of the older palaces for two nights. Each morning it was the custom of our group to have a Bible reading. We likened this great city to the city of Babylon. We visited the Eiffel Tower and the Tomb of the Unknown Soldier. We visited the place where the peace treaty was signed after the First World War. I remembered how soon war came again as I looked at this place. I also remembered that Jesus said that when they tell you of peace and safety, then sudden destruction comes upon you. Peace will last only a little while unless the Lord Jesus Christ, the Prince of Peace, is invited to sit down at the peace table.

We had eleven different denominations represented in our group. One person would have something in mind to see that would be of great interest to him, while another would have something else he wished to see. We all tried to be fair and went with the group as much as possible, so that each one would be satisfied. I told the guide, if it were possible and not too selfish on my part, I would like to see some of the dress shops where the elaborate clothes were sold. He assured me that this was included in the tour, and he took us to a very elaborate dress shop. We saw coats for women as high as $8,000, and it was very common to find dresses marked from $1,000 to $1,600. We saw the price tags but it was hard to believe. I thought in my mind that Jesus had told me He would give to me His robe of Righteousness. What we have today is like filthy rags compared to the garments that shine with the glory of God.

There are many stories which, if I were to put them in a book, would perhaps cause someone to want to sue me, but I saw many things in the city of Paris which no man has ever put in writing. I found one night, along with my companions, just what Paris was like after dark. I remembered the prophets of old said they had visited the city when the sun had gone down, when the nobles did not know that they were around. The same sin which one finds in Chicago, New York, Los Angeles, and Akron you can find in Paris. However, I believe the larger the city the larger the sin. We left Paris and went on to Switzerland.

Switzerland, the land of watches, is a beautiful country. No words could possibly describe the mountains and valleys of that country. We noticed how very clean the cities were. There was not one noticeable piece of paper anywhere on the streets. It looked as if someone had just come through the streets and given them a morning bath. Of course, I remembered it was the people of Switzerland who had said, Let us have peace. They had said, Have no wars. They had invited representatives from the whole world to come and talk of peace. They were a small nation who wanted to be left alone to live in peace. War is a thing that is forced upon us. If a heart is honest, it wants no war.

It was unbelievable the watches that we saw, and it was my pleasure to purchase a watch right from the place where it was made.

Our next stop was Rome, Italy. Rome is a place known to every school boy and school girl. A large bus met our plane, and we learned that the guide on the bus had been educated in the United States. All of our guides had been able to speak perfect English, which made our trip much more enjoyable. The guide shut off the motor of the bus and told us certain things which we might look for as the bus moved along toward the great city. Rome has always been a magnificent city. It was known throughout Bible days and through the years that have come and gone as a great center of culture and power. This city has figured greatly in the history of all countries. Many favorable and unfavorable stories have been written about this city. It would take too many words to repeat all the things that have been said about Rome.

The month was April, and spring flowers were in bloom. I could not help but think of the many who had gone into Rome to die, including Paul, the writer of fourteen books of the Bible. "For I am now ready to be offered, and the time of my departure is at hand. I have fought a good fight, I have finished my course, I have kept the faith: henceforth there is laid up for me a crown of righteousness, which the Lord, the righteous judge, shall give me at that day: and not to me only, but unto all them also that love his appearing." II Timothy 4:6-8. These were the words spoken by Paul perhaps the night before or the morning before his execution, before his head fell beneath the sword. Paul asked them to bring him his cloak, for winter was coming, and also to bring him some parchment paper. Paul did not write long messages, and because his eyesight was bad, he wrote large. When he was not in prison, he always had a secretary or scribe to write for him.

These words of Paul were read by all in our party, as we realized that we too were entering Rome and into the very prison about which we had all read. It seemed like a dream that we were seeing the prison which we had talked about in Sunday school. According to books I have read, when Paul was lowered into the prison by means of loops of rope under his arms, he was left there supposedly without water. The soldiers were supposed to have teased Paul about the lack of water. Paul told them he had water which they knew not of. Rome had always had difficulty getting water. They got water by means of aqueducts from the Mediterraean Sea. An aqueduct had a big water wheel with great cups which lifted up the water and poured it into troughs; another wheel below picked the water up in like manner. The aqueducts stretched from the sea into Rome, bringing in the water. To dig a well was unthinkable because of the rock and limestone under the city. When Paul did not ask for water and said he had water they knew not of, they became curious and lowered a soldier into the prison with Paul. The soldier found a hole with water bubbling up for Paul to drink. No one could believe it, and after Paul drank of the water to show it was not poison, the soldier tasted it.

When the guard told his superior officer that there was water there, he was threatened for telling an untruth. The story tells that the superior officer was let down into Paul's prison to see if it was true. The soldier wet his uniform with the spring's water to show everyone above that water was really there.

Our group saw the water in Paul's prison. We do not know how it came there, but people say it has been there since Paul was put in prison. We do not have this story in our Bible, so we cannot vouch for its truth. But this we do know, that nothing is impossible with God, and if God wished a spring there, it would be there.

Paul had his trial before King Agrippa, and now he was ready to cross over from time into eternity. He was getting ready to cross over onto Heaven's shores. He was writing these words to a young preacher called Timothy, who was half Jew and half Greek or Gentile. Little did Paul think that I, a Baptist preacher, wanting to see where these wonderful words had been written, would visit the prison two thousand years later. A preacher was willing to come many miles just to see where Paul had spent his last moments on the cold slabs of stone. I pictured in my mind how the guard was lowered into the prison to put the straps around Paul to bring him out for execution. Paul was lifted up through the trap door, where many Roman guards were posted so that he would not escape. Perhaps they said to Paul what is commonly said to one who is about to die: "Do you have some last words?" I can hear Paul as he said he was ready to be offered up and the time of his departure was at hand. I could imagine him, stooped and tired, saying he had fought a good fight, had kept the faith, and had finished the course.

My prayer has always been that when the day comes for my crossing I can say with Paul that I have kept the faith, fought a good fight, never dipping my colors for one moment for what I believed. I know not what lies ahead of me, for Christianity is fast being closed in on in America. People today can buy nationwide time on the networks to sell beer, wine, and cigarettes; but not the gospel of Christ. I myself had to be told that my religious broadcast would have to be moved from nine in the morning to five in the morning. Needless to say, there would be very few listeners. While I was not put off the radio, still they gave me the time when I might as well not have been on the radio.

People who do not know Jesus do not love Him. Those who do not believe in God are called atheists; the Bible calls them heathens. Paul was perhaps eighty or ninety years old when he was beheaded by those who would not believe in God.

The guide who was with us was easily touched, and on one occasion as I talked with him he said that, although he did not believe as I did, he did believe that Jesus Christ was the Son of God. As I stood there I wondered what I would do if someday I would be called upon like Paul to deny God or be faced with the martyr's death. Have you ever thought about this? Just think for a moment about Cuba, Russia, and many other places on this earth where I would not be allowed to worship the way I believe is right. I would have to follow a pattern or die. I would have to be in exile from my home and friends; I could not worship there as I do in America. I would not be permitted to write this book, proclaiming that the only way a person can be saved is through the blood of

Christ. I could not tell people of a Saviour who was crucified, buried, and rose again, and who is coming back someday. Jesus will come someday in the clouds of Heaven, in the same manner in which He went away.

I wish all of you could visit Rome. You should see the Colosseum, where the early Christians died. You would be humbled to see the place where Paul spent his last days, where he taught us not to deny our belief and faith. I believe with all my heart that Paul lives in the City of God and looks the same as he did when he walked the streets of Rome, or climbed, as a young rabbi, the Judean mountains and out on the shores of Galilee. When his life was taken, his work was completed. He never faltered on his journey home and even at death sang praises to God. Is God's grace that strong in your heart?

Paul wrote these words to the Romans (1:7-17): "To all that be in Rome, beloved of God, called to be saints: Grace to you and peace from God our Father, and the Lord Jesus Christ. First, I thank my God through Jesus Christ for you all, that your faith is spoken of throughout the whole world For God is my witness, whom I serve with my spirit in the gospel of his Son, that without ceasing I make mention of you always in my prayers; making request, if by any means now at length I might have a prosperous journey by the will of God to come unto you. For I long to see you that I may impart unto you some spiritual gift, to the end ye may be established; that is, that I may be comforted together with you by the mutual faith both of you and me. Now I would not have you ignorant, brethren, that oftentimes I purposed to come unto you, (but was let hitherto,) that I might have some fruit among you also, even as among other Gentiles. I am debtor both to the Greeks, and to the Barbarians; both to the wise, and to the unwise. So, as much as in me is, I am ready to preach the gospel to you that are at Rome also. For I am not ashamed of the gospel of Christ: for it is the power of God unto salvation to every one that believeth; to the

Jew first, and also to the Greek. For therein is the righteousness of God revealed from faith to faith: as it is written, The
just shall live by faith."

The story of Rome is ancient. As you drive by the Colosseum with its broken walls, it is as though you were turning
the pages of time back several hundred years. It is said that
72,000 Christians perished in this arena. The story of Christ
had spread from Jerusalem to Rome. When Paul arrived
there, the people received the gospel firsthand. I could
imagine the pompous Romans as they sat in their respective
seats, screaming and shouting as the Christians were torn
by the beasts. If I closed my eyes I could see in my mind the
Christian kneeling, praying, unwilling to recant. It made me
realize how little I had been asked to do for Christ. At the
Colosseum I secured a pamphlet of pictures which an artist,
inspired by stories of those days, had drawn of the sadness
and cruelty of the deaths. The Colosseum was packed; it
could hold at least 100,000 people. The Christians were put
in the center so everyone could see them, and the beasts were
brought in cages and placed in the arena. The beasts were
turned out, and the Christians were defenseless as the beasts
came for them. The crowds appeared more wild than the
animals, as the Christians were killed. They laughed and
screamed for joy to see the blood run freely on the Colosseum
floor.

I wonder, as I think of the Christians whom I know today,
how many would face the wild beasts as these did, rather
than deny Christ. All these early Christians had to do was to
say they did not know Christ and did not love Him or believe
in Him and they would have been set free. These Christians
could accept death, for they knew that life, even if it is long,
is very short compared to eternity. Whether you die a natural
death or by accident, you must meet God one day. They
must have said, Let the beast come and, God, make it soon
over that I may be home with Thee. Eternity is forever;
prepare for it!

We visited the catacombs, where we were told a million or more Christians were buried. We walked through dim, narrow paths where the bones of men, women, and children were stacked away. These were people who had walked ahead of us, leaving a bloody trail, a living testimony to the truths written in God's Holy Bible. If you doubt the words of the Bible, you should take a trip to Rome and see for yourself what it cost our Christian forefathers to give us the heritage which is ours today.

One privilege I had and shall not forget is my being permitted to bring a message to our group as we stood in the midst of the Roman prison where Paul had died. In the days when Paul was in the prison it had no outside entrances. However, there is now a gate for people to go in and out of the prison. Paul was lowered into the prison through a hole. There was a hole in the wall the thickness of a brick and the width of a large stone, and Paul could talk with people through this hole. People on the outside almost had to lie down to get to the hole to talk with Paul. Each cell had this little hole so that the prisoner could talk with loved ones and friends. A guard always stood there to see that the prisoner would receive no weapon to free himself. The prison was a damp, dingy, ugly-looking place. To think that Paul's only crime was believing in Christ made you want to cry. This man Paul was no ordinary man, for he was well educated and high in his church. One day as he started to Damascus for the purpose of persecuting the Christians, he was struck down, and he heard a voice which said, "Saul, Saul, why persecutest thou me?" Thus Paul met Jesus for the first time, and he was told to go into Damascus to a street called Straight, and there he would learn the truth. Ananias told Paul the story. Paul believed in Christ and was saved; and then his own people, the Jews, turned on him.

I preached that day in the tomb where Paul had lived, prayed, and died. It made me feel so unworthy, and yet I felt the nearness of God to me. It made me long for faith like

Paul's. I prayed for courage like that of the early Christians. As I thought of how much they had given, it encouraged my heart to realize more than ever that God had honored their lives because Christianity had lived through every kind of man-made persecution, and I along with millions of others were keeping alive the faith for which they had so willingly died. I shall never forget my trip through Rome.

40. Athens, Greece

ACTS 17:22-27: "THEN PAUL STOOD IN THE MIDST OF Mars' hill, and said, Ye men of Athens, I perceive that in all things ye are too superstitious. For as I passed by, and beheld your devotions, I found an altar with this inscription, TO THE UNKNOWN GOD. Whom therefore ye ignorantly worship, him declare I unto you. God that made the world and all things therein, seeing that he is Lord of heaven and earth, dwelleth not in temples made with hands; neither is worshipped with men's hands, as though he needed any thing, seeing he giveth to all life, and breath, and all things; and hath made of one blood all nations of men for to dwell on all the face of the earth, and hath determined the times before appointed, and the bounds of their habitation; that they should seek the Lord, if haply they might feel after him, and find him, though he be not far from every one of us."

Athens is a great part of the Bible land. Perhaps Paul preached the greatest sermon of his life here on Mars' hill. It had always been a desire of mine to see the place where Paul delivered this great message. We traveled from Rome down through what is called the Athenian Way into the city of Pompeii, which was destroyed about A.D. 79 by Vesuvius erupting. Pompeii was so wicked that when a group is taken through the city, the group is divided into groups of women and men so that the guide can explain what is left without embarrassing anyone. People did die screaming as they perished beneath the fire and burning lava. You can hear people say they don't believe in Hell. It does not matter whether they believe it or not, for that does not change the fact. God has visited many nations in judgment in the various forms of tornadoes, storms, cyclones, volcanoes, and many other things. Paul spent his life speaking out about the judgment of those who would not believe, and at the same time he told of Heaven for those who did believe.

Mars' hill is just outside Athens. We climbed to the top of this hill; and standing where it is believed Paul stood, one man could perhaps be heard by half a million people gathered on the slopes around that spot. I am sure that would be true if the wind were blowing so as to carry his voice. God did not need a public-address system when He planned for Paul to speak. Paul declared to the Greeks that their God was a living God; he pointed out to them that they had a monument erected to the Unknown God. This God was the one he wished to discuss with them. For the God they wished to call Unknown could be as real as their own loved ones. God is unknown only to sinners. A small child too young to know right from wrong does not know God, but he is known of God for he has committed no sin. The purpose of Paul's message was to introduce God to the people of Athens, for the Greeks, with all their learning, knew not God. Paul told the Corinthians that to those who refused to believe, the cross is foolishness, but to those who believe, the cross is the power of God. God chose the foolishness of Paul's preaching to win the Greeks to Christ. It is written that God will destroy the wisdom of the wise and will bring to nothing the understanding of the prudent. Where is the scribe, the wise man, the disputer of this world? Hath not God made foolish the wisdom of the world, for after that in the wisdom of God the world by wisdom knew not God? It pleased God by the foolishness of preaching to save those who believed. The Jews require a sign, and the Greeks seek after wisdom. But we preach Christ crucified—unto the Jews a stumbling block and unto the Greeks foolishness; but unto those Jews and Greeks who are called, Christ is the power of God and the wisdom of God. Because the foolishness of God is wiser than all men.

We reached the city of Corinth, where we saw the temple of the false gods. Then we wound our way through the little towns and places marked on our tour and pointed out to us by our guide. We saw the broken-down towers and buildings, with just the pillars standing of what once were beautiful landmarks.

I declare unto you, as Paul did, that you will never find God through some wisdom of your own. You must believe through faith if you are to be saved. We must submit our lives and our very souls to God if we are to be saved. God is never very far from you. You may have said all your life that you do not need God and are not interested, but when the first loved one close to your heart leaves you, or when you yourself are faced with death, tucked away beneath the oxygen tent, God is standing very near. You just have to accept Him and believe. God is just as near as you will let Him be.

I have faced that valley when I thought I would never see the sun come up again, but three times by God's eternal grace I have been lifted up. I have been brought back to my church and I know not why, except that my work is not finished or God would have taken me home.

I had had two severe heart attacks before I decided on the trip to the Holy Land. Of course, my loved ones and friends insisted that I should not go. However, I made up my mind that if God willed that I go, then I would go for His glory. I felt that God was with me every mile of my journey, for my soul was blessed at every turn, seeing the places about which I had read in the Scriptures.

41. Egypt

WE LEFT ATHENS AND WENT TO CAIRO, EGYPT. EGYPT IS very familiar to a minister, for Egypt has had much to do with our Bible stories. Egypt is the place where Moses and his people were in bondage for forty years. Moses had been left along the Nile River, where the Pharaoh's daughter found him and took him for her own. He had been placed in a little bulrush ark and into the water under the watchful eye of his sister. So many of our stories in the Old Testament were written with Egypt as their setting. Joseph and Mary had fled with Jesus and had gone down to Egypt. It was no longer a dream but a reality that I was actually walking in the desert sands of Egypt.

As we passed through this country, I thought of the story of Jacob and Esau, of Ishmael and Isaac and the divided races. Many of the Jewish people are scattered throughout the world, but here still is the Jewish homeland. I marveled at the pyramids and the Sphinx. It seemed almost a miracle that in the days in which they were erected, those stones could have been assembled. The stones had to be brought some 300 miles over desert sand. But then I thought of the real miracle that had saved my soul. I thought of the One who died to save me from my sins and give to me eternal life. This is the greatest of all miracles.

Someone has said it was not a mystery that God could create this world, but a greater mystery by far that God could love man enough to let His only Son die on a cross. How can God continue to love man when millions, after seeing this miracle of love, doubt Him even yet?

I had spent many years reading history, commentaries, the Holy Bible; and yet none of my reading could compare with the actual visit to the places and seeing them with my own eyes. This was an education that would last all the days of my life. When I saw the places where the prophets and preachers of the Bible had actually been, then I began to see more clearly and it was as though I was living in their time. The Bible became a more real, living account than ever before. God became even more real, for I was walking, eating, and drinking water at the very same place where these men of old had walked, eaten, and drunk. How can anyone deny that God is real?

We met missionaries in Cairo, who told us stories of their victories and obstacles. The girl baby in Cairo is not loved or considered as important as the boy baby. The missionaries have done a lot toward changing that way of thinking, but girl babies are still being found uncared for and starving.

If you are a person who has enough time and money to take the Bible route, your time and money would be well spent. I promise you, if you are a Christian, you will get more than you ever hoped for. If you are not a Christian and take the trip, and can return to the United States and go on living your ungodly life, then I would say to you, you are a hopeless case. God has left many milestones to prove to everyone without a shadow of a doubt that this book, the Holy Bible, is true.

I sincerely hope that as you read my book and come across a reference to some Scripture, you will have a Bible close by and will read the verses quoted, as well as the entire chapter where the verses are found. Then you will more fully understand why I have chosen to use these Scriptures. This will perhaps cause you to become a Christian, or if you are already a Christian, then perhaps it will strengthen your faith. It would please me a great deal to hear from you, should you care to write and tell me what you think of this book. It would be worth the effort to me just to know one soul had found Christ through reading something in this book. I would be glad to answer your letter personally. I have received foolish letters that one does not take the time to

answer, but every sincere reasonable request is given attention. I pray God that I shall never get to the point where
I think I am too busy to answer someone in need. I have
received letters from all kinds of people having all kinds
of trouble. I have always tried to send each one a message of
love and hope through Jesus Christ.

As the days passed and our journey continued, I was ever
amazed at the things that I saw. We looked at the Egyptian
mummies and the intricate ancient writing upon the walls of
the tombs, which told of their civilization five thousand years
ago. We looked at the temples erected to their gods, knowing in our hearts how foolish they were to worship a dead
image, when they only had to look above them at the sun,
moon, and the stars in all their brilliance to know there was
only one true and living God. I realized as the miles were
left behind me and stretched before me how really great this
work is. God looks down upon this earth just as you and I
look at the palms of our hands, and all the inhabitants of the
earth are as open to His eyes as the fingers of our hands are
to us. God wants to help you. He wants to write your name
in the Lamb's book of life. Ask Him today for forgiveness
and salvation for your soul.

RIVER JORDAN

Many have longed to see that fast, swift-running stream of
water which has its beginning in the Lebanon mountains. It
flows down to the Sea of Galilee, and from there winds its
way into the Dead Sea.

"The beginning of the gospel of Jesus Christ, the Son of
God; as it is written in the prophets, Behold, I send my
messenger before thy face, which shall prepare thy way
before thee. The voice of one crying in the wilderness, Prepare ye the way of the Lord, make his paths straight. John
did baptize in the wilderness, and preach the baptism of

repentance for the remission of sins. And there went out unto him all the land of Judaea, and they of Jerusalem, and were all baptized of him in the river of Jordan, confessing their sins. . . . And it came to pass in those days, that Jesus came from Nazareth of Galilee, and was baptized of John in Jordan. And straightway coming up out of the water, he saw the heavens opened, and the Spirit like a dove descending upon him: and there came a voice from heaven, saying, Thou art my beloved Son, in whom I am well pleased." Mark I:1-11.

Jesus walked sixty miles to be baptized in the river Jordan. Our Old Testament told us of a forerunner who would introduce Jesus, the Son of God. No one ever was baptized by immersion until John, who was known as John the baptizer, came. Immersion means to put the entire body under the water. No one has the right to say they have been baptized if they have just been sprinkled or anointed or poured. John the baptizer had been preaching along the banks of the stormy Jordan, and he preached repentance. This was about six months prior to the beginning of Christ's ministry here on earth. The river Jordan is not a beautiful stream of water, for only during three months of the year is the water clear. The other nine months the waters are very muddy. The river winds itself through this little country, which is only 145 miles long and in some places only 37 miles wide.

My people were Methodists and Presbyterians and were converted, born-again Christian people. When I began to read the Bible, the Scripture told me to be planted with Christ, to be buried with Christ. So today I am a Baptist minister through the conviction of the Holy Scriptures and not because of some school or theologian.

Our bus had to be parked, and the guide took us down a path to a steep, rough bankside. The guide, who was an Arab (for the territory around there is under the jurisdiction of the Arab state), did not try to be misleading but told us that from stories handed down to them from generation to generation, this was the place where Jesus was baptized. As far as he or anyone living could tell us, this was the actual spot. This guide made many references to the Bible, and I believe he was a converted man for Christ. Some of the ministers who were with us baptized in the water of Jordan and were baptized themselves. I did not baptize nor was I baptized, for I do not think this water would save me any more than I was already saved. I do not believe this water is holy water. I don't believe any water is holy. Water is still water, no matter how many prayers it has had said over it. I do not think that the prayer of a priest, rabbi, or preacher can change carbolic acid into honey, any more than I think water can be made holy from some man's prayers. I live in America and can believe what I wish and you can too; however, there are countries where this is not permitted.

Every time our group would come to a place about which we had read, we would each take our Bible and read again about this place. We would read all the Scriptures we could find pertaining to this place, and then we would discuss it among ourselves.

As I stood on the banks of the Jordan I pictured in my mind the days in which Christ actually was a living, walking man just like me. He had hands just like my father's and his body was a living, tangible robe of flesh. Suppose you have a loved one who is dying of cancer or a little one who is dying of an incurable disease, and Jesus was still on earth as He was in those days. You could just walk up to Him and say, "Come, Jesus, go home with me. I have a little child whom you gave us who is very sick. Won't you heal her for me?" Jesus did this when he was on earth. There are accounts of three being raised from the dead while Jesus was on earth. He is still healing those who have been given up as hopeless by doctors. We did not anoint them or lay our hands upon them, but we did pray to the God of Heaven. We announced their names on our broadcast and asked Christians to pray for them, and God answered our prayers.

If you will forgive me for using myself for an example, the fact is that I speak the truth with God as my witness, and I lie not; I believe with all my life and being that I am living today because thousands in my church prayed for me. Medical science and my family had given up all hope, and I was not conscious enough to pray for myself. But on a Sunday afternoon many of my people stayed all day long at the church and prayed that I might be spared.

What would you give to be able to have Jesus come to your home? Have you invited Jesus? Have you asked Him to come? Only three during Christ's ministry were raised from the dead, but today we have no way of knowing how many thousands are being raised from sickbeds where they lay dying until Jesus changed things. The Scriptures tell us that Jesus healed all who were brought to Him. All power was given to Christ. I would not want you to get the impression that Christ would heal all the sick. However, Jesus has the power to heal all if He so desires. The healing will come from His divine will, not from any mortal man. I shall never ask you to send me your name and address along with money so that I may send you a handkerchief or something similar dipped in oil to heal you. Healing comes from the nail-scarred hands of Jesus and not from the hands of man. Your own sincere prayers of faith will have as much power with God as anyone's on earth. Pray "God's will be done" and believe in your heart that all things work for the best for those who love the Lord.

If you have not been buried in baptism with Christ, just read your Bible concerning baptism; you will see it is a plan that Jesus set for us to follow. You thereby set yourself apart from the world and declare your allegiance to Christ. Go all the way with Christ. If you are a Christian and have not been baptized, do as the Lord did and be baptized. God will bless your life and your testimony.

DAMASCUS

Acts 9:1-6: "And Saul, yet breathing out threatenings and slaughter against the disciples of the Lord, went unto the high priest, And desired of him letters to Damascus to the synagogues, that if he found any of this way, whether they were men or women, he might bring them bound unto Jerusalem. And as he journeyed, he came near Damascus: and suddenly there shined round about him a light from heaven: and he fell to the earth, and heard a voice saying unto him, Saul, Saul, why persecutest thou me? And he said, Who art thou, Lord? And the Lord said, I am Jesus whom thou persecutest: it is hard for thee to kick against the pricks. And he trembling and astonished said, Lord, what wilt thou have me to do? And the Lord said unto him, Arise, and go into the city, and it shall be told thee what thou must do."

There are some things in the world and on life's journey which you and I must do. They were planned from the morning of eternity, and we must do these things. As we approached the very old city of Damascus (some historians say it is the oldest city of civilization), we had to cross two rivers. These were the waters that the king Naaman wanted to wash in so as to cure his leprosy, but Elisha sent a messenger telling him to go to the muddy waters of the Jordan. These two rivers, which were not more than streams, had beautiful, clear water; and Naaman, being of that country, thought the clear water would be best. However, it is not our will but God's will that makes us whole.

It has been assumed that Saul's parents named him for the King Saul in the Old Testament. If that is true, no doubt the parents hoped that he would be a tall man, standing head and shoulders above the other men as King Saul did. However, when Paul was born, he was very small of stature and never was very large. He was called hunchbacked, with stooped and rounded shoulders. He was ugly in his form of a man. His given name was Saul of Tarsus, but after his conversion his name was changed to Paul.

The Bible has much to say about the city of Damascus and this man called Paul. Paul, as he was on his way to Damascus, was next in line to be the chief rabbi of the Jews. He was very learned in the Jewish religion and had a brilliant mind. He had heard that Christians had fled to Damascus, and Paul wished permission from the high priest to go to Damascus to bind and bring back for trial those Jews professing Christ. I traveled along the road, walking part of the way, where Paul was struck down. I went through the gate which Paul had to be led through, having been blinded by the light of God. The streets of the city are exceedingly narrow and still look ancient, much as they must have looked when Paul was there. Living in this same town was a man called Ananias, who was chosen to explain to Paul why he had been struck down on the road to Damascus. Paul received not only a new name but a new heart, soul, and mind. He became a lover, follower, believer, and trustworthy soldier for the cause of Christ. When the Jews found that Paul was a changed man, they plotted to kill him, and even the authorities in the city closed the gates, intending to take Paul's life. However, the disciples took him and let him down in a basket through a hole in the city's wall. Can you even imagine how I felt as I walked down the narrow street called Straight? It is still the same as when Paul was there. People sleep on the street at night, and part of it is covered because merchandise is left out all night, while the merchants sleep by their wares. Wayfaring men who have no home have a sheepskin which they carry about with them during the day. At night it is unrolled, and the street becomes their bed. When we read the Scripture "Take up thy bed and walk" we may be puzzled, for our people are not accustomed to sleeping in the street; but in the days of Christ, and in that country, it was a common thing. So many things that I saw in the Bible land clarified the Scriptures for me.

In the 7th chapter of Acts you will find where Paul, before his conversion, watched Stephen as he was stoned to death and lifted not a finger to stop it—and perhaps even enjoyed seeing Stephen die. How very different Paul was as he walked down the street called Straight.

We know that today it is not very wise, if you want to be popular with the world, to be an out-and-out, old-fashioned, God-fearing Christian. The kind of church member who plays golf on Sunday, who plays poker on Saturday night, who is not above drinking the social glass or even getting drunk, who pays his church dues and all is forgiven, has joined the church for prestige, to have a minister to marry his children and bury his dead, knows not God nor does he have salvation in his heart. Just being a church member will never make a Christian out of you. There was an evangelist who said you might go to the garage all of your life and never be a car, or go to the stable and never be a horse, and, sadder still, go to church all of your life and never be a Christian, and thus go to Hell. It is sad to read of a man with Paul's learning who had sat at the feet of great teachers, knowing the Mosaic laws backwards and forwards, being able to discuss the law with the highest religious leaders, yet who knew not Christ. Paul lived by the law. Some people today boast that they live by the golden rule. Yet to live by the golden rule is an impossibility for everyone. No one has ever kept the Ten Commandments except Jesus. You might say you live by the golden rule, but if your son and another boy were drowning in the pool, you would have to save the neighbor's son if you lived by the golden rule. If you say you have never told a lie and are at least ten years old, you would be the first one to have managed this. And if you have told a lie, you have broken one of the Ten Commandments. All of us have lied.

As I went through Damascus I remembered when I was a

boy and heard the story of Paul for the first time in my Sunday-school class. I remember what a changed personality Paul became after Jesus came into his heart. I have known persons who thought they lived such perfect lives that they had done no wrong. After they come to Christ, these same persons will acknowledge many things they should not have done. How quickly their stories change. They realize their way was not God's way. Christians will not talk about their own merits or how good they are, but will talk instead about the grace and mercy of God who saved their souls. They will talk not of their own righteousness, but of the righteousness of God. The glory is given to the Rose of Sharon, the Prince of Peace, Lord of lords, and King of kings, whose name is Jesus.

We left Damascus, seeing the Lebanon mountains. The Book of Acts seemed more vivid to me now and I felt so humble, so thankful. I felt as though I had lived through Paul's conversion; time will not be long enough for me to forget Damascus.

42. Lazarus Is Dead

"THEN SAID JESUS UNTO THEM PLAINLY, LAZARUS IS dead." Our bus stopped, and we were told to look in the distance for the first glimpse of the walled city of Jerusalem. Our bus took us down the long slope of the Judean mountain and across a valley into a little town called Bethany. We opened our Bibles and read the story of two sisters who lived with their brother in Bethany. Their home was a place where Jesus loved to visit; he spent many nights there. Somehow no one else ever asked Him to go home with them; but Mary, Martha, and Lazarus loved Jesus and enjoyed being in His presence. The Bible says that Jesus loved Lazarus. Lazarus was a godly man, and his sisters were fine, devout believers in Christ. They counted it a privilege to prepare dinner for Christ and offer Him a place to rest.

Word was sent to Christ that Lazarus was ill, but Jesus knew he was dead. When Jesus came to their home, one of the sisters ran to meet him, telling him her brother was dead. She told Christ, had He been there her brother would not have died.

We went to the place which is called the tomb of Lazarus. There were winding steps which led down into the tomb. The steps and tomb had been dug out of the stone. It was about ten or twelve feet below the ground. I was in the tomb of Lazarus, who had been dead four days before Jesus came to the tomb. It seemed almost like a dream that I could be in this place to behold with my own eyes the setting of the story I had read so many times.

Next we came down the side of another mountain, and reaching the bottom we found ourselves in a valley called the Valley of Kidron, through which a brook or stream of water runs. We then found ourselves winding our way until we came into the old city of Jerusalem. New Jerusalem, or Israeli, is on the other side. The old walled city with its twelve gates is today in the possession of the Arab people. Our first stop was the Mount of Olives, and just before we reached it we passed the potter's field, which was purchased with the money that had bought Christ. We got out and looked upon the old, rough, broken-down hillside known today as the place bought to bury strangers. The mountain slope beyond the potter's field was covered with olive trees. I don't believe I would exaggerate if I were to say that if you included all of the roots of some of these olive trees and measured the area they covered, some of them would measure thirty feet in circumference. Roots would die and sprouts would latch onto other roots and grow from there. The guide told us that no one actually knows what tree Christ prayed under; however, with only the information that had been handed down, there was one tree which had been singled out over the years. Jesus prayed that night until His perspiration became as blood, dripping down upon the ground.

It was a beautiful sunny day and Dr. Lakin went with me as I walked beneath the old olive trees. The trees were of many sizes and shapes, some of their branches dipped to the ground. I said to Dr. Lakin—not to be a hypocrite but to be real and genuine—that I wanted to kneel there beneath the olive tree and let him take my picture, so that I might take it to my son, my church, and my grandson. We spent close to an hour there, and then we drove into old Jerusalem.

It was not possible for all of our party to stay at the same hotel, for it was the Easter season and people from all over the world had come to Jerusalem for the homecoming time. We ate and rested at the hotel. We wrote notes about our journey. I had with me a little wire recorder which would take one-hour messages. Oftentimes, instead of notes I would record the day's happenings on the recorder. As we walked through Jerusalem, I would simply keep the microphone close to my mouth and talk, recording what I saw. However, each night our rooms became workshops where we got together our notes and marked our films. We stayed at the American Colony Hotel that night, and the next day we planned to go to Bethlehem, which is the birthplace of Christ. No one can ever tell you or make you understand in words or in song how many thoughts will flood your mind or how deeply your soul will be moved when you, as a Christian, view Bethlehem. I believe that an unsaved person could go there and look upon what I saw as so many rocks and hills, for he would never have known God in the forgiveness of sin. What manner of Christian would not thrill to know he was walking in the footprints of Jesus, looking upon the same scenes His precious eyes had beheld. You will never have your soul stirred like this. It will bless your heart as it has never been blessed before. Your life cannot be the same again. I found myself wishing I could live my life over, in order to live even closer to God and completely give myself over to God's will.

Seek Jesus with all your heart, with love, and beg for forgiveness of your sin. You will never know real happiness or real peace until you know Jesus as He is.

FROM RIVER JORDAN TO JERUSALEM

As you travel from the river Jordan, where Jesus was baptized, toward Jerusalem you pass through a place called Jericho. The old walls of Jericho are partly unearthed and are open for the public to see. I am sure that God had it that way so that we, who live today, can go and see the ruins and the covered walls of old Jericho. This is the city in the Book of Joshua which God called the wicked city Jericho, and the children of Israel, led by Joshua, crossed the river Jordan into that city. Moses was forbidden to go there because he had smitten the rock, instead of merely touching it as God had directed. Therefore, Moses was never permitted to go into the Promised Land, but instead he went to the top of the mountain and looked across to the city. The Bible tells of a rich man who climbed a sycamore tree here that he might get a glimpse of Christ as He passed through. It is believed that this was the last time Jesus would travel this road before he was crucified. Ministers like to use the thought that in the case of the rich man, Christ would only travel this road this one more time, and perhaps Christ will travel only one more time on your road. You may have only one more opportunity to accept Christ. While Jesus was on this last journey from the river Jordan to Jericho, blind Bartimaeus sat begging, crying, pleading that someone help him. He heard the shouts of joy of boys and girls singing hallelujah, for Jesus of Nazareth was coming. He cried out, "Son of David, have mercy on me." Some said to him not to bother Jesus, for He was a busy man. But blind Bartimaeus only cried more, and Jesus heard his cry and went to him. Jesus touched his eyes and the man could see. The rich man who climbed the tree had his eyesight, yet he was as blind as Bartimaeus, for he was blind to the love of God. He had rushed ahead of the crowd and climbed a tree, for he was very small in stature and he wanted to do all he could to see Jesus. Jesus said, The day you seek me with all your heart, you will find me. Zacchaeus did all he could do, and Jesus did the rest. Jesus is standing waiting for every heart that is broken, tired, and discouraged to come to Him and find rest. Zacchaeus might have been lost in the crowd. You might get lost in the crowd. Zacchaeus chose to climb a tree and wait upon Jesus. "And Jesus entered and passed through Jericho. And, behold, there was a man named Zacchaeus, which was the chief among the publicans, and he was rich. And he sought to see Jesus who he was; and could not for the press, because he was little of stature. And he ran before, and climbed up into a sycamore tree to see him: for he was to pass that way. And when Jesus came to the place, he looked up, and saw him, and said unto him, Zacchaeus, make haste, and come down; for to day I must abide at thy house. And he made haste, and came down, and received him joyfully. And when they saw it, they all murmured, saying, That he was gone to be guest with a man that is a sinner. And Zacchaeus stood, and said unto the Lord; Behold, Lord, the half of my goods I give to the poor; and if I have taken any thing from any man by false accusation, I restore him four-fold. And Jesus said unto him, This day is salvation come to this house, forsomuch as he also is a son of Abraham. For the Son of man is come to seek and to save that which was lost." Luke 19:1-10.

We live in a day when too many people condemn a man or woman because they are wealthy. The Bible tells us

Zacchaeus was rich and yet he wanted to see Jesus just as much as poor, blind Bartimaeus did. The world made fun of Jesus for going home with a sinner. Nevertheless, this man was saved, and he wanted to make right every wrong he had done to another. The *love of money* is the root of evil. Money is not evil. You perhaps have known people whose one aim in life was to accumulate all the money they could. They worshiped their money. I knew a farmer who had a good farm and could have provided his family with a good living, but he would even sell so much of the good meat and vegetables that his own family had not enough left to eat.

Jesus told the story about the traveler who was beaten and left to die on this road. A priest passed on one side and a levite passed on the other side; finally the Samaritan came and helped him. A part of that inn where the Samaritan took the injured man for shelter still stands on this road.

The good Samaritan is like the Lord Jesus Christ. The world may pass you by on every side; your own family may disown you; but God will hear your cry. The places we saw were so real that each passing moment my heart became very full and brimming over, and my Bible knowledge became greatly increased.

To us it was no longer a place in a book; now it was very real. We were traveling along the same route that Jesus had traveled many times, as He journeyed from one place to another across the little country of Palestine. Palestine was 145 miles long and in some places 45 miles wide, in other places as narrow as 37 miles. This was called the Holy Land, the Bible land, the place where God had sent His chosen people, the Jewish people, who were not strong but small in numbers, weak in power, that they might learn to lean upon God who was their Father and watched over them. Abraham had left all the idols and had turned his back on them, because he had heard the call of the only true and living God. After Isaac, his son, was born, his people grew and became God's chosen people. They were a royal people whom God had chosen for His own, that He might show His love and mercy.

You too can find Jesus along this road, if you will only believe in your heart and trust in Him.

BETHLEHEM

"Now when Jesus was born in Bethlehem of Judaea in the days of Herod the king, behold, there came wise men from the east to Jerusalem, saying, Where is he that is born King of the Jews? for we have seen his star in the east, and are come to worship him." I wish that each of you could have been with me as our group approached Bethlehem. Someone spoke up and said, "There is Bethlehem," and immediately every one of us thought of the birth of our Lord. Most people will say that the letters B.C. in our history books mean "before Christ." This is not true, for there was not a time when there was no Christ. It is only the devil who would plant that in your mind. The letters B.C. mean before the cradle. In the Book of Genesis God said, "Let us make man in our own image." "Us" meant Christ and God. God has a purpose in everything He does. He gave his Son that the world through Him might have eternal life if men would only believe on Christ. At the same time, when a mother gives up her son, she will know God understands, for He has experienced the same loss. God planned Christ's birth from the morning of eternity. We should find peace and consolation in our hearts, knowing God has experienced separation and loss, and because of this there is no separation or loss of ours which He cannot understand.

If you will notice, the revelation of Christ's coming was not given to a big Jewish school or high official of the town but to the shepherd boys who watched the stars at night and believed in Jehovah God. They had heard many times about the coming of their King, who would deliver them from bondage. Many, many years before the birth of Christ, His coming was told by the prophets. You can read the account in the gospels where Joseph, becoming engaged to Mary, found that she was already with child. Joseph, loving Mary and not wanting shame to be hers, thought of having her put away; but God spoke to Joseph and told him Mary had done no wrong, for that which was conceived in her womb was of the Holy Spirit and was the Son of God. After the birth of Christ, the next mention in the Bible of Jesus is when He is eight days old and is brought into the temple to be circumcised, which was the custom of the Jews. He must follow every lineage and every custom in order to prove Himself to be God and to fulfill all the prophecies which were written about Him. Then our Bible does not mention Jesus until he is a boy of twelve, found in the temple, confounding the learned doctors and lawyers of the day. The world looked upon Jesus as just another child and they called Mary his mother; however, nowhere in the Bible does Jesus call Mary his mother. Mary had been the door through which our Saviour had come. She had given an earthly birth to Jesus, but that was not His beginning. Jesus had no beginning, as God had had none, for both were the beginning of all things. Naturally, Mary loved Jesus, and when He had been gone from her for some time, perhaps she became anxious, not knowing what He was doing. So when she found Him in the temple perhaps she scolded Him. Then Jesus said, "Wist ye not that I must be about my Father's business?"

However, He was not yet a man; He returned with his parents to Nazareth and began the anxious years of waiting. The next time Jesus makes His appearance, eighteen years have passed and He is thirty years old.

The next few years of the life of Christ have given a story to my life. For without Jesus I would have no story to tell. I had planned in my heart to visit the Bible land one day. If ever you are permitted to go to the Holy Land, to walk the same streets Jesus did, to climb the mountain trails of the Judean mountains, and even to ride upon the Sea of Galilee,

please don't miss the opportunity. For as a Christian you
will have a deeper faith, and God will be more real to you
than He has ever been before. You will begin to say in your
heart, The things which I have read are a firm reality, for
I have seen the place myself. It is true.

The people of Bethlehem sell their wares on the street.
You can purchase a crown of thorns, and the Jew will tell
you these are like the thorns that our (not his) Jesus wore.
I bought a crown of thorns and brought it home with me.

After the baptism of Christ, His ministry began and the
world began to turn its eyes upon Him. The organized religious crowd was jealous of Christ, and for "envy" they beat
Him and sold Him. Even though they had been taught that
someday a "Deliverer" would come and every small child
knew the promise of a King who would rid them of their
burdens, yet when He came they would not accept Him.

Perhaps you will never be permitted to walk the dusty
roads that Jesus walked or sit at Jacob's well and drink the
water from it. It may not ever be your experience to look
upon the Dead Sea as I have. However, there is one thing
you can do. You can receive Jesus in your heart. The Bible
tells us in the Gospel of John that as many as received Jesus,
to them He gave power to become the sons of God. My life
for many years has been enriched with the presence of Jesus,
the Prince of Peace, the Bright and Morning Star, the Rose
of Sharon who is altogether lovely, the Son of God. Since I
have given my heart to Christ, my life has been to serve
Jesus with all my heart, mind and soul. I have never played
a round of golf. I know many ministers who are good golfers
and I do not in any way condemn them for taking this relaxation; however, I would rather take my Bible, sit down in the
quietness of my home, and find perfect relaxation and peace
through the Word of God. I would just rather take two more
"rounds" with the Lord. Jesus made home calls. He buried
the dead and comforted the sick and preached to the multitudes. After the multitudes had scattered to their homes,

Jesus would go into town and talk with businessmen. He asked a businessman to follow Him. Jesus went to the seashore and found fishermen whom He asked to come follow Him and be fishers of men. Jesus found a tax collector who wished to follow Him. Jesus was interested in the sinners and went among them that He might help them. Many times a minister is asked to go into a home where sin is obvious and no one tries to hide it. The sinful crowd knew Christ and did not expect Him to be a part of their sinful ways. A minister who remains true to the gospel will be respected. Many times I have had to go into such homes, and not once have I been asked to drink, play cards, or anything like that. Instead, they have honored the God whom I serve.

No matter where my calls have taken me, whether they were in my home town or in other states or even in foreign lands, I have always tried not to be too pious, or wear a long face, or give the impression that I thought myself better than anyone else, for I realize that what I am or ever hope to accomplish is through God's love and His grace. It is not my works but His blessings that have made the difference. I don't wear uniforms or dress differently from other men. I wear ready-made suits just like everyone else. My hat is no different from other men's. My tie is tied just like theirs. Jesus wore garments just like all the other men of His day. However, He did have a robe which had no seams. If you were to look at it, you would think it the same as all other robes. You had to examine the robe to find the difference. You have to watch a Christian and examine his life to see the difference. You might look at two men and see no difference in them, but one may have Christ in his heart and this makes the difference. You don't have to be around him long to determine this.

"Then cometh Jesus with them unto a place called Gethsemane, and saith unto the disciples, Sit ye here, while I go and pray yonder." Not many young people today of high school or college age have any conception of the meaning of the word "Gethsemane." Oftentimes you might hear an elderly person who has been a Christian for many years say of a trying time he was going through, that it was a Gethsemane. According to the Holy Bible, Gethsemane was the place where Jesus died. Being God, He could not be killed, only punished. Jesus had to give up his life, for it could not be taken from Him. Having eaten the last supper, where Jesus had told His disciples that one of them would betray Him, Peter had vowed he would not betray Jesus but would die for Him. Jesus told Peter that he would deny Him three times before the cock crowed.

Judas, who had walked with Jesus like the rest for three and a half years, who had had the same wonderful teaching as the rest, who had had the honor of being called one of the Twelve, knew that the religious crowd were anxious to put their hands upon Christ. The high priest knew that if they should try to take Jesus from a public meeting they would have trouble. Judas went to the high priest and bargained with these wicked men that he might get as much as he could for selling Christ. Most historians will say that around fifteen to sixteen pieces of silver was the common price for a Hebrew slave; Judas demanded thirty pieces for Christ. This man who had watched Jesus heal the sick, open blind eyes, and raise the dead was willing to sell Him for twice the price of a slave. For the love of money and greed for silver and gold, Judas bargained for the life of Christ. In the 26th chapter of Matthew, the Scripture tells us that it would have been better if Judas had never been born. It is far better never to be born than to be born and live only to die and go to Hell. If you are reading my book and have never accepted Christ, having no intention of ever accepting Him, then it would have been better had you not been born. I say this because life is so short and eternity is forever. The little span of life that you have upon this earth with its pleasures is not worth an eternity in Hell without God.

Judas told the priest and others to come and He would

show them where Jesus prayed. To me, the most cruel thing that I can think of could not be worse than seeking the place where a man prays and from there begin to take his life. Jesus spent much time in prayer. The Bible says that Jesus spent all night in prayer before He chose His twelve followers. Now, one of those twelve was going to take the enemies of Christ, not to a dwelling, or eating place, or even an auditorium, but to the holy sanctuary where Jesus talked with His Father, and there seize Him and inflict upon His human body extreme torture. Judas took them to the Garden of Gethsemane, where Jesus prayed beneath the old olive trees. Jesus was praying only a stone's throw from the disciples, and his sweat became like drops of blood. He went further than the disciples, for He alone redeemed our souls without the help of the disciples, the Virgin Mary, or anyone except Jehovah God. They bound Jesus and brought Him before Caiaphas, the high priest. They brought Jesus there before daylight, and the trial was illegal; however, Jesus was charged with treason. Nevertheless, Jesus opened not His mouth; the Scripture has said that He came like an ox to the slaughter. Jesus came to this earth to die on a cross as a sin-bearer, a substitute for your sins and mine. Jesus took our place that we might go free.

As Jesus was being tried and Peter was warming himself by a little fire outside, one of the women told Peter she had seen him with Jesus. To this Peter answered that he did not know who Jesus was. After a while another person came by and told Peter he surely was one of Jesus' disciples. Peter said, "Woman, I know not what you say." It was not long before another told him his speech betrayed him as one of Christ's followers. Then the word of Jesus came into Peter's mind, for he had denied Christ three times as the cock crowed.

Judas watched the trial and remained hidden in the background. Finally, when his conscience would let him have no peace, he took the silver back to the temple and offered the money to the priests, saying he had betrayed innocent blood. The Bible says that he cast down the money and went out and hanged himself.

Jesus was then brought before Pilate, who pleaded and reasoned with the people to release Jesus; but they would not release Jesus. Someone told Pilate that Jesus came from Nazareth, which was under the jurisdiction of Herod. Pilate, wishing to be rid of Jesus and knowing Herod was in Jerusalem, sent him to Herod to be tried. Herod made mockery of Christ and put on Him a tattered, torn robe which had been worn at one time by a king. They put a reed in Christ's hand and laughed and made fun of Him. Then Jesus was returned to Pilate and was whipped at the whipping post. Many years ago the old prophet of God, Isaiah, had said, "He was wounded for our transgression, he was bruised for our iniquities; the chastisement of our peace was upon him; and with his stripes we are healed."

One morning while we were in Jerusalem, our group went to see Calvary. When we were almost there, the bus stopped and the guide said that when the bus turned again we would see Mount Calvary over to our left. This is called "the place of a skull" and is just outside the gate north of the city. We saw the old bald skull place that actually looks like the forehead of a man, and we were told that we could get out of the bus and look around as long as we wished. Not a word was spoken by our group as we got out of the bus. You have never been at a funeral service where there was more reverence. As my feet went onto the steps taking me down to the ground, the squeak of the steps seemed to cry, "God have mercy." The rocks seemed to roll under my feet and it seemed as if I could hear the groans of the Son of God. There was a deathly silence all about us as if we could actually hear the blood of Christ as it dripped upon the ground.

I wish you could have been there with me. It makes no difference who you are or whatever your profession, I believe if you had never known Christ as your Saviour you would have accepted Him then. If you are a Christian, I believe you would have been closer to Christ than you had ever been before. The experience which is mine for having visited the Holy Land is priceless to me. God is very real to me. I know Him as my Saviour, as my Lord; and everyday I try my very best to make Him my Master. When I was asked to write a story of my life, I knew the only life I had to write about was one with Jesus. If you take Jesus out of my life, then there is nothing for me to write about. When you watch the sun set, and there are clouds above the sunset and the sun has gone behind the mountain, the sun will reflect its beauty and its glory in the clouds above it. You can let Jesus be seen in His beauty living in your life and in you.

If you are not a Christian, I beg of you to be saved today, that it will never be said of you, it would have been better had you never been born. Be saved today, through the blood of Christ.

IV

The Harvest Years

43. Building of
Million-Dollar Auditorium

IN 1946, AFTER THE WAR HAD ENDED, WE BEGAN TO TALK
to our people about a new building. However, we were
unable to get anyone to talk to us about finances for the
building. We had had the same trouble before, in building
our first and second buildings. Several estimates were given
to us on the cost; the lowest estimate was $1,300,000. Our
church treasury only had about $75,000 to $80,000.

By May, 1947, we began to talk urgently about building
this large auditorium. It would have a horseshoe balcony
extending over the second and into the third floor. We
wanted a babyland with soundproof windows, so that, while
the babies were cared for, the mothers would be able to see
and hear the service. (This new auditorium was covered
in the Encyclopaedia Britannica yearbook of 1950. A picture
of our church was shown there along with a full-page story
on the church and its growth.)

I say with great humility that the hand of God was upon
me and my church, for since we had begun our church there
had always been a problem of getting enough room and seats
for our crowd. God was leading, inspiring, and instructing
me to build. I consulted about ten or twelve loan companies
and was told we had to have at least $600,000 of our own for
the banks to grant the balance needed to erect the building.

We knew that if we contracted the separate jobs instead of giving it all to one individual, the building would cost a great deal more. We had in our congregation an expert contractor, Ray Chilton, who said that he would supervise the building by doing all the buying and being responsible for all craft. His wages were to be those of a foreman. However, when we were ready to build we still did not have enough money in reserve for a loan the size we would need. We had $180,000 and tried to get a company to lend us as much as they could and we would go as far as possible; but not one loan company would consider it.

When our building plans were completed we needed a building permit, and it was then we were told that Washington still had restrictions on building, especially where steel was involved. We were not granted a permit. My congregation voted that I be given full power of attorney and do what I thought necessary to get the building started. I went to Washington and was told I could not get a permit for a building which would cost a million dollars. Instead, I was granted a permit for $250,000 to start the basement. No contractor would take the job because we could not pay him the full amount of a contractor's bid. However, Ray Chilton, the contractor in our church, agreed to work from day to day. I wish you could have seen the hand of God upon us as we began our new building.

Nehemiah 2:19,20: "But when Sanballat the Horonite, and Tobiah the servant, the Ammonite, and Geshem the Arabian, heard it, they laughed us to scorn, and despised us, and said, What is this thing that ye do? will ye rebel against the king? Then answered I them, and said unto them, The God of heaven, he will prosper us; therefore we his servants will arise and build: but ye have no portion, nor right, nor memorial, in Jerusalem." Our enemies did laugh at us and ask how we could build such a building with only $180,000. Some of the local contractors thought we were wrong in trying to build and they called a contractors' meeting. They

had not wronged anyone, but he had heard the sermon I preached on Sunday, in which I said that each one of us while we are on the earth and on this side of the grave had to make our own, individual peace with God. He reminded me I had read from the Book of Romans, and he asked me to find the Scripture for him. We turned to this Scripture and read it together. Romans 14:11, 12: "For it is written, As I live, saith the Lord, every knee shall bow to me, and every tongue shall confess to God. So then every one of us shall give account of himself to God."

He told me that I had also mentioned in the sermon "being saved or converted," and he said that he was not sure if he understood the meaning of these words. I turned my Bible to the 10th chapter of Romans, where the 10th verse says that with the heart you believe and the 13th verse says that whosoever shall call upon the name of the Lord shall be saved. Then we read a few verses from the 3rd chapter of John, where it tells us we must be born again if we wish to see the kingdom of God.

As we prayed together in the quietness of his office, the tears flowed freely down his cheeks. He was a real man's man, and he shook my hand and thanked me for coming.

He had a big heart and freely gave gifts to his friends. On Christmas he called me over to his office where he had gifts for me, my wife, my son, and my son's wife. The following Easter, he spent the sunrise service with us, and while he did attend other churches, the last few Easter sunrise services before he went to be with the Lord he spent with us here at the Akron Baptist Temple. He gave checks to our church, and we loved him and believed that he loved us. Buck, with his sons, Bruce and Richard, spent his last sunrise service with us, which was made more beautiful because of the lovely floral contribution which the Buchholzers had furnished for several years.

I remember well how Mr. Buchholzer appreciated hearing our soloist, Joe Thomas, sing "Sunrise with Jesus throughout

All Eternity." He came by and said it was wonderful to listen to that song. He said, "Won't it be wonderful when we see that sunrise in Glory?"

I have met many men in business and got to know and love them. They have helped me, and by God's grace and His holy Word, I have been able to help many of Akron's businessmen.

We meet many friends on life's journey, and some of them are buried deep in our hearts. The memory of them and their introduction to God makes life worth living. I believe with all my heart that if ever a man found Christ, Mr. Buchholzer found Him that day in his busy office.

If you are a busy man and seem to have all your time taken, I beg of you to stop long enough to read your Bible and attend church, for spiritual food is necessary if you are to find peace.

Mr. Buchholzer was a busy man, but he found time to worship and hear the hymns sung, and he died in a Saviour's love, beloved by his family and friends.

45. Are You Ashamed of Christ?

WE FIND IN THE GOSPEL OF MARK 8:38: "WHOSOEVER therefore shall be ashamed of me and of my words in this adulterous and sinful generation; of him also shall the Son of man be ashamed, when he cometh in the glory of his Father with the holy angels." I have studied God's Word, the persons in the Bible who were willing to stand for Christ, and also the persons who denied Christ. I have read the accounts of the old prophets, seeing that some sold out to Balaam and others stood true to the calling and purpose of God, even unto death.

I have seen the old Colosseum at Rome where the Christians, unwilling to give up their faith, were thrown to the wild beasts as sport for the unbelievers. These Christians were mocked and imprisoned and finally brutally slain; yet they held on to Christ and His teachings.

We have all read of what it cost our forefathers to come to this new world, leaving everything they loved, and many dying from starvation, bitter cold winters, and Indian attacks. If it had not been for their grim determination to worship God the way they chose, where would America be today?

I often wondered in my mind what I would do if I were put to a real test of my faith. Now, I realized in America this would not happen, perhaps, but the thought lingered in my mind. I wondered if I would stand up and declare myself to be a Christian, or would I keep my seat. I doubted if ever my life would be in jeopardy, but would I have the courage, if I had to make myself conspicuous and invite ridicule, to champion Christ?

It is easy to confess Christ in a church. It is easy to sing in a choir in a church where everyone, for the most part, comes to sing and worship. It is not hard to be an usher or to take an active part in a local church, for while you are in the church, it offers a dignity and a prestige, and most of those attending church are your friends.

In 1951 my wife and I went traveling with a good friend of mine and his dear wife and were gone about a month. Our trip took us through many of the western and midwestern states and on to the West Coast. While we were in Phoenix, Arizona, we stopped at a very nice restaurant. It was a large eating place, both inside and outside. There was a swimming pool and tables on the outside to serve the people. It seemed to me that every seat was taken inside. You entered at one door, and when you had eaten and received your check, you went out at another door. In between these two doors, near the entrance, was a nice marble-top table, which was plenty large enough for four people to be served. However, there was an elderly couple sitting at this table. When we entered, I did not notice the couple, other than as dinner guests such as we were. Shortly after we were seated, the elderly gentleman rapped his glass to gain attention, and with the aid of a microphone which was heard inside and out, he welcomed everyone there to the restaurant and to Phoenix. He told us that when he was a boy of fifteen, he went home with a boy one night who attended the Methodist church and who asked him to attend with him the next Sunday. He stated that the preacher preached on the 9th chapter of Mark, where the fire is never quenched and the worm dieth not. He said he was scared so badly by the message that he did not sleep well for a month, and he assured himself that he would not go back. Then he related how he had been asked to go to church with a Baptist boy. Sarcastically he said, "Lo and behold, if that preacher didn't preach on Hell." The message came from the 16th chapter of Luke, where the man died and was buried, and in Hell he lifted up his eyes. He repeated twice that he still had this message in his heart and he could not forget it.

When he became nineteen he went to Boston, where he heard a Unitarian preach. He learned that the Unitarians believe there is no judgment after death and that they do not believe in Christ. He decided then and there to become a Unitarian minister. He finished his schooling, became a Unitarian minister, and served in that capacity for more than thirty-five years. Being retired, he acted as the welcoming host for the guests who came to this restaurant.

He took his seat, having accomplished his welcoming speech, and there I sat, having the largest church in the United States, with 16,000 Baptist members. I rapped my water glass and stood to my feet. I asked the people to bear with me for just a few minutes. Silence fell over the room as I began: "I have read in the Bible about a man who sold Jesus for thirty pieces of silver, and they called his name Judas. I have also read the account of one called Peter, who denied Jesus when he only needed one character witness, and even cursed when one girl said Peter was with the crowd. Jesus stood in Pilate's judgment hall without a friend. As I read those accounts, I wondered what I would do when called upon to sell Christ or claim Him as my own. This is the day to make my choice. I would like to say to the gentleman seated over at the door, he has stated twice that from a boy of fifteen there remains fresh in his mind the message on Hell, where the fire is never quenched and the worm dieth not. I am a Christian and have been saved. I have read the books of the Unitarian doctrine, and I have also read the Book of God, the Bible. It would depend on whether you want to take the words of man-made religion or the words of Christ, who bled and died on Calvary that you and I might be saved. Forgive me for taking your time, but I could not deny Jesus nor sell him for thirty pieces of silver."

People in that restaurant applauded and tapped their water glasses as I took my seat. Someone shouted, "Hoorah for the stranger!" The elderly man got to his feet and quoted one of Longfellow's poems. When he had finished I rose to my feet and said, "Forgive me but I must say this one thing: Jesus said, 'Except we repent, we shall all likewise perish.'" An old gray-haired man seated next to me took hold of my arm and said, "Young man, I don't know who you are, I have never seen you before, but I would like to say to you that I was gloriously saved in an old Methodist church when I was about seventeen. I live here in Phoenix as a banker, and I want you to know that Phoenix is proud of you and men like you."

We had our meal, but before Mr. and Mrs. Tell and my wife and I could leave, many came to our table, wishing to know more about us. I was happy that God had given me the grace to stand to my feet, a humble Baptist preacher, and declare my loyalty to Christ. God had given me the courage to tell them Jesus had died for every one of them, including the elderly host.

Our Scripture tells us that if we are ashamed of Christ, He will be ashamed of us. Jesus will come in the clouds of glory, declaring judgment. In Matthew 10:32,33 it says, "Whosoever therefore shall confess me before men, him will I confess also before my Father which is in heaven. But whosoever shall deny me before men, him will I also deny before my Father which is in heaven."

I left that restaurant unashamed that I had told the story of Christ when the opportunity had been given me. I wonder, when you have some golden opportunity to let perhaps strangers, persons whom you have never met, know whether or not you are a Christian, will you be ashamed of Jesus? There were perhaps people in that restaurant who had never heard any gospel until that day. I believe God sent me to that place for a purpose: to tell them the truth. I asked the gentleman host why he remembered the two stories of Hell so well. His belief does not satisfy, merely eases, a conscience that is still burning. I talked with him personally and told him that I did not wish to offend him, but it was my prayer that he would change and accept the Lord Jesus. I respected his age and his silver hair, but I wanted him to know the best friend he could ever have.

I was told that the restaurant could seat around five hundred persons, and from the response that I received, it warmed my heart to know that there were people who loved to hear the story of Christ, no matter where or when. I left there that day, happy as I could be—happy in a Saviour's love.

46. Doctor of Divinity

GOD HAS PROMISED IN HIS WORD THAT IF WE TAKE THE back seat of life, be humble, pray, and trust in Him, one day we shall be invited to have a front seat, having deserved that place, according to God's standards. God out of His mercy judges all men honestly.

It has not been my privilege to have had the formal education which many of my preacher friends and others have had. However, in April, 1955, I was invited to teach and preach for several days at the Bob Jones University in Greenville, South Carolina. The teaching was to be during school hours, and then at night I was to bring a message to the student body.

While I was there it was my happy privilege to confer several times with Dr. Bob Jones, Sr., and Dr. Bob Jones, Jr. I talked with many of the college's staff and learned to love them. They questioned me very thoroughly concerning my background as a Bible student. They wished to know how I had become a preacher and teacher of the Bible.

After I returned home I received a letter from Dr. Bob Jones, Sr., and his son inviting me back to the university in June. They wished to confer upon me at that time the honorary degree of Doctor of Divinity. Surprised and very much pleased, I returned in June to receive this honor. I count this occasion as one of the greatest moments in my life. It was with great humility that I accepted this degree from the Bob Jones University. I thank God, who put the idea in their hearts and made possible for me this great honor. Now by God's grace and mercy I am permitted to use Doctor of Divinity as my title. I do not think the degree makes a person any better nor does it make a minister a better preacher, but it does encourage his efforts and perhaps allows him to talk with people who before would not have listened.

Since that hour I have been given many opportunities to speak in places where I doubt that I would have been asked had I not had the title. I had not changed, but this is man's way and not God's way. Man will judge a person for his outward accomplishments; God examines his heart. God made it possible for me to enter circles otherwise closed to me that I might glorify His name.

I left the university that day saying in my own heart that the Bible teaches us to love God and to serve Him. I remember reading once that Abraham Lincoln said, "I will study and get ready and, perhaps, someday my chance will come."

I would like to take the next few paragraphs to talk to ministers and Christian leaders. It has been my great and happy privilege to meet and help close to seven hundred ministers. Many of them had been preaching for several years, and yet from some of the experiences that I had had I was able to show them how God had proved Himself over and over to me and would do the same for them if they would only have faith and work. It was a joy for me to watch their churches double in size and see them grow in grace and strength in Christ. Some of these men, with the help of God, were able to increase their church attendance to four times what it had been. They were able to secure finances to enlarge their churches, through the strength of their own good name and the freewill offerings of their faithful members. In time I saw many of them sent by their own congregations to the Holy Land, which always enriches the life of anyone, especially of a minister.

There will come a time in your life when you will have to make the decision whether to go forward or remain still. You may think that you can remain still, but in time you will find yourself going backward. The Christian life is always a forward life. In the Bible the word "exceeding," which is so often used, means to move on.

There will come a time in your life, if you live right and trust God, when you will be permitted to help others. When you reach the place in life where you are not helping others, then your life is at a standstill, and before long you will start going backward. If you work and pray, many times you will be asked to take perhaps a small job. That job might be as a Sunday-school teacher. Some people don't rate a Sunday-school teacher as very important. However, I have learned through the years that this job has great importance, whether you teach a class of two or three or two or three hundred. For instance, suppose you were asked to teach the class of children who were two and three years old. You might keep them for a year. In that year you would have a precious chance to instill in their hearts and minds things about Jesus that they would never forget. You remain in your class, and perhaps years would pass; and one day you would receive more responsibility—you would be asked to be superintendent of a department. All the knowledge of the years would make you confident, with God's help, to organize and lead.

Here at the Akron Baptist Temple no literature is used to help teach our lessons. The Bible alone is brought to class by our teachers. Flannel graph is used in the lower grades, and at the end of class a paper is passed out to take home. We ask our teachers to bring the Book of God to class and read that to the boys and girls. We have found it impresses them far more in their minds and hearts to know that they are studying the actual Word of God. When an evangelist comes and says where his Scripture is to be found, it is wonderful to watch the youngsters in our congregation as they take their Bibles and follow along just like Mother and Dad.

You will perhaps find contentment in serving as a superintendent, but one day you will find yourself wanting to do more. One day you will find yourself saying that God is calling you to preach the gospel. Looking back over your life you will see how God has blessed your work and has continually given you more responsibility and the wisdom to see it through. You began with the little tots and went on to the teen-agers. You have been prepared by God, and now you feel the call to preach to everyone the precious Word of God.

It is so wonderful to work in God's vineyard. Perhaps you may not have a son and have chosen a young man to help along life's way as if he were your son. You live your life honestly before him and freely show your love and affection for him. Perhaps having no children of your own, you show your love in a gift at Christmastime and at his birthday. As the years pass and a close bond grows between you, you have a great satisfaction in knowing your life has influenced this young man. One day this young man will perhaps come to you and say that he has felt God calling him. Just a little time when he needed it, a word of encouragement when he was low, and countless prayers when he was gone from you, have finally borne fruit. No greater thrill can come to a Christian's heart than to know he has had a small part in molding someone's life for Christ. What a thrill to live so that someone will want to be like you, will want to make you proud of him. Perhaps you have had the glorious privilege of leading this young man to Christ and now he wants to lead others to Christ.

I enjoy a football game and get a thrill when the ball goes over for a touchdown, and I can stand and cheer with the rest when the baseball clears the fence for a home run; but I say to you there is no greater thrill than to see a young man in the prime of life willing to serve Christ, knowing full well what a part you have had in his life.

I have heard Dr. Bob Jones, Sr., and Dr. Bob Jones, Jr., speak of men on whom they had conferred degrees and of whom they were very proud. They were kind enough to say that they were proud of me. It made me want to study even harder than ever, for they had exalted me in the eyes of man and more would be required of me. My study should not be haphazard but, if possible, more diligent and with much prayer. I wanted to be worthy of the honor which they had given me. It made me want to be a better servant of God. I like the name "servant," for if a minister is what he ought to be, he is a servant first of God, then of the people. His job is to serve when the death angel visits, when the wedding bells ring, at social gatherings where there is joy and laughter, at the sickbed when hearts are worried. He is there to share with you whatever comes your way, whether it is joy or sorrow.

When we leave this world we can take nothing with us. Our wealth, lands, houses, and loved ones we must leave behind. However, in my profession as a minister, if I remain true to God, long after I am gone my influence will remain and not die in the hearts of those I have tried to help. It is easy to be a part of someone's happiness but it takes grace to share his sorrow. Somehow I think the sharing of sorrow is the part you never forget. You must walk into a house where a loved one has died. There you will find the wife to whom you can give hope of reunion through Christ. There is a mother and father who have watched their baby being taken away. You can take your Bible and read to them where David said his baby could not come to him but he could go to his baby. A minister's job does carry with it a lot of sorrow, but with it are many privileges and many joys. My work, God's work, will live on long after I am gone, simply because GOD IS REAL.

47. Associated Press and Akron *Beacon Journal*

IN APRIL, 1960, OUR CHURCH CELEBRATED THE TWENTY-fifth anniversary of its foundation and organization. Our local newspaper, the Akron *Beacon Journal,* one of the

Knight publications, whose executive editor is Mr. Ben Maidenburg, gave us the entire front page of section "F" and the story carried over into another column of another page. Mr. Lloyd Stoyer, who writes most of their feature articles, prepared the story. Our local paper has a circulation of about 135,000.

The Associated Press ran parts of this story in an article, which appeared in many newspapers across the United States. In my opinion, this article was very well written: they had followed our history truthfully without exaggeration. After the story broke across the nation, we had clippings sent to us from newspapers in foreign countries. They, of course, had received their information from the Associated Press.

God said in the Bible to write the article and to send it, and there is no greater way to reach people than through the press. We as a church and as individuals have always been grateful to the Knight newspapers, not only here in Akron but also in Detroit, Florida, Chicago, and many other places. I believe life is a journey and we all walk together. We do not live alone nor do we die alone. From a boy of twenty-two, when I turned about-face and put my faith and trust in Jesus, I can truthfully say that all I am or ever hope to be I owe to God, Christian parents, and the girl I married, Nell Stokes. It pays to serve Jesus. God has said in His Word that He would never leave you or forsake you. This means me and everyone who will put their faith in God. Many things may happen to us and we will wonder why, but someday we will understand. Too many of us plan for this life only, and yet if we would plan for God and eternity, this life would be so much greater. Do you suppose for one minute that I believed or thought as a youngster of twelve that one day, through God's love and faithful friends, that which God had used me to do would be national and international news? Do you think that it ever crossed my mind when I was saved at the age of twenty-two that one day I would be permitted to travel to many foreign countries and preach the gospel of Christ? It never crossed my mind that one day I would see Jerusalem, even though I had nourished the dream in my heart. But God said in His Word to seek first the Kingdom of God and His righteousness and all these things will be added. Before I rest and many times during the day I thank God for His goodness to me. I thank Him for the good friends He has given me, for God has used those friends to glorify Himself. Jesus said He would honor even a cup of water given in His name. Before we are saved, all our efforts to obtain salvation through good works appear as filthy rags in the nostrils of God, but after we become sons of God and trust in Him, all these good works become a reward. Just as you receive pay for your earthly services, you will receive peace and happiness which are the rewards that last throughout the endless ages. There is a reward for loving Christ and trusting in Him. You shall miss the dark abyss of the regions below, where there is no peace and only sorrow. Our payday will find us in the streets of Glory, safe throughout all eternity, because our Saviour prepared a place for us.

Our church had such a humble, small beginning. Life itself is like that. The little baby born in the hospital lies helpless and dependent upon someone to care for it. Yet, in a little while, the baby begins to turn over in its crib and, holding to the crib, is able to pull itself up to the side and stand. One day this same baby turns loose from the chair and takes its first step. The jibberish becomes words. Years pass before he is recognized as an adult who can vote. Young converts, don't become discouraged when, after you are saved, you find that you are just as weak and dependent spiritually as this little baby is physically. So many things can happen to a young convert. Just as the little one will fall and stub his toe and cry, you in like manner will stub your toe spiritually. As the mother or father hears the child cry and rushes to help, so will your God and mine hear your cry and hear your prayer. It may be at the midnight hour in total darkness or at high noon when the sun is shining the brightest when your cry will go out to God. However, the time matters not to God, nor is the trouble so small or so great that God is not equal to the job before Him. Steal away and pray, for Jesus told His disciples to ask what they would in the name of Christ when they prayed to God, and it would be granted. God is more real to you than any loved one or friend you can ever know, for no matter how great their love, they are still subject unto death, while God is eternal and is everywhere. Miles can separate loved ones, but you are only a whisper away from God. Days and weeks of travel may separate you from someone you trust and love, but God is as close as your honest prayer.

I believe with all my heart that because of God's great love, my willingness to let Him govern my life, my adherence to the dictates of the Holy Spirit, and my desire to serve God and His people, the story of my church was given to the Associated Press. God is no respecter of persons. He will listen to you, as a child of His, as well as He listens to me. If you are sick, get your Bible and read. Jesus said every herb was given for our benefit. Yes, I believe in medical doctors and their ability. Their knowledge was given them to benefit mankind and end suffering if it is God's will. You have no idea what God can do for you if you don't give Him the chance. I know men who began life with practically nothing. They loved God, served Him, and tithed from their earnings. From men with few dollars in their pockets they became millionaires. Without God you can do nothing. God holds your very breath in His hand. I am sincerely thankful for the Associated Press and the Akron *Beacon Journal* for the part they have played in my life and in God's ministry.

48. Church in Tucson

IN THE MONTH OF MARCH IN THE YEAR 1961, MRS. Billington and I left Akron, Ohio, for Tucson, Arizona, where we were to help establish a church. Since my conversion at the age of twenty-two, most of my time has been given to God's work. The Bible tells us in the 35th chapter of Isaiah that the desert will blossom like the rose. It also tells us in that chapter to lift the feeble hands and the weak knees and be strong and courageous, for God will come and help.

I had been asked to visit Tucson to look over the possibilities of starting a church in that area. There I met the Johnson family. Brother Johnson had two children who were polio patients. They had contracted the dread disease when they were only three and five, and now they were about eleven and thirteen.

If it be God's will, in this year, 1961, the building will be finished. This church is one of five building programs which were started in 1960 and will be completed in 1961. There are large churches being finished in Youngstown, Cleveland, and Dover, Ohio. I can think of no better way to spend God's money than to build churches where people can worship and find Christ.

I remember the Sunday that the two precious children of Mr. and Mrs. Johnson sang a song in which they said they knew not what the future held but they knew who held the future. Whatever tomorrow brought, God would be holding their hands. It makes do difference who you are, I believe that song would break your heart. No one could ever be hardened enough to hide the tears, looking upon two children burdened with polio, singing praises to God.

Many things happened to my wife and me on our journey to Tucson. For instance, a man died on the plane and we had to return to Chicago. There seems always to be something to hinder one in doing the will of God. We found so many things wrong as we tried to get into Tucson. We met with several men to discuss the new building. After much prayer and careful planning, the completion of the church in Tucson is in sight.

The reason that I decided to put this chapter into my book is that there are many men in these United States who have in their possession more money than they will ever be able to use. They let it multiply in stocks and material things, and yet they could use it for God and be so much happier than they ever dreamed possible.

Many men who have great wealth want to do more for God, but they are just waiting for a worthy cause or for someone to persuade them to do what they wanted to do in the first place. Our Saviour, Jesus Christ, said that it is more blessed to give than to receive. How true this is, and how well I know this. By being instrumental in getting someone to give and watching their blessings, I have had just as great a blessing myself. The Bible tells us stories of rich men. Many of them were saved. Abraham was very rich; Job was richer than all of the men of the East. The Bible says King Solomon made silver and gold like the leaves of the oak trees.

Now, my life has not been perfect, nor will your life be perfect. But when you come to the end of your life and look back over the journey, will your last hours be full of remorse and regret or will you be happy for the things you have done?

We took money from Ohio and put it into Tucson so that a church to glorify God might be built and because we believed that Louis Johnson had been called, not by man but by God Himself, to preach the gospel. He had no friends with money enough to help him. God's money was taken into the desert, and the desert bloomed like the rose. It is an old-fashioned church with an altar. People are saved in that church. The desert is blooming in Tucson, in Jerusalem, in

China, in Old Mexico, and far and wide, wherever Jesus is being lifted up.

What are your plans for tomorrow? Are they to help someone? I believe it was Abraham Lincoln who said that a day spent helping no one but yourself is a day wasted. Someday you will meet your loved ones for the last time: you or they will step from the scene of time into Eternity. There is another meeting place in Heaven, and we gain this place through the blood and cross of Christ. He was nailed to a cross, and in so doing He nailed your sins and mine to the cross. The precious blood of Christ gave me, this preacher, a heart of love, that I would leave my home in the month of March, although I was sick, and journey all the way to Arizona to meet a young preacher, his wife and fine children. There in the desert is a church for the wayfaring man or the desert dweller, the Indian on his trail, the passer-by, even the man or woman there for reasons of health.

The Bible says of your soul that it never dies. The soul lives on forever. You have an eternal destiny. The Johnson family believed so strongly in the Christ of Calvary that they were willing to go to the desert, make it their home, and establish a church. God then laid upon my heart to go there and help with the building. It is a beautiful church. If you are ever in Tucson, it would bless you to see this church.

You might ask why I take the time to tell you this, but I realize life is a short journey; it will soon be over and done. You will have a lot of pleasure in your last days, your hair white with the frost of many winters, if you are able to say you helped that man, that church, that mission, that missionary, that family. Whatever joy those you helped have, you too have that same joy. Joy is abundant to share.

God saved me and called me to preach to others the story that Jesus saves. Therefore, by God's grace, by God's calling preachers, by God's still putting His hand on men and changing their lives and directing their paths, one day His family will be complete in Glory. Sometime, according to

Scripture, the last soul will be converted. It will complete God's family, and time shall be no more. God knows your heart and mine, and He knows those who will never trust Him. We ask you to reason with yourself. Are you satisfied? Does the life you are now leading make you happy? Are you afraid of dying and meeting God just as you are? If you would be honest, many of you would have to say you are afraid of dying. Do you know what to do if you are afraid?

None of us has the promise of tomorrow nor do we know what tomorrow brings, but if our hands are in God's hand we need have no fear, for God knows and holds the future in His hand. Jesus, the Rose of Sharon, hung on a cross while darkness covered the land that you and I might have a Saviour and a hope of eternity.

My days upon earth are fast drawing to a close, and I am happy to tell you that the way of the cross leads home. I know of no other life, of no other profession that I would choose should I be allowed to live my life over. I would not exchange my life of helping others. God let me help a mother at the casket of her baby. God let me comfort a son whose father had no time for him. God let me help a man whose business failed and who was lost in a sea, not knowing which way to turn. God let me lead men in the sunset of life to Him, just before they stepped over into eternity.

Somewhere, someone is needing just you. There is someone whom I shall never see or meet, yet you will, and you can do for him what no one else can. You can be a blessing to that person if you will; but you must first know the Lord yourself before you can introduce Him to others.

It will be such a comfort to you to remember those you have helped on this journey home.

49. All Nations That Forget God Shall Be Turned into Hell

I HAVE BEEN ASKED BY STATESMEN OF OUR LOCAL GOVernment and of the state of Ohio and members of the United States Congress, along with other individuals, to prepare a message for this day in which we live. It will be written so that statesmen, presidents, and rulers will at least know what the Book of God has to say. We have found several Scriptures which we plan to use. The first of these is Psalms 9:17: "The wicked shall be turned into hell, and all the nations that forget God." As I have already mentioned in another chapter in this book, in 1945 I warned the President of the United States and Congress not to give Russia our secrets. That message became a part of the Congressional Record.

Though we call ourselves a great nation, whatever we have that other nations do not have is through a gift of God and through the minds of our own God-loving leaders, whose leadership has made us different. We find all through the Old Testament that in time of war the leaders who were known as God-loving men turned to the prophets for advice, because they were known as prophets of God. They were asked to come and pray that God would be with them in their endeavors.

We find in the 18th chapter of the Book of Genesis that the cities of Sodom and Gomorrah were taken, and Lot was also taken in the capture of those cities. Men went to Abraham and told him the plight of Lot, his nephew. Abraham was a godly man and prayed. He took with him a small group of men, about three hundred in number, and recaptured the city, because Abraham was God's man.

We also find the story of Gideon, who had thousands of men. But God told him he needed only a small part of them and told Gideon how to pick those whom he should take with him into battle. Gideon was told to send the married men back behind the lines. When the others came to a creek, those who lay down to drink all the water they wished were to be left behind. However, those who took water in their hands and lapped it like a dog he was to take with him into battle. Thus God gave Gideon a pattern to follow to win the victory, and Gideon harkened to every word of the Lord.

You will find in the Bible where thirty-two kings became drunk, and even though they combined their armies, they were badly defeated. In II Kings the 6th chapter you will find that God used the old prophet Elisha to tell where the enemies would be, and they were told what should and should not be done. Our book, the Holy Bible, tells us plainly in the Book of Malachi that God said, "For I am the Lord, I change not." We must, of necessity, accept God's Bible as the only guidepost for soldiers, sailors, presidents, kings, and leaders if we expect to be on the winning side with God. We must read our Bible. There are too many statesmen, including presidents, who will read all the literary works of other great men but will leave the Bible alone. It has been said more than one time by great men of great learning and in all professions that no man is properly educated until he has at least read the Bible through one time. The Bible tells everything that is coming.

Elisha, Elijah, Isaiah, and the other prophets of old were used to warning and guiding the people. God says the nation that forgets God will be turned into Hell, which means total, final annihilation and destruction. There are kings and kingdoms mentioned in the Bible who, God tells us plainly, drifted so far away from God that they were destroyed and no seed was left.

When I visited the Holy Land I saw the great mountains where Esau and his people stayed. Today none of his lineage can be found. They were in the rocks, hidden securely from all mankind; but Gold told them if they were against Israel, they would be defeated. In the end this was what happened.

Today it is time for our statesmen, presidents, and leaders, whoever they are, to turn to God and read their Bibles—to realize that God still lives and rules in battles. Whether we believe it or not does not change this.

In the 6th chapter of Revelation, beginning with verse 3, we read these words: "And when he had opened the second seal, I heard the second beast say, Come and see. And there went out another horse that was red: and power was given to him that sat thereon to take peace from the earth, and that they should kill one another: and there was given unto him a great sword." At the time these words were written, the fastest thing on the ground was the horse, and the swiftest thing in the air was the eagle. Although God was the author and dictator of the Holy Bible, the prophets of old used terms which their people could understand. When we take the reference of the red horse and its rider and trace it all through the Bible, it paints such a direct picture of Russia that it prompted me as far back as 1945 to warn our statesmen to beware of Russia. I do not claim to be superior in any way or endowed with prophecy, but I know that I am God's man and, being God's man, it is my duty to search the Scriptures that I might warn my nation and my people. God tells me, in Ezekiel 33, that when He sat someone over the house of Israel as the king He expected that king to warn the people and tell of the danger; and if he did not, the destruction which fell on God's people would be because of this king, who sat by and let destruction come.

I know that God has called me to preach the gospel, and the only claim I have is that God has given me grace to warn my government that He is still with the nations who will trust in Him. It is for this reason that I am pleading with government officials to begin reading their Bibles and to pray. They should seek those men who know the Bible and know God to help them make the right decisions. I maintain that every weapon which we have today which other nations do not have is God-given, just the same as our well-being is God-given. It would be worth any king's or president's time to sit down and read II Chronicles in the Old Testatment. Chapter 15 begins, "And the Spirit of God came upon Azariah the son of Oded: and he went out to meet Asa, and said unto him, Hear ye me, Asa, and all Judah and Benjamin; The Lord is with you, while ye be with him; and if ye seek him, he will be found of you; but if ye forsake him, he will forsake you."

God teaches us that He does not force Himself on any king, leader, or individual. Isaiah, another prophet, tells us that the day in which we seek the Lord with all our hearts we will find Him. As a minister of the gospel, it has always been astonishing to me how scientists and great leaders with abounding intelligence can look at the heavens crowned with a million stars and see the great lights which God made to rule the day and night and still make foolish statements about the Book of God. Recently I read in a national magazine where an outstanding religious leader said he did not believe the story of Adam and Eve. This man said he did not believe in a high Heaven or a hot Hell. In other words, while wearing the cloth, he himself said he believed not in life after death. For this reason, it is easy to see why presidents, leaders, congressmen, kings, and rulers are confused and know not whom to turn to when in search of an answer. Here is a man who is recognized nationally, and yet he denies the existence of God.

The only thing which I have ever asked of a president, a vice-president, or a statesman is that he just sit down and reason. If it is logical that water runs downstream, if it is logical that when something is dropped it falls, if to our medical doctors there is life in the blood, then there is reason in the Holy Word. Don't we plant a grain of corn and then wait ninety days to have corn? Don't we by faith plant a dried soup bean in the ground and wait for it to bring forth its harvest? Don't we believe in the law of nature when we set a broken bone to let it knit together? When we have a wound in the flesh, we wait from nine to sixteen days for it to heal. The scar remains but the wound is healed. Why is it that men of such great learning become so foolish as to think they have accomplished great things through their own knowledge? It is true they may be great doctors, lawyers, scientists, or statesmen; but they too come to the end of life's journey. They die and we carry them out for their funeral services. If there is no God, there is no need for a funeral. We might as well take them to the common dump and burn them. Do not let your heart be troubled, for there is a God. The Jewish people call Him Jehovah.

How many of you have heard our boys tell how they prayed in the foxholes? How many recall the plane that managed to return, even though the fuselage was shot to pieces? You might say it was luck. But I ask you, why do we drive along the highway and find a car turned upside down and yet the occupants are scarcely marked? God is everywhere. God rules in all times and He rules in battle.

I pray for our President, for I know in my heart that if a man is close to God he does not need anyone else close by but can look to God in the face of seeming defeat—like George Washington, who led his men with bloody feet across the Delaware, he can lead us to victory, through the grace of God.

Our forefathers came here seeking a place to worship God in spirit and in truth. We can keep our country such a place if our leaders will put their trust in God and if we as individuals strive to make America what God wants it to be. Let us make God first in our hearts, for God said the wicked shall be turned into Hell, and all nations who forget Him.

50. My Own Immediate Family

GOD SAID IN HIS WORD IN THE BOOK OF GENESIS, "AND THE Lord God said, It is not good that man should be alone; I will make him an help meet for him." I believe that when God gave to me Nell Stokes for a wife I received one of the best girls God ever gave to any man. We were married and began immediately to attend church, for my wife was reared to go to church and was a saved Christian girl. We were married in Paducah, Kentucky, but after our marriage we moved to Akron and rented an apartment. In due time, God out of His mercy gave us one son, whom we named Charles Franklin Billington.

When our son was very young we started him in Sunday school, for God had said in the Book of Proverbs: "Train up a child in the way he should go: and when he is old, he will not depart from it." Inasmuch as I had been reared in a Christian home where prayer was had and the Bible read, I began to teach my son what my father had taught me. It was said that a young woman came to Dr. H. B. Riley and asked him how soon she should begin teaching her child about God. He answered her saying, "Three generations before the child is born." The Old Testatment tells us to teach our children, and they in turn will teach theirs, and on into many generations. My parents lived to see all their children saved and in church, living the best they could for God.

I remember well the day I sent my son off to kindergarten and then to first grade. I was at home in bed with a heart attack when he graduated from grade school. The day that he received his high school diploma is still fresh in my mind.

One day he walked in and told his mother and me he had found the girl whom he loved and wanted to marry. He discussed with us his helpmate for life. Charles and Eileen were married, and our son hurried off to war. Uncle Sam was calling young men, almost as soon as they finished high school, to put on uniforms and serve their country. He was no different from the other boys we knew and he had to serve as they did. He spent his days at training bases in Indiana and Texas. He returned home for a few days, and then we were told his training was over and real duty was ahead. His mother, his dear wife, and I followed him to the train depot. His destination was overseas into action. It was during these months when my son told us that God definitely laid it upon his heart to become a servant of God.

One day the war came to an end. We received word from Charles that he would be sailing home from Germany, and he gave us some idea of when to expect him. One night the telephone rang, and the voice I heard was my son's in New York. It is not necessary for me to say to you fathers and mothers how we felt, for many of you have experienced this wonderful time. We met him at the airport, and we were content just to have him home again. However, another night he told us he was thinking seriously of going to Bible school at the Seminary of Fort Worth, Texas. He and Eileen packed their bags and left for school.

We received a letter some time later carrying the news that we would be grandparents. I shall never forget the night we waited for the doctor to come out of the closed doors. He walked with a smile on his face directly to my son and said, "You are the proud father of a fine son." It was not long before this grandson was old enough to attend his Sunday-school class all by himself. He grew rapidly, and when he was five years old, another son was born to Eileen and Charles. Our first grandson was named Charles Franklin Billington, Jr., and the second grandson was named after his two grandfathers: Dallas Robert Billington.

One night when Chuckie was sitting in church with his grandmother, he said he wished to be a Christian and walked by her and down to the altar, where he told one of the church deacons, Mr. Hott, "I want to be a Christian." Tears dimmed his eyes and he stood to his feet. I had preached that night, but his father was out of town. We met his father at the airport, and one might expect a child to question Dad about what he had brought him, but instead Chuckie's first words to his father were, "Dad, I have been saved, Jesus has saved me." He told his dad that while I was preaching he had just felt in his heart he had to go. He said he wanted his dad to baptize him, but if he were to be out of town Grandpa could do it. A week later we saw our first grandson wade into the water, where his own father waited to baptize him. The privilege which had been mine to baptize my son was now my son's privilege with Chuckie.

Our family has stayed in church. Like other families, we have had our times of trial together. Illness has caused great heartache. I myself have been near to death's door. My own dear wife has been very sick in the hospital with private nurses around her twenty-four hours a day. My grandchildren have been very sick in the hospital. But we knew God and we knew how to pray.

I would like to suggest to anyone who may read the lines and pages of this book that when you get married, you will promise God as husband and wife that you will invite the Lord to be present with you always. Begin at the table and offer thanks for the food He has given you and yours. Read the Bible yourself and to your family. Pray beside your bed at night. The family who prays together will stay together. Prayers must be honest and sincere, and when we say "Our Father" we must be children of God and in His will. There are many people who will pray and yet take God's name in vain. Unless they are converted and born again, their prayers cannot be sincere. If parents would begin early to read the

Bible to their children, they would give them a heritage no one else could take from them.

You cannot take children and isolate them from the world. You cannot keep children from sin—sin is all around us. But you have a weapon which can overcome the world and its sin, and that is the Word of God planted deep in the hearts of your children. The seed which you plant will take root and grow as the child grows. He shall be strong through God. God holds you, as parents, responsible for the religious training of your little ones.

I am not alarmed about what children are or are not to be taught in school. I would hate to think that some public school teacher or other outsider had more influence over my son than I do. However, I believe that if a father and mother are true to their children, correcting them when they need it —for a child uncorrected will bring his parents harm and shame with disgrace—teaching them the ways of God and living that teaching before their children, they need not be afraid those children will forget God.

I would like to think in my own heart that we have one of the most happy, peaceful, joyful homes and families on this earth. Nell Stokes Billington is and always has been a precious companion to me. If I were asked to write a hundred pages of what a daughter-in-law should be, I would describe Eileen. There is not a man living who is more proud of his son than I am of mine. Of course, I am proud of my two wonderful grandsons. I think Charles Franklin Jr. is the finest boy of his age in the world, besides yours. Little Dallas, who is not yet five years old, is boss of our family.

We love our family, we live together, we visit together, and we travel together. Our holidays are spent together, just as you spend yours with your loved ones; but I never fail to thank God for having given me Christian parents. What is important to me is that I know my family are doing their best to live for God.

V

How the Bible Can Remake Your Life

I wish it were possible for me to sit down in the home of each one of you who reads this book. I would like to hear your story and point out to you the appropriate Scripture in the Book of God that is yours. The Bible has a message for every circumstance, every sorrow, every fear, and every joy. There has never been a man born, living today, or yet to be born for whom God has failed to put a message in the Book. If you will read and believe, it can change your whole life.

Since it is not possible for me to visit your home, I decided to write this book, hoping that my experiences and some of the stories of people I have met will help many of you to find Christ. After you read this book, you may think of others who might need what is written in it. Perhaps a friend, loved one, or business acquaintance will find all answers here. God has said that one soul is worth the whole world.

In the chapters that follow in this section, come and share with me some of the experiences I have had, making my rounds as a preacher and trying to help those in trouble to get out of it with the aid and guidance of God's Word.

51. Born Again

JOHN 3:1-8: "THERE WAS A MAN OF THE PHARISEES, named Nicodemus, a ruler of the Jews: The same came to Jesus by night, and said unto him, Rabbi, we know that thou art a teacher come from God: for no man can do these miracles that thou doest, except God be with him. Jesus answered and said unto him, Verily, verily, I say unto thee, Except a man be born again, he cannot see the kingdom of God. Nicodemus saith unto him, How can a man be born when he is old? Can he enter the second time into his mother's womb, and be born? Jesus answered, Verily, verily, I say unto thee, Except a man be born of water and of the Spirit, he cannot enter into the kingdom of God. That which is born of the flesh is flesh; and that which is born of the Spirit is spirit. Marvel not that I said unto thee, Ye must be born again. The wind bloweth where it listeth, and thou hearest the sound thereof, but canst not tell whence it cometh, and whither it goeth: so is every one that is born of the Spirit."

I was holding a revival meeting in the Southland. We were having evening services and also morning services, which were Bible study hours. We were taking each chapter, teaching verse by verse. God blessed us with a good attendance, and many professional people in the town were coming regularly. Our Bible study hour, from 10:30 to 11:30 each morning, was drawing more people than the services at night. The people seemed actually hungry for the Word; it pleased and yet surprised me to see the interest grow.

I shall never forget the morning I used the above Scripture. Our story involved a fine businessman, namely, Nicodemus, who was a ruler of the Jews and like the pastor of a church. Nicodemus came to Jesus at night and told Jesus that he believed Him to be a good man. Miracles could not be done by someone not knowing God. Jesus pointedly said to Nicodemus, "You must be born again." Immediately, with all of his learning, Nicodemus questioned Jesus on how this could be. How could a man, when he is old, be born a second time? Jesus told Nicodemus not to marvel but he must be born again. Jesus always referred to the Old Testament Scriptures and said, That which is born of the flesh is flesh, and that which is born of the Spirit is spirit. Unless you be born again, you cannot see the kingdom of God. The Gospel of John tells us that if all that Jesus said were written, the world could not contain the books. Therefore, we must imagine, or read between the lines, what the conversation might have been.

Jesus probably asked Nicodemus to sit down so that they could talk freely. Jesus told Nicodemus that he must be born of the water and of the Spirit. There are people today that will tell you that water birth is to be baptized or wet with water in the several ways in which different faiths baptize. But we can disprove this if we look at the Scriptures. The Scripture says that what is born of the flesh is flesh and what is born of the Spirit is spirit. Water is not mentioned. Jesus did not say that you had to be born twice more, but only once more. Jesus discussed with the ruler how the children of Israel, having sinned and disobeyed God, were punished by the poisonous serpents sent into the wilderness by God. The Scriptures say 23,000 people died from serpents' bites in one day. God told Moses to raise up a serpent, and those looking upon it would be saved if they believed. If they refused to look and believe, they would continue to die of snakebite. As Moses lifted up the serpent in the wilderness, even so must the Son of man be lifted up.

While I was teaching this lesson, a well-dressed gentleman came in and took a seat in the back. After the lesson, the
pastor of the church told me this man followed revivals and
always had a lot of questions. I was no different from the
others, so at the close I found this man before me. This man
was from England and held a doctor's degree in chemistry.
Having introduced himself to me, he asked me to come to his
home that afternoon. I agreed to come, but the pastor told
me I was in for a session, for this man liked to argue the Bible.

After lunch the pastor and I drove out to the man's home.
It was a typical old southern mansion—a beautiful place with
a long front porch. Large swings and comfortable cane chairs
decked the porch. We went up onto the porch and took a
seat in one of the swings. His wife and two children were
seated at the opposite end of the porch. The man drew a
cane-bottom chair over to our swing and sat down beside us.

He apologized for taking up my time but there was only
one thing which he wished to discuss and that was being born
again. He asked me very humbly to explain to him the Scripture which said you must be born again. I read that verse to
him again and called to his mind the two babies who sat opposite us. "If they were to die today," I said, "you, a grown
man, would never see them again. If your wife, a Christian
girl, were to die, you would never see her again. When the
Scripture speaks of flesh, it means where you got your name.
I was born a Billington in the flesh and I remain a Billington."
I asked him to look at the tall Lombardy poplars, as the wind
stirred the branches and leaves. The silver maples were
softly swaying in the breeze, and the shrubbery and the rose-
bushes offered no resistance to the wind. The wind bloweth
where it listeth. You hear the sound but you cannot tell
where the wind comes from or where it goes. So it is with
every person born of God.

I noticed tears in the doctor's eyes, and I asked him why he
had emotions. He did not know why. I explained to him that
the Holy Spirit of God was dealing with him and that if he

would offer no resistance and bow to the wind, like the trees, he could be born again. Would he resist God all the days of his life? He did not know how to pray, but like a child, he dropped to his knees beside his chair and we read together the third chapter of John. I begged him not to resist God. He prayed with me, repeating after me, "Dear Lord, forgive my sins, save me, I pray, in the name of Jesus." I asked him to give me his hand and God his heart and stand to his feet with Christ as his Saviour. I saw him stand and slowly walk across the porch to the swing where his little girl, about four years old, and his son, about seven, were seated. First of all, he took the little girl in his arms and kissed her as though he had been gone from home for many days. He stroked his son's head and kissed him. His wife stood weeping, and embracing her, he said, "I know what it means to be born again. I won't drive you to church any more and then leave, but I'll go with you and be baptized." This was a scene that must have made the angels weep. This one man was worth my trip.

A skeptic might ask me why I do not mention the names of my converts. I have given my word to many professional men, as well as to alcoholics and fallen women, never to reveal their secret. However, if you would like to come to my office I can show you documented stories with all the facts. Jesus always said, "A certain man or a certain woman."

The day when I prepared to return home, this man and his family came to bid me good-by. They extended an invitation to visit them anytime I might be near. He thanked me for not mistaking his curiosity for mockery and for taking time to explain the Scriptures. He shook my hand and said if we should never meet again on this earth, he would meet me on Heaven's shore.

Perhaps one of my stories or experiences will be told for you. My prayer is that as you read your heart will be blessed. Have you been born again?

52. The Unwed Mother

I RECEIVED A TELEPHONE CALL ONE DAY FROM A YOUNG woman who asked if she could see me in my office. We made an appointment for the same day. She was ushered into my private office, and, after the door was closed, she asked me if anyone would hear her story except God and me. I assured her that I would keep her secret. She told me that she did not believe in confessing her sins to any man and she did not believe that I could save her from what had been done; but she had to talk to someone who might perhaps help her straighten out her life.

Her parents had both died when she was very young. They had lived in another state; and she came to Akron after they died. She tried to obtain a job in the factories but failed. There was an ad in the paper for a housekeeper who would have to care for two small children. Answering the ad, she found that, either because of death or divorce, the mother was not there. The man was very kind and seemed to be a very nice gentleman. He had to be gone from home a great deal and wanted her to move into the home, so that the children would not be left alone. She was only nineteen years old, and, inasmuch as this seemed to be her only hope of a job and a livelihood, she accepted the position.

It was not long until she learned to love the children and they her. After a year had passed, the man whose children she loved began to tell her that he cared much for her. Step by step was taken until she found herself expecting a child. This man was well thought of and respected by everyone in the neighborhood, and when she could no longer hide her sin, the blame was laid entirely upon this young girl. Disillusioned, condemned, with hope and fight gone from her, she had boarded a bus. She had only stopped long enough to

tell me her story, for her mind was made up to continue from
my office to a bridge downtown, known as the High Level
Bridge, where more than one have taken their lives by
plunging to the street far below.

I listened intently to her story and looked upon a face that
was beautiful. That face was wet with tears. She had no
home, for this man who had claimed love now demanded
that she get out. She had no loved ones to turn to or friends
to take her in, especially one so sinful.

I asked her if she was a Christian. She said she knew what
it meant to be a Christian and she was not one. She had gone
to revivals in the state where she was born. She had been to
our church, and because it reminded her of home and the
messages she had heard there, she had thought of me and
come to see me. One of the neighbors had told her that I
would listen and be kind to her. They had told her not to
be afraid, because I often said on the radio that I would help
any woman for the sake of my own sisters.

I asked her if she had ever read in the Book of Genesis the
story of the unwed mother. Hagar stayed in the home of
Abraham. Abraham's wife, Sarah, had never had any children, and she thought it would be better that there be
children by the maid Hagar than for her husband not to have
any children at all. Even his own wife suggested—in those
days there was no condemnation of such a thing—that the
young maiden be used to bear children for Abraham. However, when Hagar conceived, Sarah became jealous and ordered her out of the home.

The maiden was driven out. She cried out to God and He
heard her prayer. God told her to return home and He would
take care of her. Her son was born, and they called him
Ishmael. When the boy became thirteen years old, a son was
born to Sarah, and Ishmael was cast out; for Sarah would not
have her son share his inheritance with Ishmael. Hagar went
with her son into the desert land, and this thing grieved
Abraham. Wandering, hungry for food and water, and seeing

her son's life slipping away, Hagar placed him by a shrub. She moved away from him, not wishing to watch him die, and lifted up her voice, weeping. The angel of the Lord called to Hagar and told her not to fear, for God had heard the voice of her son. She was told to get up and hold the child, for God would make of him a great nation.

I advised the young girl in my office to go back to the home where she had been staying and tell the man that she had talked with me. "Tell him," I said, "that this pastor is asking him as a gentleman either to marry you or to make some provision for your care and the child's."

She wept her heart out in my office, and I saw her accept Jesus. She read that Jesus loved her and would forgive her, and she believed in Him. Jesus did not excuse or condone her sin, but He forgave it. Jesus knew more about her than anyone did. He knew her when she was a little child, as pure as the dew of heaven. He knew of the heartaches and insecurity of her childhood.

She returned home, and the man agreed to make provisions for her until the child would be born. A few years passed, and once again this girl came to me. This time her story was different. She had met a Christian man whose wife was dead and who wanted to marry her. She asked me what she should do. I advised her to tell him the whole truth and hold nothing back. "Tell him that Jesus has forgiven you and has saved you. If you love him and he loves you, there is no reason why you cannot be happy."

They were married, and she is a wonderful mother to her child and to his three children. Bear in mind, this story was told because there are none righteous, no, not one! It would have been easy for me to point an accusing finger at her, but the Book of God says there is none without sin, not one. All of us who think we stand should take heed, lest we fall.

One hour was spent with a girl who grew up without father and mother, brother or sister, to tell her how to live. I count it a privilege to be able to help someone. To want to help someone is a Christian attitude. Even since I was a young man twenty-two years old, I have tried not to point an accusing finger as the world will do, even though the accusers themselves might be guilty, but instead, to take God's Word and find the solution.

I do not know why I was twenty-two years old when God saved me. I have often wished I had accepted Jesus earlier in years. I know that God convicted me of my sins, as clearly as He did this young unwed mother, when I was only eleven years old.

I would like to say to all you young girls or women who may need the Lord Jesus that God will never glorify your sin or excuse it; but if you turn to the Book of Isaiah where it says, "though your sins be as scarlet, I will make them as white as snow," you will find forgiveness for your sin, whatever it may be.

God wants to save you; you cannot hide your sin from Him. You may hide it from everyone near and dear to you for a little while, but you won't always. The God of Heaven says to all of us that if we say we have not sinned, we make God a liar and His Word is not in us. He tells us to confess our sins and be forgiven. You don't have to confess your sin to me or anyone on earth. You can be alone in the darkest hour— in a lonely hotel room or in the most isolated little shack— with despair all around you and no human being to hear your cry, and yet God will hear and answer. He saw Hagar out on the Arabian desert with a starving child.

If you are an unwed mother, read carefully the story in Genesis of Hagar, whom God saved and whose son became the leader of a mighty nation.

53. He Died in the Electric Chair

"FOR THE WAGES OF SIN IS DEATH; BUT THE GIFT OF GOD is eternal life through Jesus Christ our Lord." Romans 6:23. I would like every young man to read Proverbs 9:13-18: "A foolish woman is clamorous: she is simple, and knoweth nothing. For she sitteth at the door of her house, on a seat in the high places of the city, to call passengers who go right on their ways: Whoso is simple, let him turn in hither: and as for him that wanteth understanding, she saith to him, Stolen waters are sweet, and bread eaten in secret is pleasant. But he knoweth not that the dead are there; and that her guests are in the depths of hell." The following story is about a young man who died in the electric chair because of a wayward woman.

I was told that this young man kept company with a woman without knowing that she was married. One day he discovered the truth, and because of the great conflict it caused, he decided to take her life. He took a revolver and, meeting her on the street, shot her to death. Needless to say, he was arrested and brought before the courts. He admitted planning her death. His reason was that he loved her and she had played him for a fool. It is of no value to the story to tell you the man's name or in what town or state this happened. I have had many experiences dealing with men in death row or in shameful circumstances who have asked my help and wished me to keep their confidences. I would not betray their trust in me. The reason I am telling this story now is that I pray it will cause someone to stop and think. Perhaps it will save someone from the same fate as this young man's.

The young man's attorney called me and told me the story. The attorney said the young man had listened to our broadcast and wanted to talk with me. I visited him in prison, and he asked me if one who has killed another wished to be forgiven, could he be saved. I assured him that if he were sincere, he could be saved as well as anyone. God does not ever glorify sin or condone it, but God does and will forgive sin. He told me he did not know much about the Bible and had gone to Sunday school very few times in his life. His mother and father had not gone to church, and they did not send him. I told him in the Book of Exodus there is a man by the name of Moses, who killed a man. At the time Moses did this thing, he thought he was right, but too late he knew he was wrong. The young man said he, too, found out he was wrong only too late. We read together about Moses, who repented of his sins. Moses, who had the wealth of the land at his feet, had to flee into the barren country, where God molded and shaped him for the great work he had for him to do.

I opened my Bible to Isaiah 1:18: "Come now, and let us reason together, saith the Lord: though your sins be as scarlet, they shall be white as snow; though they be red like crimson, they shall be as wool." I explained to him that the Scriptures tell us that the harlot, whose sin is a sin of scarlet, can be saved. The sin red like crimson is the sin of a murderer.

The young man had two fine attorneys sitting there with us, and he turned to me and asked, "What must I do to be forgiven?" I showed him the passage in Matthew's Gospel which says, "Whoever will confess before men, him will I also confess before my Father which is in Heaven." Jesus did not say that he had to confess to a man but, rather, tell the Lord of his sins. I asked him to pray with me and ask God to forgive his sins. He did pray and asked God to save him from all the sin of his life. Romans 10:13 says, "For whosoever shall call upon the name of the Lord shall be saved." "Whosoever" meant this young man or any of you reading this. Then, it did not say maybe you will but *you shall be saved.* I John 1:9 says, "If we confess our sins, he is faithful and just to forgive us our sins, and to cleanse us from all unrighteousness."

It was not Dallas Billington or the lawyers sitting there who promised to forgive, but Jesus; for He is the faithful one, promising to forgive and cleanse from all unrighteousness. The young man said that he believed.

He was found guilty of murder in the first degree, which meant the electric chair. I visited him several times before he paid his debt to society. Finally the hour came when he would take that last walk to the death chamber. Before he was taken, he was allowed to eat his last meal with anyone he wished. I had learned to love this boy, and I could not bear to watch him die. A good friend of mine, who was also a minister, went with him to the death house. The hair had been clipped from the boy's head, and the pants leg was split so that the electrode could be placed on the calf of his leg.

The last time I talked with the boy he asked me to preach his funeral. He asked me to take the little Testament which I had given him the day he was saved and give it to his mother. He wanted me to talk with his brother and sister. I looked at the face of this fine-looking man, with strength and youth in his body. He was not dying of cancer or any other affliction, yet the life within him was to be taken because of his sin.

It is an old, old, story, and even King Solomon in his old age followed strange women. I plead with men of all ages to count the cost, for the wages of sin is death.

He died on the appointed day, and his body was brought to Akron, where I had his funeral. I was told by my minister friend that this boy hummed an old hymn, "Safe in the Arms of Jesus," and carried his Testament as his life was snuffed out. The guards told me that he had been a model prisoner and would not even play cards to pass the time away in death row.

This young man told me he had never heard his mother pray or call his name in prayer. "She corrected me, fed me, clothed me, but she never told me about Jesus." I wonder, are you a mother like this one? A child needs spiritual guidance and spiritual food. How can you pray for your boy or girl if you know not Christ? Have you ever knelt beside their bed and prayed that God take care of your girl, your boy? Did you know that the first prayer a child hears should be that of its mother? She should teach him to pray. It is a God-given privilege. Someday, according to nature, children are left by themselves. Have you given them a Christian heritage? Is Christ so much a part of you that they must have Christ too? They must face their own troubles. If they have Jesus, the load won't get too hard to bear. They will always remember Mother's prayers.

This young man paid with his life, but because he trusted Jesus he lives today with a gift of eternal life through Jesus Christ.

54. She Had Five Husbands

"JESUS SAITH UNTO HER, GO, CALL THY HUSBAND, AND come hither. The woman answered and said, I have no husband. Jesus said unto her, Thou hast well said, I have no husband: for thou hast had five husbands; and he whom thou now hast is not thy husband: in that saidst thou truly. The woman saith unto him, Sir, I perceive that thou art a prophet." John 4:16-19.

I want you to believe the Scriptures and know that, regardless of the degrading depths to which a woman can go, the hand of God will be able to reach her and bring her forth from despair. My sole purpose in writing this chapter is that I might help some fallen woman or wayward girl. Countless women have taken their lives, not being able to live with their sins. We read in the papers of girls dying of poison, jumping from bridges and high buildings—anything to blot out the sin which is grieving and eating at their hearts. The saddest thing of all is that death is not the end of their grief if they die without a hope in Christ.

If you will read the 4th chapter of John you will find that a certain woman came to the well to get water to drink; but Jesus told her to go call her husband. He did this to let her know that he knew her life. She said that she had no husband, to which Jesus said she did not have a husband, she had had five. He forced her to look at her guilt and her sin. He also brought her the promise of salvation if she would trust in God.

God has much to say about the midnight sin throughout the Old and New Testaments, perhaps more than is said about any other sin mentioned in the Bible. God mentions the midnight sin many more times than He does murder.

Oftentimes man looks upon murder as being the worst sin of condemnation before God. Here we find that Jesus told this woman to believe in Him and receive living water. He wished to keep her all the days of her life and throughout eternity, with a joy and a peace in her heart which she had never had before. This Scripture was put here for a purpose. Jesus wished to impress upon fallen women that they need not take their lives for their sins; in believing in Christ, they would be freed of the guilt and sin. There will come a time in your life when you will have no one great enough, powerful enough, or rich enough to help you in your trying hour. The sorrow will be too deep or the sin too great for money, prestige, medicine, human knowledge, or human love to help your grieving heart. What has happened will be beyond the reach of man or woman. In that hour, try to say "I will pray" and, containing yourself, believe in Jesus, who has all power to control all things. The storms will never be too much for Jesus.

If your life is wrecked by sin, stop and be humble. Accept your shame, but do not take your life. Taking your life would not solve your trouble. You would meet yourself in an endless eternity, where the soul and memory never die. Jesus told the woman of her sin, but He told her to believe in Him and thereby relieved her of all her burdens. The woman believed and was saved. She left her waterpot at the well and hurried to the city to tell others what Christ had done for her.

Whatever the sin is of anyone, Jesus, out of His mercy, can forgive. A little boy once asked his teacher what mercy meant. The teacher said that mercy is grace, which is something for nothing. God has mercy on us when we are guilty. Grace is God's gift to us, not because of anything we might have done. It is free, just for the taking, to everyone. God gives us grace because of His love for us. It is not the will of God that men and women live and die in sin. God does not wish us to play with sin until it becomes like a rattlesnake, with poison enough to wreck our souls. It is the will of God that the whole human race turn to Him and lean upon Him in time of trouble.

Suppose we have two women. The one has had five husbands, has lived with a man who was not her husband, has gone to the very lowest depths of sin. The other woman has lived a straight, moral life, and the only thing that she has in common with the first woman is that neither woman is saved. One has known sin in all its ugliness and has drunk from the bitter cup, while the other has all the material blessings and has lived comfortably in society. If the wayward woman would turn to God and beg for mercy, ask for forgiveness, and take God's unmerited favor of grace and believe, she would be saved. On the other hand, the morally good woman would say she had done no wrong and had no need of Jesus. She would refuse to pray and trust in Jesus. The good woman would be separated forever from God, because she trusted in her own righteousness as being good enough for her to enter into the City of God. While the wayward woman, on the other hand, declared her guilt and trusted in Jesus, and the Bible says her sins of scarlet were made white as snow.

The song writers have written, "Lord, I'm tired of sin and straying, Lord; now I'm coming home." They have also written, "Just as I am without one plea, but that thy blood was shed for me." Until you reach a time in life when you realize, as did the wayward girl, your own sin and turn to Jesus, you will have no peace. Life is so short, and this world will soon pass you by. Why not prepare for eternity, which has no ending? Come just the way you are, for all of us have sinned and come short of what God expects of us.

It is not your church, your kind deeds, your material possessions, or your own goodness that will save you and give you a home in Heaven. Jesus alone, abiding in your heart, brings salvation.

What has happened to others can happen to us. The things we plan often do not materialize. We have our hopes and dreams shattered and many times in our lives only the grace of God keeps us going. Our children can break our hearts. Their shame is our shame; their joy is our joy. It is easy to share in the joy, but it takes God's grace to share the shame.

When I look into the faces of men and women who have been degraded and tormented into despair with their own sin, I whisper a prayer: Except for the grace of God this could be my son, my brother, my sister. We don't sit way off somewhere where sorrow cannot reach us, for sin is all around us. Despair will come, and it may not be our own doing—we don't live alone in this world. Our lives touch many, many others. We are different from others only through God's grace and His love. We are kept by His wondrous, watchful care; and when storms strike, if Jesus is the captain of our ship, we will find a safe harbor.

There were two men crucified besides Jesus. One of those men made fun of Jesus and turned away, separated forever from the only hope, Jesus Christ. The other was saved because he believed and wanted to be with Jesus when He came into His glory. If you go through life declaring that you have no need of God and die without accepting Christ, then you are lost forever in Hell. This woman who was saved was not in church when she believed. You can find Christ anywhere you seek Him. Of course, I believe it is right to go to church, but I know personally many who were saved at home and in the hospital. If a man gets right with God, you will find him in church, for he likes the fellowship of God's people and the preaching of God's Word. However, if you feel that you would like to be saved, just get out your Bible and read and ask Jesus to forgive you and save your soul. He is faithful and just to forgive your sins and will save you.

My book will tell of many experiences. I pray that in it there will be a pattern for the life of everyone who will read it, that not one unsaved person will read my book and turn away from Christ.

55. Dead on Arrival

ONE FALL NIGHT, ABOUT 2:15, MY TELEPHONE RANG, and a man's voice at the other end said, "This is Sergeant ———— of the State Police of Medina, Ohio. We have two families here. An ambulance has just brought in a boy and a girl who have had a serious wreck between Akron and Medina. Both of the families have told us that they know you. Could you come to the hospital right away?"

As my son, Charles, lived only two blocks away from me, I called him to go with me. We lost no time in getting to the Akron General Hospital. The state policeman met us and said, "In this room is a D.O.A. (dead on arrival)." The family of the dead girl were down the hall in a waiting room. The boy, who had survived the crash, was in another room, and his family were in another waiting room down the same hall.

I ask you, what would you do? You may have asked, Why does God call preachers? It was my lot to tell this family that their daughter was dead. I told them I had some bad news for them, whereupon the mother asked if her daughter's condition was serious. Then, like Jesus, who had to say, "Lazarus is dead," I had to tell this family the truth. I had to tell the mother that she would not see her daughter's body, for her face was so mangled that it could not be prepared for a showing at the funeral service. I took from my coat pocket the only comfort at a time like this and read, "Let not your heart be troubled: ye believe in God, believe also in me." No poems, songs, or writings which I have ever read have the comfort that the Word of God has in a time of trouble. We had prayer, and my son and I ushered them across the street and into their cars. Then we returned to the other family in the hospital, who did not know of the girl's death.

The doctors told me there was a good chance that the boy would recover. His family would not be permitted to see him, however, and I persuaded them to go home. The boy did recover, but we had the funeral services for the girl three days later.

The mother of this girl, like many other mothers, asked me the question, "Why did my daughter have to get killed?"

There is no one living who can answer that question. One thing I am certain of is that Jesus is the resurrection and the life. He that believeth in Christ, though he were dead, yet shall he live. Whosoever shall believe in Christ shall never die. Mary and Martha, sisters of Lazarus, told Jesus their brother would not have died if He had been there, and Jesus had compassion on their sorrow. Lazarus was raised up physically from death; but Jesus is telling us, even though we die physically, yet shall we live in Christ, never lost.

This is the preacher's work. Wherever grief calls—it makes no difference what time or place—it is his duty to God to give comfort through His Word. I used to pray much about writing a book. I wanted to tell people everywhere that, while they are clothed and in their right minds, and not in a hospital with a dead loved one, they should read carefully the words of God, to learn what to do at a time like this. There comes a time in every family when death comes to one of them. What would you as a mother or father do if you were called to a hospital, like these dear people, and told that your daughter was dead upon arrival at the hospital? The Bible tells us so plainly that death is sure. Life is the most uncertain thing that you will ever know.

There is a Scripture in the Bible which says, "Today is the day of salvation, and behold, now is the accepted time." I believe there are persons who will read this book and not understand the word "salvation." Salvation means to be forgiven of your sins. It literally means to believe on the Lord Jesus Christ and be saved from your sins. Millions of books have been published, yet a great number of them are fiction. Although my book is the truth, some of you perhaps will be skeptical. May I give you one fact and implore you to stop and think about it? Someday you are going to need someone other than loved ones, friends, doctors. You will need a special friend, a godly friend who will take God's Word and bring you peace and comfort in your trying hour. This man is a preacher called of God, who can introduce you to a

Christ who has endured every suffering or sorrow which you might be asked to bear. Jesus did not come and stay on earth as an angel, but put on a robe of flesh, that He might understand our sorrows. Jesus was born into a humble family in a humble home. Jesus sometimes had no home to go to, and the Bible tells us that He often went to the mountain alone. Jesus knew what it was to be hungry, tired, and sad. Whatever your burden, Jesus will understand.

There is a way to have joy and peace, even in death. The mother of the dead girl looked at me and said that her girl was a Christian and someday they would meet again. She had a hope in Christ. Could you say this about your daughter or your son? Should you be called tonight under similar circumstances, could you be sure of meeting them again? To every mother I say this: God has placed this precious child in your care. Because of the duties of a mother, it is usually she who remains closer to a child, especially during the maturing years. Her influence, whether it is good or bad, is strongly rooted in her child. A little child does not grow very old before it can tell if its mother is sincere or playing with her scoldings. Will the child be taught from the cradle to love God as mother does? Will the Bible be read in the child's home or just dusted and put out when the preacher comes? A child's first taste of faith must come from its mother. Only God can give you, a mother, grace enough to give up your child. Only God's love can keep you together forever. Believe in Christ and teach your child to believe.

There are many, many people who do not go to church. They will turn off a gospel broadcast and never listen to a preacher. Once in a while God will send a warning. They will not take time to listen to the preacher, but they will read a newspaper or listen to a broadcast. This story was carried about the girl, and Heaven alone knows how many young boys and girls took time to pause and wonder if it would happen to them.

People will not read their Bibles, but perhaps they will

read this book. I pray God will let me use the right Scripture that they will know they are lost without hope, unless they accept Jesus and be saved. My prayer to God is that someone, tired and weary of sin, perhaps feeling the loss of a loved one, will pick up his Bible, wherein is the answer he is seeking. God is too wise to make mistakes. Because He loves us, He permits things to happen, that we may turn from a life of sin and turn instead to peace and hope in God.

No one could die a more horrible death than Jesus. When He bowed His head and said, "It is finished," He meant my salvation and yours was completed in Him. If you are called upon to look into the face of a dead loved one, can you be sure of your salvation and his, that there will be no separation? Only believe as it tells you in the 16th chapter of Acts and be saved today, now.

56. Preacher Turns Detective

ONE DAY MY TELEPHONE RANG, AND ONE OF THE *Beacon Journal* reporters told me there was a man in jail who was charged with murder. The reporter had been listening in on the questioning of the prisoner. Up until now the police had not been able to get him to tell what he did with the gun he had used. He had admitted to killing the man with a gun but would not tell them where the gun was. During the questioning he said that Rev. Billington was his pastor. The reporter had talked with the prisoner and asked him if he would like to see Rev. Billington.

I went to the police station and asked permission to speak with this man. The chief of police granted this to me, but one of the detectives said I would never be able to get anything out of him. The detective said he was one of the most stubborn men he had ever talked with.

The police left me and the attorney alone with the prisoner. We bowed our heads and had prayer. Then I told him the police were not his enemies and would treat him fairly, but that he must cooperate with them. They were just trying to find the murder weapon. They had not told him that the man whom he had shot had died, and when I told him this, the tears came into his eyes. I asked him which of his brothers had the gun. He asked me why did his family have to be brought into this. I assured him that the newspaper had told me that his family would not be mentioned. He told me exactly where to find the gun. I went to the place of business where his brother was, and I asked the brother if he knew me.

I told this brother where the gun could be found, and then I went to the basement. There in the scattered paper and boxes lay the gun. I took a handkerchief from my pocket and dropped it down over the gun. I then wrapped it and put it in my pocket. The detectives had brought me to this place of business, and when they saw me come out the building, one of them kidded me and said, "I suppose you are going to tell us you have the gun." Humbly I say this, but the police had had this man in custody several hours with very little information, while with God's help I had his full confession in five minutes; and now I had the murder weapon in my pocket.

The paper took my picture and "Preacher Turns Detective" was printed under the picture.

This man who had trusted me was divorced from his wife and had several children. He was granted permission by the court to see his children on Sundays and Wednesdays. Once before, he had asked help of the authorities because the present husband of his former wife was threatening him with a knife and a gun. When the man went to see his children, the stepfather would threaten to kill him. One Sunday evening he went to see his children, and the stepfather opened the door and reached for him with a knife in his hand. The stepfather was a big man, while the prisoner was very slight in build. The father ran off the porch and onto the porch of another home, screaming for help. He warned the stepfather that if he came any closer, he would kill him. The man paid no attention to the warning and the gun was fired.

On my broadcast I related the facts of the story. I expressed the hope that this man would not have to spend time in the penitentiary. If we were living in a country where a man could not protect his home, then where was justice? If this man had to serve time because he was trying to see his own children, then something was wrong with our laws.

The judges got together and decided that he would be given a five-year sentence and then put on probation. The Bible says plainly, "I was in prison, and you visited me." No man or woman can condone murder, but the Bible says that the man who does not provide for his own household is worse than an infidel and has denied the faith. If any of you had been threatened as this man had, would it be too farfetched to say you would have protected yourself? Jesus said they who are whole need not a physician but they who are sick. Too many times a preacher will not take the time he should for the man or woman who needs him the most. I have made it a practice, should I be holding a week's revival in a city, to visit the jail; and I have been in many of the state penitentiaries. I have visited two federal prisons.

You ask me, Can this murderer be forgiven? I say to you, Yes. You can be forgiven for murder the same as you can be forgiven for lying. We put so much stress on murder and we should, but we all forget that Jesus said we must be born again or not see the kingdom of God. One would not commit murder, but it is alarming, the number of college girls who, according to statistics, are guilty of committing adultery. The same Bible which tells us that no murderer can enter Heaven also tells us that no adulterer can enter. When you are forgiven of your sins, you are no longer a murderer or an adulterer in the eyes of God. You are cleansed by the blood of Christ.

When we are saved through Jesus the past is blotted out, and we are given a clean white sheet to begin life over again. Each morning we must seek Jesus in prayer for renewed cleansing. Someday, when we have reached the end of the journey and have had our last prayer here on earth, we will come to the crossing. We do not cross on our reputations, deeds, or goodness, but only on the blood of Christ.

The man whom I have written about is now living a happy Christian life, because God pardoned him and gave him peace in his heart and mind.

57. Marriage Counselor

IT WOULD BE SHOCKING TO THE PUBLIC TO SIT IN A pastor's study and listen to the husband-and-wife problems that are brought to him. It is amazing how very small their reasons can be for not getting along. Their excuses for getting a divorce are many times not even logical.

I remember one story in particular. The husband came to our altar and was saved. He talked with me after the service and asked me to talk with his ex-wife. He was at least sixty years old or more, and he and his wife had been separated for more than twenty-five years. Neither of them had ever married again. They had married when they were very young, and through the years that followed five children had been born to them.

I made arrangements through their oldest son to talk with the man's wife. The man and his wife each told me, when the other was not present to hear, that they still loved each other. The wife told me she had not married again because she had always loved him.

I would have a meeting with the husband and we would read the Bible together to see what God had to say about marriage and a home. When I met with the wife we would do the same. I proved to be just a go-between for these two people. Finally, God convinced them the love they had in their hearts was real, and we arranged a wedding day for them.

Their own children gathered around that day to see their mother and dad remarried. They had grandchildren, who attended their wedding. I reasoned with them and quoted these words: "For this cause shall a man leave father and mother, and shall cleave to his wife: and they twain shall be one flesh. Wherefore they are no more twain, but one flesh. What therefore God hath joined together, let not man put asunder." It was a great and happy privilege to remarry this couple.

In my ministry I have married at least fifty-three couples who had been married to each other and then divorced. I believe in court counseling; however, I believe a minister who is truly a man of God can take the Word of God and find a way to hold that marriage together, if there is any love there at all. Brothers and sisters coming from the same family will fight and then make up, but somehow when two people get married, coming from different homes, without the aid of an impartial friend, they are blinded to the solution. A man of God will search for a practical solution but will give them spiritual blessing and spiritual reasoning, which makes the union stronger. Not only is the fleshly companionship satisfied but a deeper, mutual respect is created by trust given through Christ.

A couple came into my office and said they had a little baby boy just eleven months old. Their quarrels were mostly over their parents, rather than over anything they did not like about each other. They had decided that if their parents did not like the marriage, then they would just get a divorce.

I asked them several questions, and learned they had been sweethearts ever since grade school. I asked them if they had quarrels when they were going steady. They assured me they did but it was soon over. Before they knew it, they were telling me how much they had thought of each other over the years. They had been very happy, and their life had seemed complete when the baby came. I asked them, as they looked back over their lives and remembered, how was it possible that they who had stuck to each other through ups and downs and who now had what they had dreamed about, were willing to call it quits because of their parents.

The wife told me she was not a Christian. The husband said he had never made any pretense of being a Christian. I let them read my Bible together where it said men ought to love their wives and wives, their husbands. They read in my Bible that God loved the whole world enough to give His only Son to die for them. "Now you have a little son," I said. "Because of an argument, you are willing to give up each other, and the home that he deserves will be taken from him."

I saw that fine couple kneel side by side in my office, weeping like two children who had been whipped and had seen the error of their ways. They accepted Jesus and rose to their feet and embraced each other. Now they are in church every Sunday, and the little boy is perhaps seven years old. I know that every time they see me they think of that day, and I shall cherish that memory all the days of my life. Just a little time and patience mixed with the clear word of God can salvage any home if the two involved are sincerely in love.

Over in one of Akron's hospitals, I got a call from a young intern to come to the hospital. He said they had a baby there who, from all indications, would die perhaps that night. The father and mother had been divorced for some time. The father had been living in California, and when he heard the baby girl, about four years old, was seriously ill, he left for Akron. The mother had refused to go home and had already been at the hospital forty straight hours without any rest. So far as the intern knew, the mother had never closed her eyes but had been sitting, silently grieving for her baby, never even leaving the room where the child was lying.

The father was expected to arrive at 2:00 A.M., and the doctor had called me to give me the picture, hoping that something might be said or done for the couple. When I arrived at the hospital I found his parents and her parents there with the young mother. The father arrived close to 3:00 A.M. This man was not a Christian, and when they were divorced, he had left Akron and had been paying alimony toward the support of the wife and little child. The mother, however, was a wonderful Christian girl, and she had prayed day and night that the Lord's will be done to bring back her husband and the father of her baby girl. She had told God she was willing to pay whatever price she had to pay. Little did she realize the price might be her own baby girl. Her husband had been gone almost a year, and this had been her constant prayer. The doctor had called me on the case because this mother had said she wanted to talk with me.

When the young father came into the room where the sick child lay, he walked over to his mother and kissed her on the forehead and patted his father on the shoulder. He was very courteous to her mother and dad, and then he looked at his wife, who was standing at the foot of the bed gazing into the face of the dying baby girl.

He walked up behind her and put his arms around her shoulders and said, "Sweetheart." She did not answer but, as if someone dead, slipped from his arms to the floor in an exhausted faint. She was put to bed and given a sedative so that she would rest until sometime the next morning.

The miracle of the story was that little baby started to rally about daybreak, proving once again that doctors can go so far and then God takes over; for that little child got well.

After this couple took the baby home, I went to visit them one night, and we sat down and talked about them. I asked the young man why he did not still love Nancy, his wife. He told me he did still love Nancy, and no one would ever know what anguish he had suffered because he had gone away and left her. "I was just too proud and contrary to call her and tell her that I still loved her," he said.

It was not hard for me to prove to them that God plants little ones in homes to keep that tie and the love green, rich with promise and hope. God never planned that anyone married because of true love would ever be separated from one another except in death. Even then, if they were saved, they would be united in a Saviour's love in eternity. I had the joy to help them obtain a marriage license. They stood before me with the grandparents, and I asked them to promise to hold one another and care for one another all the days of their lives, through sickness and health, until death should part them. Heaven broke out in their faces. It is times like this that make the sorrows of a minister's life seem unimportant. My heart was full and I was so very thankful to have been used in this happy moment.

It is a very happy experience to see a home reunited. This home had been reunited because Christ intervened. Perhaps your home is broken. Perhaps there are little children in that home. They love Mommy and Daddy and it is hard for them to understand. Jesus said what He has joined together no man shall put asunder. Make your home happy through Christ.

58. "Man Has No Soul"

THAT STATEMENT WAS MADE TO ME BY A VERY PROMI-
nent doctor in the state of Tennessee a few years ago at a
revival meeting. After he had heard me preach that evening,
he came to me and said, "I have been to surgical and medical
schools and have been a practicing surgeon for more than
twenty years, but I have never found a soul in the human
body." He asked me to come to his office the next day around
eleven, when his office calls would be over, and talk with him.

He assured me the next day that he was not a Christian,
for he could not be if he did not believe in a soul. I read to
him from Genesis 2:7: "And the Lord God formed man of
the dust of the ground, and breathed into his nostrils the
breath of life; and man became a living soul." This man was
thoroughly convinced that man had no soul, but he plainly
told me that if he had not been interested he would not
have asked me to come to his office. He said that if there was
a Heaven, then he wished to go there; and if there was a Hell,
then he surely wanted to miss it. If there was a living place
for us when we die, he wanted to live with God. That was
his reason for asking me to come.

I had to reason logically with this man, and I first said to
him that he had gone to school to learn the human body and
its physical life. I told him that I had planned and even
bragged about becoming the youngest governor of Kentucky before I was saved. I borrowed, begged, and bought
every book I could lay my hand on about political science or
government. When I became saved, I began to study the
Bible, that I might understand the spiritual science and
government. If the doctor was to understand the spiritual
body of man, he too would have to read the Book that con-
tains the truths.

The Bible says, "In the beginning God"; therefore, God was the beginning of all things. I asked him if he believed that someone greater than man created the mountains. He believed God created the whole universe. He believed that someone very special, greater than any man, created the seas and the oceans. I asked him if he followed the theory of evolution, being a medical doctor. He said that he had truly tried to believe in it, but he had cast it aside. The doctor said, "I am just a man groping in the darkness." I asked him had he ever felt while he was in church or anywhere that if he were alone he could just sit down and cry. He said he had felt that way in the service last night. I asked him if monkeys ever cry. He said, "I think not." If you should read a message of judgment to any animal, would they have any fear concerning their future or the hereafter? The doctor again said, "No." I asked him if he had ever gone out at night and looked into the heavens at God's star-lit canopy. Did he not think it was a wonderful, awesome sight? Had he seen the trees in the woods and the flowers of the field? He had observed all these things and was convinced of a High Power. Then I asked him, if I brought him a dead mouse, could he restore it to health; and of course, he said, "No." Life comes from somewhere. I turned to the Book of Leviticus, and we found there where the life of all flesh is in the blood. He believed in the blood transfusions and that there was life in the blood.

The doctor read from the Bible for himself where it reads, "But whosoever shall lose his life for my sake and the gospel's, the same shall save it. For what shall it profit a man, if he shall gain the whole world, and lose his own soul? Or what shall a man give in exchange for his soul?"

This is God's Word. In the Bible, in the Book of Genesis, God tells us who we are, where we came from. He gives us an account of two different people at death. One goes to a place where they cry for water and there is none. They beg that someone be sent back to earth to warn their loved ones, but they who remain must listen to the preachers on earth. If they will not believe one, they would not believe someone else.

"In your own mind," I asked the doctor, "are you convinced that somewhere there is a God who is real?" He answered, "Yes." He had watched people die praying and in peace, while, on the other hand, there had been those who died screaming and cursing. He had searched, as he operated, for the human soul; but in the dissecting room he had never found a soul.

"Then shall the dust return to the earth as it was: and the spirit shall return unto God who gave it." Ecclesiastes 12:7. In Genesis the doctor had read where God had made man a living soul; in death the soul had been changed to spirit. I explained that he was a man born with flesh, being tangible, having ability to walk and talk; but should he die that night, he would no longer talk or walk, and the feeling of the flesh would be gone. Now, when our body molders back to dust, it has the same sixteen elements which it had in life, and this dust can be found in the garden. The doctor believed me. I asked him, "When the body is dead and you can freeze it or cremate it and it cannot feel, where is that which gave us our sense of touch, smell, emotion, and conscience? It is gone, but where?" The soul, the spirit, that part of you that made you walk and talk and feel is alive. Where the soul is, is up to the individual, for God said the soul that sins shall die. God also said those who call upon the name of the Lord shall be saved. Because Jesus is the resurrection and the life, those who believe in Him shall never die but shall be eternal living souls through Jesus. The body is placed into the grave, but the soul goes back to God. Christ gave His soul, not His body, as an offering for sin. His body was pronounced dead and put into the tomb, but He came out on the other side.

Being a doctor, a logical, methodical man, he read the Scriptures and searched carefully for the truth. He needed to know Christ just as much as the farmer, laborer, or the heathen of the jungles. He had all the learning of this day, yet his conscience would not be satisfied. He had never had anyone to sit down and explain Christ to him, and he was like a child, eager for bread. Your doctor is no different from you. Perhaps you should be the one who tells him of Jesus. He may be a stranger to God and just waiting for you to satisfy his heart.

Talk to your doctor. We had a secretary working for our church, who took sick of cancer, but before she died she talked with two doctors about their souls. One of the doctors told me she was the finest person he had ever known and the only patient who had ever asked him about his soul. I remember the day she gathered her books and walked into my office and said, "Well, preacher, I have come to say good-by. I am sure that I shall never come back to my desk"; for she had some nursing training and was well aware of what was coming. She said, "I am on my way home." She did not mean her earthly residence but a house not built by hands. She told me how much she had enjoyed her work at the church and that she had learned more about her Saviour by working here. She walked away from church that day with the pain noticeable in her face but in her eyes a peace that only God can give. Both of the doctors whom she so earnestly pleaded with about their souls were saved after her death.

It makes no difference what profession a person has or what job he or she labors at from day to day, each one needs to have Jesus in their hearts. You may be the only opportunity that person will have to meet Jesus.

59. A Criminal Lawyer Saved

WHILE I WAS HOLDING A REVIVAL IN OKLAHOMA CITY, the minister at the church where I was had to see a lawyer on some business. Of course, the minister chose the lawyer who he thought was the best in town. This man had law offices in several counties with younger lawyers under him. We went to the office of this criminal lawyer, and he jokingly said that preachers needed smart lawyers to keep them out of jail. Before I left the office with my preacher friend, I turned to this very learned lawyer and said, "Tonight I am going to preach on 'When Court Convenes in Jerusalem.' I dare you to come and hear my message."

When the service began that night, I was told that the lawyer was there with one of the town's common pleas judges. I set up a table like one sees in a trial court and placed a chair at the front to represent some attorney and a chair at the back to represent the one accused. I read the following Scripture (Luke 23:1,2): "And the whole multitude of them arose, and led him unto Pilate. And they began to accuse him, saying, We have found this fellow perverting the nation, and forbidding to give tribute to Caesar, saying that he himself is Christ a King." Carefully I went through the Scriptures and proved that Jesus was taken in the Garden of Gethsemane and before daylight, which was all contrary to the customs and laws of the Jewish people. The Jewish people, not in power, could not take any civil action. Nevertheless, Christ was arrested by a religious mob and brought before Caiaphas, where false witnesses were brought in. Since they could not condemn Him, the whole mob led him in to Pilate.

History tells us that they brought Jesus to Pilate before court hours. Pilate examined Jesus and asked if he was a Galilean. When he found out Jesus was in Herod's jurisdiction, he sent Jesus to Herod. Herod was in the city of Jerusalem for the Passover days, so Herod tried Jesus. Jesus was mocked, and they put upon Him a torn, tattered robe and sent Him back to Pilate. Pilate then asked questions of Christ concerning who He was and all about His life. Jesus told him that His work had been no secret. Pilate said to the people that they should chastise Christ and then let Him go. The people would not have this, but cried out to crucify Jesus and let Barabbas go free.

After four unfair trials Jesus was sentenced to die on the cross. I wanted to show the congregation, as well as the men of law, how unfair this was, and yet Jesus willingly died for everyone. We had people forward that night accepting Christ, but the lawyer and the judge did not raise their hands, even for prayer.

However, a few weeks later this attorney wrote to me, telling me of his salvation and asking for the outline of the four unfair trials. He said that he would use it throughout all of the country to tell the story of the Lord Jesus Christ. This attorney used these trials in his cases and had great influence wherever he spoke as a lawyer, perhaps more influence than any minister might have in his lifetime. Speaking to the different legal bodies (which was quite often his job) as a man who declared his faith in God, he could present to them our civil law and then present the trials of Jesus.

The lawyer kept the title "When Court Convenes in Jerusalem" and used it far and wide to tell of a Saviour's love. Our Bible tells us that all Christian men, regardless of their race, creed, or profession, should use their lives and testimonies to tell of Christ and His love.

God may send a minister into a certain town for just one man's soul. When Jesus was sentenced to die, He was fulfilling all the prophecies of the Old Testament. Even in

Genesis 3:15 it states that Satan would bruise the heel of Christ and Christ would bruise his head. This meant that Jesus would not stay in the tomb: one day Satan would be bound forever. The Bible says that not one jot or tittle of the law, meaning the law of the prophets, should fail to come true in the birth, life, trials, death, burial, and resurrection of the Lord Jesus.

That night in my message I pointed out in the Word of God and proved from past history what Jesus did while on earth, how it was said of Christ that when He should come, He would raise the dead, set the captive free. This message was taken and used in his life by a criminal lawyer who was past sixty years old when he gave his life to Christ.

Whether you are a criminal lawyer or whatever your work might be, God wants you, and He wants you to be a witness for Him. Jesus only asks us to live for Him; but He died for us.

Even though a minister can travel the world over, witnessing for Christ, even if you spend all of your days living for Christ, you and I can never repay the debt we owe to Him. Every time you hear the story of Christ or hear an old hymn like "The Old Rugged Cross," reminding you once again that Jesus is your Saviour, and you reject Him, Christ is on trial again in your heart. Anywhere, whether it is on the radio, on television, or in this book, that Christ is offered and lifted up and you turn away, Christ has once again been crucified by you. If you will not accept Him, then you are just as guilty as Judas, who sold Him, or the angry mob; as guilty as Pilate, who tried Him; as guilty as Pilate's wife, who said, "Have nothing to do with this man."

You cannot be neutral in the story of Christ. You make a stand either for Christ or against Him. Jesus asked the question Himself when He asked, "Whom do men say that I am?" Every individual must answer for himself. No father can be saved for his son, nor can a mother be saved for her daughter. A daughter or son cannot take the place of a parent. You must make your own decision. Salvation is a personal thing between you and Christ. What you do with Jesus is absolutely up to you. You can never say that you might have been saved had you been told, for that is not true.

"How can I be saved?" you might ask yourself. Read John 1:11,12 where it says of Jesus: "He came unto his own, and his own received him not. But as many as received him, to them gave he power to become the sons of God, even to them that believe on his name." Then, very clearly, Romans 10:10 says that man believes with the heart unto righteousness, and then with his mouth confession is made unto salvation.

You can be in a hospital alone and sick unto death, without a preacher, priest, or rabbi, and without oil or water poured on your head, without the Ten Commandments, but if you are rational, if you are sincere, you can ask forgiveness and, believing, you can be saved. No door can ever be closed that Jesus cannot enter if someone calls for Him. You alone can close your heart's door and Christ will not enter, for Christ demands that your will accept Him. Jesus stands at the door and knocks. But you must open the door. I have heard people say that they have sought the Lord for years but they just could not find Him. This is not true, for Jesus is seeking us. We keep Him out because of our own stubborn unbelief.

When Jesus knocks at your heart again, won't you let Him come in?

60. My Largest Love Offering

I WAS IN A MINING REGION OF A SOUTHERN STATE, HOLDing a revival meeting. On the first night of the revival I saw a boy, perhaps eleven or twelve years old, sitting on the front seat, dressed in overalls and a blue shirt. He badly needed a haircut, and he wore a faded cap which he brought in under his arm each night. As he came through the door each night, immediately he would remove his cap. He always came by himself and sat on the front seat.

As I read the Scripture and preached, his eyes would follow me; and the very first night he raised his hand denoting that he wanted to be a Christian. This was a rather large country church, and several of the townspeople were driving down every night for the service. There was a large bell on top of the church, and every night when the bell was rung to begin the services, this young boy would come in and take his seat.

We planned a prayer meeting for the men and women. The men would meet out under the trees, while the ladies would remain inside and have their prayer for the services that night. My wife took charge of the ladies' group while I met with the men and boys outside. My son, Charles, was about eleven years old then, and he was with us on this revival meeting, since school was out for the summer. There were about fifteen or twenty men and a few teen-age boys who met with me that night. One boy fifteen years old stood to his feet and asked prayer for the boy who had been sitting on the front seat. These boys were cousins. Their mothers were sisters. The little boy's mother had been in a hospital for about six years, and the father, who drank a lot, had arranged for the boy to be sent to an inexpensive boarding school. When the aunt heard of the revival, she had gained permission from the school to let her nephew stay with them so that he might come to the services. The fifteen-year-old cousin said that on the way home that night the younger boy said he did not believe the preacher liked him. When the older boy asked why he thought this, the boy said for two nights he had raised his hand for prayer. Others had raised their hands and the preacher went and talked with them, but he never came to him.

I asked his cousin how old he was and was surprised to learn that he was going on fourteen but was very small for his age. I thanked him for the information and we went on with our prayer meeting. At the close of the Wednesday night message I told them that it made no difference who they were, how rich or how poor, Jesus loved them. It made no difference who their families were or what station in life they might have or how far away from God they might have drifted, Jesus loved them. As an individual it was necessary that each one trust Him for himself. I read in Luke's Gospel where Jesus, at the age of twelve, said that He must be about his father's business. Carefully I tried to explain, especially for the young boy, that at the age of twelve one knows how to love and trust Jesus. There were two other besides this young boy who lifted their hands, so saying that they wished to be saved.

I walked to the front seat where the boy was standing and asked him how old he was. He told me when he would be fourteen years old. I knew of his sick mother and his almost drunkard father. I did not question him about his parents but went with him to the altar, where we knelt and prayed. I showed him the Scripture where God loved us so much that He gave his only son to die for us. I asked him if he would trust Jesus as his Saviour. He prayed, asking forgiveness of his sins and salvation of his soul. He was supposed to return to the boarding school the next day, but now he wished to stay for the rest of the week and be baptized. This was granted by the school.

On Saturday night the minister told his people that it was always customary to take a love offering for every preacher who held a revival for them. He had mentioned it also on Wednesday, so that they could perhaps put away a little something for the preacher's love offering, which would be taken on Saturday.

The offering plate was passed, and the people gave their love offering. After the service, I noticed the young boy waiting until everyone had gone except a few, and when I was standing there for the moment by myself, he came directly toward me and reached out his hand to give me something. I opened my hand and he dropped one quarter into the palm of my hand. He looked straight into my eyes and said, "I love you. This quarter my aunt gave me for spending money, but I just kept it so I could give it to you for my love offering. You use my quarter and preach to other boys who need you as badly as I did." I did not want to take his quarter and asked him if I could take it in my heart and let him keep it. He would not have it that way.

On Sunday he was baptized out in the creek close by the church. After the services my family and I were to drive about fifteen miles to town, stay there all night, and then leave Monday for home. The boarding school was on the way into town, and the aunt asked us if we minded dropping the boy off at the school. We started to get into the car, and the boy who was almost fourteen but not nearly as big as my eleven-year-old son, said to Charles, "May I ride up front with your dad? You can ride with him all the time and this will be my only chance." Charles agreed and said he would sit in the back with Mom.

He sat in the front seat with me and talked freely as we rode along. I remember it was a beautiful summer night and the moon was shining brightly. When we got to the school, we had to walk across a creek on a plank walk. I left my wife and Charles in the car and walked across to the school with the boy. I had noticed that this boy admired a Precious Promise Testament that I had used while preaching there, so I took the Testament and slipped a dollar bill between the pages of the book. The light was on, and as we walked up on the porch a gray-haired lady met us. I gave him the Testament, and quickly he kissed me as if he were my own son and was gone.

Three years later I went through this same town, and I stopped to inquire about the boy. They told me he was in high school and gave me directions for getting there. I went in and asked to see the boy. They told me he was playing ball. I told them just to let me go to him and see if he remembered me.

When we got near enough to be seen, a boy threw down his glove and made for me. I knew it was this same boy, and he hugged me and, unashamed, told me he still loved me and that someday he was going to be a preacher just like me.

His vision and dream came true, for this young man lives today in the Southland, a prominent and successful minister. It should not be hard for you to understand why I have always thought of this boy's twenty-five cents as being my greatest love offering. It was from a boy who loved me, gave his heart to Jesus, and today is a great soul winner for Christ.

61. The Alcoholic Ward

ONE DAY I RECEIVED A CALL FROM A PERSON WHO ASKED me if I believed that God could save men and women from a drunkard's grave. I told him that I believed and knew for a fact that God could do just that. I told him I could believe it from past experiences in homes where I had been called. These homes were completely broken and ruined because of drink. The drinkers' jobs were gone, scarcely anything remaining, not even their self-respect. By the grace of God I had been able to convince them of their need of God, of putting their faith in God. I watched the beer, whiskey, and wine go from their homes, because Jesus had come to live in their hearts.

The person at the telephone gave me the name of a man and his address, which was an alcoholic ward. He asked me to go and see him. I found a man past fifty years old, who was an educated, a college man. His education was far above the average. At one time he had held a very good job in the city and was known to be a smart, shrewd business-man.

I told this man that I had a friend who I knew could help him. When I told him this friend was Jesus, a doubtful smile came over his face and he said, "I don't know if anyone can help me." We read the Bible together. Proverbs 23:29-35: "Who hath woe? who hath sorrow? who hath contentions? who hath babbling? who hath wounds without cause? who hath redness of eyes? They that tarry long at the wine; they that go to seek mixed wine. Look not thou upon the wine when it is red, when it giveth his colour in the cup, when it moveth itself aright. At the last it biteth like a serpent, and stingeth like an adder. Thine eyes shall behold strange women, and thine heart shall utter perverse things. Yea, thou shalt be as he that lieth down in the midst of the sea, or as he that lieth upon the top of a mast. They have stricken me, shalt thou say, and I was not sick; they have beaten me, and I felt it not: when shall I awake? I will seek it yet again."

God begins by asking who has sorrow, woe, and so on. Then God answers by telling us what happens to those who drink too much. Those who have redness of eyes and seek the mixed wine have trouble, contention. I told this man that in my church there were many men who were living testimonies of what God can do with those whose lives have been wrecked by drink. These men were drunkards, and that is what this man had become. He had only one enemy, but that enemy was keeping him from holding any job that he wanted and was keeping him from being a decent, moral individual. Strong intoxicating drink was his bitter enemy, and yet he was caught as if in a vise with no hope in the world of getting free.

I showed him God's plan for salvation, where the blood of Christ would cleanse him from all sin. I showed him that the Bible said he could be cured from drinking and go back to his business life a straight, sane, sober man, happy in a Saviour's love.

He prayed for his salvation, that Christ would save and cleanse him from a drunkard's life. The following morning he came down to the office of the home where he was staying and asked for his car keys. This was several years ago, and to my knowledge he never returned to the alcoholic ward again. Just a few Sundays after I had talked with him, he came forward and publicly confessed Christ. This is like many stories which I have witnessed myself.

Most of America will agree with me when I say that the greatest crime is selling this drink everywhere we look. There is hardly a restaurant or public place where it is not displayed. Drink is the biggest curse on America today. It damns men's souls and makes them do the most sinful acts, which if they were sober they would never dream of doing. That our government makes it legal does not make it any less sinful in the eyes of God. Its legality will not keep God from judging it and our nation.

In at least 75 per cent of the homes which I am asked to visit and of those persons whom I counsel, where the home is being destroyed and the children are going without, the origin of the trouble is in beer, whiskey, or wine. In years past, men were the primary victims, but today women as well as men are becoming hopeless drunkards.

When our country was very young there were saloons for the men. The women who worked in them were seldom respectable, and certainly no decent woman who cared for her good name would even be caught near a saloon. However, now there are as many women as men who crowd the beer joints. It seems to me, being guided by my own experiences, that the woman who degrades herself with drink will continue on into the deepest sins one can imagine. Perhaps we are remembering all the good women whom we have known, which makes it seem that a degraded woman is worse than a degraded man. The Bible likens a good woman to a jewel or precious stone. The pedestal that womanhood has had has become very shaky and worn. The great respect she once had has been trampled and made dirty. I think drink has done that to her. Of course, to God it makes no difference whether you are a man or a woman, for sin is sin and God is no respecter of persons. It seems to man, however, that a drunken woman is more sinful, and it is especially disgusting that children have to look upon their own mothers in this sinful condition. There is a hope for you who are held in the clutches of drink. That hope is in Christ. You can be saved and turn aside from such a life to the glory of God, but you must trust in God, not in yourself. There are persons who will say that they will taper off and just take one drink a day for a while. God never does a job halfway. When you come to the Lord, the job is complete. When you trust God, sin is gone. The past is gone. God not only forgives a drunkard, but He cleanses him or her. It is true that if you willfully wanted to go back to drink and wanted your appetite satisfied, you could return to drink. Even Paul said that if he were of a mind to return to a life of sin, he could; but he stated, inspired of God, that he had grace (God's given power) to conquer those things which he dreaded most.

Paul did not mention his sins by name, but he was like you

or me in that he had many sins. Perhaps like us he had a chief sin from which he was saved and which had remained uppermost in his mind. You know which sin is your greatest, and believing in Christ has set you free from this sin. The Scripture has told us that the man who has woe is the man who is drinking and stays too long at the wine, until he goes out and beholds strange women. Of course, that is what destroys the home. Oftentimes you will hear a man say he is not jealous of his wife. If there is no jealousy, there can be no love. We can be foolish in our jealousy without a cause or reason, which in itself will destroy a home. A little child will be jealous of a new baby in the home, because it is taking some of the love and attention which used to be solely his. If you love your wife, you will be jealous to see her with another man, and the same goes for a wife who sees her husband with another woman. If you can say that you do not care, then I would say you do not love him or her. The Bible says that God is a jealous God because He loves you and me. He loves all the human race, for He gave His own Son to die to prove this to all the world. God planned a way of redemption through the death of His son, to keep us from the drunkard's grave and make us whole.

Read the Bible carefully, then you will turn and trust in Jesus, who alone can save you. I have known persons who have spent at least six different intervals in alcoholic wards and could not conquer drink. All they needed was one sincere trip to Calvary, where God's grace is sufficient.

It always breaks a pastor's heart when he is called to a home where the person died while drunk, to arrange for a funeral service. I remember the funeral of a man who had been so drunk that he had fallen down the stairs. His friends and family believed strongly that he had been shoved down the stairs, but no proof was ever given. However, he was dead at the bottom of the steps, full of strong drink.

At such a time a pastor can only mention the day this man was born and the day he died. You cannot tell of his life, for it does no good to embarrass his wife and children. I am one preacher who does not preach all people into Heaven. I cannot preach the same funeral for sinners, drunkards, as I can for consecrated Christians and saintly sweet mothers and fathers. I preach to those who remain that death comes in a day when we are unaware, and those who are warned and still harden their necks will be cut off, and that without remedy. I preach to the living, making just as little reference as possible to the one lying dead before me. I try with all my heart to warn those sitting there that while there is time left they should prepare for eternity.

This is a hard job for a minister, but we must take the sorrow and the tears to make us appreciate the happiness that is often ours. It is a joy to see a drunken father trust in Jesus and be saved. We watch him as he grows outside as well as inside. The old car is traded in for a better one. His clothes take on a new look. The haggard, bleary-eyed expression is gone from his eyes. He has been released from the prison of drink. He can walk past a place of sin and turn, by God's grace, the other way and walk hand in hand with Jesus into eternity.

62. Going West

I REMEMBER ONE AUGUST WHEN MRS. BILLINGTON, MY son, Charles, and I were going west for some meetings. While we were in Illinois we stopped at a big drive-in service station. You could get ice-water there, and they had room for several cars, with big dividing ramps to stand on while your car was being serviced. As we stood there we could see the cars coming by which were headed east. When we pulled into the station and up to one of the pumps, we had been told that it was 96 degrees. Everyone's face was noticeably covered with perspiration. Our shirts were limp and wrinkled from the heat.

A car pulled in opposite us. The car was headed east, and we noticed that it was driven by a chauffeur, the man and his wife sitting in the back seat. It was a beautiful car and shining like a mirror, so it was easy to notice. The elderly man got out of the car and stepped upon the ramp, where the cold water and machines with candy, nuts, and cigarettes were handy. He began to curse and take God's name in vain while speaking about the weather. He was not angry, but he was so used to swearing that swear words were a part of his vocabulary. He seemed to be a very happy-go-lucky kind of fellow who could take life in his stride. You could tell when he spoke that he was a well-educated man, having no conscience, however, about taking God's name in vain in front of everyone.

There must have been at least six cars lined up at our station, and there was another station directly across from us. All of these people could easily hear his remarks. It made no difference to him that there were women and young children hearing what he said. I looked at him and thought to myself that God had said for me as a preacher to warn every creature, even this stranger. Finally, in an almost fearful manner, I put my hand on his shoulder and said, "Dad, if you will permit me to call you Dad, do you realize that when you curse and take God's name in vain you are cursing the best friend you will ever have?" I talked to him quietly, and he looked at me and asked me who I was. I told him I was a Baptist preacher who was going west to hold some revival meetings. I told him that I had listened to him curse, and feeling that perhaps our paths would never cross again, I felt that I must talk with him. I told him that God had certainly been good to him, for he was driving an elegant car with a chauffeur, and he looked like a man who had just about all of this life's goods that God could bestow upon him. I asked him if when he cursed had he ever realized how much the One he cursed loved him.

He looked at me and, as if remembering years gone by, told me he had not been reared to talk that way. I asked him would I offend him if I were to show him the Word of God. He listened as I read from the Testament which I carried in my pocket. There in the presence of others, not trying to attract attention, we quietly read together where God said if we believe in Him, He will forgive us our sins and save us.

He said he would pray with me. We bowed our heads there, with the sounds of the cars going and coming on the big highway. He raised his head and thanked me for talking to him. The tears came into his eyes, and he reached for his wife's hand and told her he was glad they had made the trip. Even the chauffeur thanked me for talking to his boss.

I travel life's journey only one time; in my feeble way I hope to reach God's heavenly city and say to Him that I did my best to tell everyone I met of a Saviour's love. I did not pass up the criminal lawyer, businessman, industrial head, or any man, woman, or child who needed Christ.

Sometimes it takes strong language, and we have to choose Scriptures which are a direct judgment upon those who have forgotten God. The county and state, as well as the federal government, have their own institutions for punishment and judgment. God too has judgment. The true civil laws of America were taken from the Holy Bible, and if they are used righteously, then the judge is called of the Lord. Some people will not listen to the love, for they do not understand the language of love. Therefore, we are compelled as ministers to turn from love and point them to the Scriptures of judgment which clearly indicate the wrath of God upon men. If they will not turn to God because of love, then the fear of God must be planted in their hearts. The fear of God is the beginning of wisdom. Judgment is sure for all those who willfully sin against God.

The rest of the hot, humid day driving through Illinois over into West Kentucky was an enjoyable time, as we rejoiced in the memory of our delay on the gas station ramps. We felt that even if we made our trip and came home without another person being won for Christ, this one man was worth the trip. We knew there was a new name written down in Glory.

The Scripture which I read to the old gentleman was John 3:17,18: "For God sent not his Son into the world to condemn the world; but that the world through him might be saved. He that believeth on him is not condemned: but he that believeth not is condemned already, because he hath not believed in the name of the only begotten Son of God." I asked this man if he believed that Jesus died for him and that God would save him just as he had saved me. Jesus did not come to condemn but to save. He trusted Jesus right there, and I believe someday we will meet again in Heaven.

How about you? What has your life been? How have you spent the years God has given you? Have you lived just for fun? Have you taken the Lord's name in vain? If you are guilty of taking the Lord's name in vain, you will have to be saved from that sin. God put a warning in the Ten Commandments when He said we should not take His name in vain. This man had silvery-white hair. His shoulders were stooped and he had come very close to the end of his life, but God saved him. Will you have time? Are any of us sure of tomorrow or that we will have a tomorrow? Will you have time to prepare for eternity? Will you waste all the years God will give you? God will save you any time you are ready to accept Him. Why put it off another day, another minute?

How much more wonderful it is to come to Jesus when you are young and have all your life to live for Christ. You have time to gather crowns of service to lay at the feet of Jesus. You can be saved in the evening of your life and cross over into eternity the way you have lived—empty-handed.

Won't you take what is left of your life and live to glorify Christ who died for you? Jesus died for you; He only asks that you live for Him.

If you go to Heaven empty-handed, you will be happy, but there will be tears which God will wipe away. You will have no reward. An aged father saved at death's door will have to look back and see lost sons and daughters whom his careless life had influenced. This is sorrow. Had he been a Christian early in life, he might have won them all for Christ. There is a story in the Book of Genesis about a careless man named Lot, who lost all his sons and daughters because of his own life.

Be saved in your youth and give God the best of your life. To believe in Christ is to be saved; to deny Christ is to be lost (John 3:18).

63. God's Way Is Best

"FOR MY THOUGHTS ARE NOT YOUR THOUGHTS, NEITHER are your ways my ways, saith the Lord. For as the heavens are higher than the earth, so are my ways higher than your ways, and my thoughts than your thoughts." I closed a meeting on a Sunday after I had spoken four or five times that day. The meeting had been held in Loudon, Tennessee. I was weary and tired and longed to go home. A young man who lived in Akron and had come down to see relatives had agreed to drive me home. I told him that I would get into the back seat and sleep while he drove us home. He drove into Knoxville, Tennessee, and there he took the wrong route. About midnight, instead of arriving in Corbin, Kentucky, as planned, we found ourselves way up in North Carolina, at least 115 miles off our route to Akron.

God had said in His Word that His ways were not mine. We saw the lights of a little town. I told the young man to drive into the town. As we neared the suburbs we knew that the lights which we had seen were those of a big night club. Inside there were many people eating, drinking, and dancing. Thinking we might get some information as to where we were, we entered the club, taking a seat at a table very near to the door. These tables were used for the restaurant part of the night club. While we sat there, a young girl came to our table and put her foot on the chair beside me. She asked me to dance with her.

I told her that I was a tired, worn, Baptist preacher and that perhaps because I had been sleeping and was not as neat as I should be, she had thought I was just someone who had come in for a good time and whom it was her job to entertain. I told her that I had sisters whom I loved and I wondered if she was a Christian. She looked at me and her eyes filled with tears. She told me she was not a Christian. I asked her how old she was, and she asked me why should I care. I explained to her that I had been in a meeting in Loudon, Tennessee, and had started home. Our course had been altered for some reason and we were far off the route to Akron, Ohio. I had a little Precious Promise Testament in my pocket; I took it out and slowly read to her. She removed her foot and leg from the chair and sat down. She wept, and someone told the owner that one of the patrons was talking to one of the girls and making her cry. The owner came and threatened to throw me and my companion out, but I told him that I was not his enemy. I told him I was his friend and was just a preacher trying to get home. I did not know why God had sent me this way, but I was beginning to find out. I persuaded this man that I had not been offensive to the girl and had just simply asked her if she was a Christian. "In this great country," I said, "where men have died for the freedom of religion, why would you become offended if I talked to this girl for a few moments about Jesus?" The man sat down at our table, and I noticed others pulling their chairs closer. The dime had played out in the jukebox and all was quiet and still. I told them how we had lost our way. The girl said she would like to be a Christian. I asked her if she would pray with me and trust in Jesus. She prayed the sinner's prayer, "Lord, save me and forgive my sins," and accepted Christ right there. Her mother had died when she was nine years old, and she had needed Jesus for many years.

I turned then to the boss and asked him about his soul. In the quietness of the room, I saw the boss and two other men accept Christ. The big fellow promised that he would get rid of his night club and live for the Lord. After I returned home I received a note from him saying he had kept his promise and was happy in the Lord.

How many times have you said to yourself, "Why did this happen to me?" We do not understand why many times, but one day perhaps we shall. I have found that since I have been a Christian many things which I wanted and things which I wished to do have been permitted by God. I realize that the things which were for the glory of God, like buying the steel or winning the lost, have always been permitted. However, many things which I honestly thought would bring me happiness God has kept from me. Time and knowledge of God will teach you that God's way is best always. I well remember that when I was very young in the ministry I dearly wished to be the pastor of a certain church here in Akron. It was a beautiful church, and was without a pastor. My wife and I prayed earnestly that God would give us that church, but it was not for me. I thought that God had forgotten me and had not answered my prayer. However, I know this church will not seat more than two hundred people. Humbly I say that the choir loft of my church seats that many people. God gave me fifteen auditoriums, and any one of them will seat more than the church I had wanted. God withheld my desire that He might do something over and above anything I might have imagined. Oftentimes we as Christians are guilty of thinking that our prayers have not been answered, and we ask "Why?"

I thought we had carelessly lost our way here in North Carolina and had lost precious time, but God in His infinite wisdom had found precious souls. I was discouraged, tired, and perhaps a little aggravated that we were delayed, yet God's ways were not my ways. I believe God had directed us to make the wrong turning. Now we had to retrace the miles back to Knoxville, where we had turned away from our route home, and begin again. Jesus said a man's soul is worth more than the whole world. I did not get the rest I had intended to get in Corbin, Kentucky, but being delayed about five hours, we could stop along the way only long enough to freshen ourselves at a barbershop. I was due to have a funeral service that day. I changed shirt and tie in a room back of the barbershop and then continued on to the funeral. This story seems hard to believe, and even as I tell it, the wonder of Jesus floods my heart. Wouldn't it be awful if a Christian were not willing to tell someone about Jesus and lose a few hours' sleep, when he remembers what Christ has done for him? Many a soldier has lost sleep on guard against the enemy. Shouldn't we be willing to fight and guard against sin any time?

I believe God has a way in my life. I remember well one time when my wife and I were traveling by plane. Because of a delay, a friend of ours insisted that we spend the night with him in his home and then go on by train the next day. We canceled our plane reservations, and the plane which we would have been on crashed and burned the next day in the mountains between Oklahoma City and Nashville. All aboard were killed. I don't think for one moment that I am better than any one of them because they died and I am still alive. However, I do believe that God has a mission for each of us. Rev. J. B. Watson and his dear wife are still living, and it was their home where we spent the night.

I told myself, the good Lord, my people, and those who have insisted that I just simply write a book of the things which have happened to me, that I will document every story and give a sworn statement that it is not a book of fiction. More than half of the book may sound like fiction, and some will say it could not have happened that way; but each story in the pages of this book, from the time of my illness at two weeks old, through my school days and all the years up to the present time, I swear to you is the truth. Many of the people concerned are still living and would swear under oath that what I say is true. These stories have been written that you might believe in Jesus, that you might trust Him as your Saviour and know Him to be real.

You cannot read this story and not realize how important one soul is to Jesus. Just imagine if that girl of seventeen in North Carolina had been your baby sister. Here she was in a night club, asking everyone to dance with her and buy her a drink, only to meet Jesus and watch all change. Now she can leave this world without fear because she trusted in a Saviour. What I thought was a badly mistaken route turned out to be God's Way for the salvation of four young people on an early Monday morning. God's Way is Best!

64. She Was Just Thirteen

IF THERE IS ONE GROUP OF PEOPLE ON EARTH TODAY OF whom I might say I have the greatest burden, I think perhaps it would be the present-day teen-agers. I may sound a bit radical at the outset of this chapter but I do not mean to be. There is so much difference between these days and the days in which I grew up as a teen-ager. When I was a teenager I was not allowed to go to the swimming hole on Sunday, nor was I permitted to go to the ball game on Sunday. My parents were very strict and godly.

Around midnight on a Thursday in 1961 my telephone rang. A girl at the other end of the line with a very sorrowful voice asked if I were Brother Billington. She apologized for having called me at such a late hour but she simply had to have help. I told her that I had never refused to listen to anyone's story and I would be glad to hear hers. She told me that she was still a teen-ager; in fact, she was not yet eighteen. From about the age of ten until around the age of thirteen she had come to our church with friends. However, she had not attended regularly. She told me that one night when she was about twelve and a half she came to the altar and believed in God and was saved. Her mother had died when she was two years old, and after that she had endured two stepmothers. After the first stepmother died and the second marriage ended in divorce, her father had no one to care for her, and she stayed with neighbors or with a friend—just anywhere was home. She matured rapidly, and when only thirteen, weighed about 130 pounds and was 5 feet 2 inches tall. She easily gave the appearance of a girl eighteen or nineteen years old.

A man who was quite a bit older than she asked her to marry him. Out of a desire to belong to someone and to have a home, she persuaded her father, through threats, to lie about her age; and they were married. Her first baby arrived, a baby girl. It was someone she could love and call her very own. She worshiped this baby girl; and perhaps for the first time the love she had buried deep within her heart was turned loose and happily showered upon this precious child. She was like a child with a lovely doll at Christmastime. A year and a half later, another child was born to her; this time it was a boy. When her son was only six months old, her husband left her and sued for divorce. She did not tell me the reasons why the divorce was granted. Her husband's parents took the baby boy to raise as their own, and she managed with jobs here and there to keep her baby girl. No one knew her real age, so the court allowed her to keep her daughter, even though she was not of age, as long as she could support her.

This young girl did housework and worked in restaurants, and now her little girl was three years old. Then she told me that she was expecting another child and she was not married. The man with whom she was going had offered to marry her in order to give the child a name, but he would not live with her.

However, she was quick to tell me this was not the reason for her call. She had called me because her true age had been determined by the Welfare Board, and unless she had a husband, her daughter would be taken from her and put into an orphanage. The baby that she would give birth to would in time be adopted out. She asked me pitifully was there anyone who could help her.

I told her that the same God who had saved her soul when she was only twelve and a half was able to help her now. God never has and never will ignore sin, nor will He excuse it; but God will forgive a truly repentant heart. She asked me if God could forgive one who had so thoroughly ruined her life. I asked her if she loved her little girl, to which she replied, "Yes, but she is mine." I said, "You took Jesus as your Saviour and you are His."

I convinced her that she still belonged to God, even though she had sinned against God, and that He still loved her and was just waiting for her to be truly sorry and ask forgiveness.

I told her the story of the prodigal son, how he left home and how he returned. He wanted to seek the forgiveness of his father, and while he was yet afar off the father ran to meet him. This is an example I give to all the backslidden Christians who are out of fellowship with God.

I asked her if she remembered some of the stories which she was taught while attending the Baptist Temple. When Jesus was on trial, Peter cursed and said, "I do not know him." When Peter was accused for the third time of knowing Jesus, he cursed vehemently. But when Jesus rose from the dead, He said to go tell his disciples and Peter. God had forgiven Peter. Moses came upon two men fighting, and he killed one of them and hid him in the sand. However, one day God called his hand and forgave him. Peter was used greatly of God as was Moses. God forgave them, and He will forgive you if you will only trust Him.

It is so hard for teen-agers, especially those who have no parents, who are left with friends and many times on their own, to have to make decisions which even an adult would find difficult. Sometimes these youngsters, robbed of parents by death or divorce, are taken by an uncle or other relative to rear and educate. These children more times than not seem to be misfits. They have lost a feeling of security, living in a home where they appear to be the outsiders. This is especially true in a home where the benefactors have children of their own. Children are sensitive, and a casual remark to a neighbor, such as "We just had to take him, he had no one else" makes a boy or girl feel like excess baggage. This is certainly not an ideal background for rearing a good, level-headed citizen.

In the state of Tennessee today there lives a man who is very near my age. At the age of sixteen he and some other boys committed a crime. His father was a groceryman and owned several stores. They were a family who were highly respected, but sin had made its mark in this family: their only son was put on trial for a very hideous crime. He was found guilty and sent to the reform school. At that particular time it was said that no boy ever returned to that school, for the man in charge took it upon himself to break boys of committing crime. He believed that if, instead of giving the boys nice treatment with decent food and good books to read, you made it rough enough on them and punished them severely enough, they would never wish to return, once they had been released. This young man was punished often, and a friend whom he had made at the reform school was punished often too. One day this young man's friend was beaten unmercifully, and seeing this, the young man prayed that if God would help him to get out of there, he would live by God's standards and with God's help would never return to prison.

This boy was released, and he kept his promise to God. And as far as I know this day, he still lives with God as his partner. He runs a large grocery business with many new stores. I am telling you this, if perhaps you are a teen-ager who has slipped by the wayside: God is still on the throne; many have drifted away from Him, but if you have enough courage to ask forgiveness, God can show you the road back to happiness again. You cannot go so deep in sin that God's hand cannot reach you. The prison bars are not strong enough to keep God from entering, if you desire His presence. This young man walked away from prison and stayed out and made good. He knows the grocery business as few men do and has gained the respect of everyone who knows him.

Please, young people, don't give up. When you have reached the end of your strength, just look up. Man's extremities are God's opportunities. Put your hand in God's once again and walk back up the hill to where there is light. Trust in Him, He will never fail you.

It has been my pleasure to have worked with several teen-agers during the past thirty-one years in Akron. I have a son who is now thirty-four years old. I come from a large family. From the very beginning of my ministry I started working with young people who were in trouble. Judge Hunsicker, who was at one time over the juvenile court of

Akron, was kind enough to sit down with me and discuss many of their problems. (Judge Hunsicker is now judge over the Ninth District Court of Appeals in Ohio.)

Whenever I read in the paper about boys and girls in trouble, I would go to this judge to see if anything could be worked out, so that it would not be necessary to send them to reform school. I wanted to talk with them and reason with them. Of course, I wanted most of all to get them to church.

About seventeen or eighteen years ago two boys, twins, were brought into court for questioning. Times were hard and money was nearly impossible to get. Their dad was a very heavy drinker, and the boys were perhaps on their own most of the time. I took them out in my car, and after we had driven a short distance away from the bustle of the city, I stopped the car and began to talk to them. I told them that I wished to be their friend: whenever they were in trouble or needed advice they should feel free to come to me, and I would try with all my heart to help them. They knew I had very little financial help to offer, but somehow through God's grace they knew I was sincere in offering to be their friend. Many times this feeling of having a friend is worth more to a young person than gold and silver.

In all these years there hasn't been one teen-ager whom I regret having helped. When these two boys went into service, I received letters from them which were a real treasure to me. I believe with all my heart that there is not one of you who, if he wants to change and do right, cannot find someone to give him that chance. Of course, you must prove yourself. I don't care what you have done, who you are, or what your religion is, if you will put God first, ahead of everything and everybody (even though you are behind prison bars where other boys laugh at you as you pray), God will hear your prayer and answer. God will hear a whisper as well as He would hear a shout.

If you, a teen-ager, have never owned a Bible, please get one. Your own family, if they are unsaved, may make it rough on you if you want to read God's Word. But in determination, very slowly turn the pages of the Holy Bible, starting with the story in the Book of Genesis about a man called Jacob and his twelve sons. Joseph, one of the sons, was hated by his brothers, for Joseph had found great favor with his father Jacob. Joseph, as a teen-ager, was sold into slavery down in Egypt. One day that teen-age boy, hated by his brothers, became the prime minister of the entire country of Egypt. Joseph became a tool for God and was used mightily for God. All faiths still tell the story about the teen-age boy who was sold by his own brothers when he was about sixteen or seventeen years old.

Another teen-ager in the Bible, whose name was Daniel, was taken in captivity when only fourteen. He became the president of a strange land and of a strange people. He refused to drink with the crowd.

There are so many children without a home today, with not enough to eat and barely enough to wear, because their father or mother drinks. But you, a teen-ager, need not give up hope. Joseph vowed he would live for God, even though his home was a damp, dingy cell; and although there seemed to be no way out, his faith was rewarded. Daniel refused to compromise and stood firmly upon his belief in God. They both saw dark, discouraging hours, and you will too; but God says we are to pray and not faint, which means not be easily discouraged and give up.

Please let me write to you as if you were my own child. I am past fifty years old and have a son and two grandsons. Being a preacher, I have had many stories told to me and I have many stories to tell, myself. You might perhaps say they sound fictional, but they are very true.

You, yourself, must do something about your condition. Like Daniel, who made his decision not to drink, and Joseph, who said he would trust in God come what may, you must make a decision. You might lay down this book and say this preacher is a religious fanatic. But I don't care what your past has been and how badly sin has wrecked your life, think of Peter, who cursed Christ, and Moses, who committed murder, and notice that God still loved them and forgave them. God did not excuse their sins but He forgave them.

In the 11th chapter in the Gospel of Luke there is a story illustrating the power of prayer, about a man who came to a friend at midnight asking for help. I cannot explain the power but I understand it, for I have seen what prayer can do in my own life.

The God of Heaven, who puts the sun in its circuit, who crowns the skies with a million stars and places the moon to shed its light, who sends the rain that the grain of corn which you have planted may have a drink and increase its yield, this same God still sits on the throne. He heard the prayers of Joseph and Daniel, and He will hear your prayers too.

Perhaps you are called the roughest boy or the wildest girl in the neighborhood. There was a time when this reputation made you proud. Now you feel ashamed and wish with all your heart that you had been more careful of the precious character which God gave you at birth. You were spotless then, but there has since been a great change.

Just turn your face to God and, as millions have done, leave the old crowd and their worldly ways; for they have brought only sorrow and disgrace. Trust in God. Pray and read your Bible. You will find yourself wanting to help others who are living in sin. You as a teen-ager can have more effect on another teen-ager than anyone else, for he knows your life and he will see the change.

The youth of our land are the strength and the future of our nation. What a wonderful place it would be for them to live in if our young people would look to God and never find they had to trade their names for numbers and live within prison walls like animals.

There is a Scripture in the Bible which says there is nothing impossible with God. There is a verse which says there is nothing too hard for God to do. The thirteen-year-old girl whose life was wrecked was restored again through faith in God, and a young boy who had ruined his reputation found strength through a Saviour's love to face his sin and became a partner with God. God delivered both of these teen-agers, and He wants to deliver you. If you do not believe, then truly all hope is gone for you. Can you say that God does not care? Why, He knows the number of the hairs on your head. There is not even the death of a sparrow, that God does not attend the funeral. Then you whom He loved so much that He willingly gave His own, only Son to die that you might live, would you think that He does not care? If God be for you, then who would dare to be against you? If you cannot look yourself in the face any more, if your nights are troubled by your conscience, then there is hope for you, because the quickening that you feel is the Holy Spirit pleading with you. If it scares you when you think of facing God, then realize that the fear of God is the beginning of wisdom. Open up your heart; Jesus is knocking. Let Him come in.

Whatever your sin, tell Jesus about it. You don't have to tell anyone but Christ. He alone can save you and forgive you of your sins. God saves, forgives, and cleanses. You can salvage your life through Christ and live so that you may once again hold your head high. God can, if you let Him, change your whole life.